SEASONS OF OUR JOY

A HANDBOOK OF JEWISH FESTIVALS

ARTHUR I. WASKOW

ILLUSTRATED WITH PAPERCUTS BY
MARTIN FARREN AND
JOAN BENJAMIN-FARREN

seasoned with recipes by
Rose Gertz, Hannah Waskow, and
Rose Sue Berstein

SUMMIT BOOKS
NEW YORK

Papercuts by Martin Farren and Joan Benjamin-Farren
Photographed by George Vasques of Fine Arts Photography
in Boston, Massachusetts
Calligraphy by Shel Bassel
Copyright © 1982 by Arthur Waskow
Papercuts Copyright © 1982 by Martin Farren
and Joan Benjamin-Farren
Published by SUMMIT BOOKS
A Division of Simon & Schuster, Inc.
Simon & Schuster Building
1230 Avenue of the Americas
New York, New York 10020
Originally published in 1982 by Bantam Books, Inc.
SUMMIT BOOKS and colophon are trademarks
of Simon & Schuster, Inc.
Manufactured in the United States of America
1   2   3   4   5   6   7   8   9   10
Library of Congress Cataloging in Publication Data

Waskow, Arthur I.
   Seasons of our joy.

   Reprint. Originally published: Toronto ; New York :
Bantam Books, 1982.
   1. Fasts and feasts—Judaism.   2. Cookery, Jewish.
I. Title.
[BM690.W28 1986]   296.4'3   85-30280
ISBN 0-671-61865-2

Said one chassid to another: "Have you come to the Rebbe to hear him teach Torah?"

"No, I have come to watch him tie his shoelaces. From his life I will come to understand living."

For Max Ticktin and Zalman Schachter-Shalomi, who have taught me both tying and Torah.

And in memory of
Rose Honigman Osnowitz Gertz, my grandmother,
Who taught me the rhythm of the blessings for a storm of sneezes:
May you grow long and broad as Purim challah!
Who saw in our joyful sit-in band an echo of the rebels of 1905;
Who insisted against my skepticism—surely at 90 she was too old to get it right—that at Purim you ate chickpeas. . .
And was right.

And Hannah Hilda Leah Osnowitz Waskow, my mother,
Who fought for breath for half her life
And taught me that the Breath of Life is holy;
Who fought for justice all her life
And taught me that the struggle is unending;
Who ate pistachio ice cream with a passion;
Who loved with fierce and open eyes
And at the end was fierce and open-eyed . . .
And loving.

Together they seasoned this book with their joy in good food and their skill in cooking it.

◆》》 CONTENTS 《《◆

◆≫≫ INTRODUCTION ≪≪◆

The rain. The dew. The dryness. And then rain again, and dew, and dryness. The story of the circling year. From the rabbis, mystics, and farmers of sixteen centuries ago we have a book that tells the story of the circling year. That teaches us what to do if the delicate machinery should stop—if the rain that lubricates the circling year should stop, and the movement from warm to cold, from dry to wet, should end. The book begins when the rainy season in the Land of Israel begins—at Sukkot, the harvest festival—and it ends with Yom Kippur, the holy day that comes just before the harvest. So the book itself circles through the round of the year. The book is part of the Talmud—a gigantic collection of profound conversations, legal debates, and tall tales. It is called Fasts, or *Ta-anit*.

And in that book there is a story that is five centuries older still.

The round of the year was broken. The lubricant had failed, and the delicate machinery was stuck. For months and months there had been no rain. The people sent a message to Honi the Circle-drawer, "Pray that rain may fall." He prayed, but no rain fell.

So he drew a circle and stood inside it and said to God, "I swear by Your great Name that I will not move from here until You have mercy on Your children." Rain began, but only a drizzle. Honi's followers said to him, "We look to you to save us from death; but we believe this drizzle comes only to clear you from your oath."

So Honi cried out, "I prayed not for this drizzle, but for rain that would fill cisterns, ditches, and caves." The rain then began to come down with

· ix ·

great force, every drop as big as the opening of a barrel. So his followers said to him, "Rabbi, we look to you to save us from death; but we believe this torrent comes to destroy the world." Honi cried out to God again: "I prayed not for this torrent but for a rain of benevolence, blessing, and bounty." Then rain fell in a normal way until the thirsty land was full, the streams abrim, and floods coming. So Honi prayed again, "Your people cannot endure too much punishment nor too much benefit. May it be Your will that the rain may stop and there be relief for the world." Immediately the wind began to blow, the clouds dispersed, and the sun shone. The people went out into the fields to gather mushrooms.

But the head of the rabbinical court sent word to Honi, "If you were not Honi, I would have you excommunicated for forcing the hand of God. But you!—you act like a petulant child before God and He does what you want, as a father grants the desires of his favorite son."

What was the circle in which Honi stood to force God's hand?

At the end of the book of *Ta-anit*, a rabbi glimpsed the future: In days to come the Blessed Holy One will hold a circle-dance for the *tzaddikim*, the righteous men and women. God will sit in their midst in the Garden of Eden, and as they dance around, every one of them will point a finger toward God, singing, "You are our God, for whom we waited, that You might save us. You are the Lord for whom we waited, we will be glad and rejoice in Your salvation."

What is this circle that the *tzaddikim* will dance in?

These circles are the cycles of the year. Honi was telling God, "If you have stopped the circle I will stop the circle. I will not leave here until you release the round of the year." The *tzaddikim* were telling God, "We rejoice in a circle because You rejoice in a circle. We waited and You sent us the circle of Your seasons."

This book is about the circle of the seasons, the round of the year, the festivals of joy with which the Jewish people dance our praise of God. There are moments of dryness, sadness, in the cycle—but beneath them there is a deeper joy in the circling of the year. So all the festivals, even those of sadness and solemnity, are seasons of our joy. Let us learn together how to dance them.

◆>>> HOW TO READ THIS BOOK <<<◆

This book is about the circle of the year, and also about the points along the circle. It can be read two ways. One way is to read straight through it—as a kind of biography of a Jewish year. The other way is to focus on one particular chapter—on the holy day or festival that is approaching, to help you get ready for it.

Even if you want to use the specific chapters in the second way, you may get a better sense of each festival if you read the Preface first. The Preface—entitled "Seasons of the Sun, Seasons of the Moon"—is about the circle as a whole. The festivals are built upon the cycles of the sun and moon; so a sense of the round of the year and the round of the month will be useful if you want to concentrate on—say—Sukkot, the harvest festival, or Hanukkah, which lights a candle of hope against the winter night of dark despair.

After the Preface come twelve chapters. Each is about one festival, one holy day, or season. Each chapter is divided up this way:

· A brief passage on the underlying mood of that holy day. This section shows how the mood applies not only in the nature cycle of sun and moon, but also in the history of the Jewish people and in the spiritual experience of a single human being.

· A history of how that holy time emerged and developed. This section shows how many of the festivals grew out of the holy times of other peoples, and how the Jewish people shaped and modified their practices, their patterns, and their meanings till today.

· A section on the formal preparation period that leads up to the holy days, if there is one. This section shows how to get ready for the festival.

· A section describing how the holy day is observed and celebrated now, in the present practices of different Jewish communities. This section explains prayers, Bible readings, ceremonies, foods, songs, and other practical details.

· A section on new approaches to the festival that are emerging now and that may highlight some newly understood meanings in it. These new approaches are often especially connected with the "mood" in the first part of the chapter and with the phase of that particular festival in the cycle of the month and year.

· A section of recipes.

· A section suggesting books and guides that are especially useful in regard to that one festival.

There are really three important threads woven into each of these chapters. One is the history of the development of the festival. One is the guide to current practice among various different Jews. And one is the new approaches that are beginning to emerge.

Most previous books about the Jewish holy days have focused either on the history of their development or on the current practices. Why is this book different? Because it emerges from a special kind of Jewish consciousness—the movement for *Jewish renewal*. From the standpoint of Jewish renewal, the past, the present, and the future are all important. We must learn from the history of the holy days how Jews have renewed Judaism over and over in the past. We must learn from the present and its glimmerings of the future how we might go about renewing Jewish life today.

What is the movement for Jewish renewal? In the 1970s it began to gather together the scattered sparks of Jewish life. This movement began in *chavurot*—small fellowships, participatory congregations where leadership was shared and rotated instead of being handed over to hired rabbis; where people prayed and studied the Jewish tradition by sitting in circles and talking with each other instead of sitting in rows behind each other; where people danced and breathed and sang and chanted. But Jewish renewal spreads far beyond the *chavurot*.

For all of us involved in it—in *chavurot*, synagogues, Jewish Y's and Centers, for unaffiliated Jewish singers and actors, young lawyers at the UJA and dogged liberal precinct workers—for all of us there has been great joy in beginning to repair the shattered holy vessel of Jewish peoplehood. Precisely because we have let ourselves experience deeply the pain and grief of the Holocaust, we have been able to renew our Jewish lives.

For us, for me, the way to renew Jewish life has been to wrestle with the Jewish past and present. Not to bow down before it, not to turn away from it. What is wrestling? It is a close grappling that has some elements of fighting and some elements of embracing in it, at the same time and *in the same process.* There are both love and anger in a wrestle. In a wrestle I do not pretend my partner is the same as me—and I do not pretend I am the same as my partner. We are two; I, who I fully am; and the other, fully other. The name of the people Israel—Yisrael—means the Godwrestler, and this is our best path of living. So this book is built by wrestling with the Jewish past and present.

This is how the festivals grew through the millennia and still are growing. Our most ancient forebears took festivals of the sun and moon, the birth of lambs and the harvest of barley—and wrestled with these nature festivals to create history festivals, celebrations of political liberations, and observances of military disasters. They wrestled with history and nature to create festivals that evoked and embodied the deepest yearnings, fears, and even clownings of the human spirit. In the Biblical age, they focused these celebrations on offering up plants and animals at a sacred site.

After the Holy Temple was destroyed and the sacrifices were ended, the ancient rabbis wrestled with the festivals again. They developed prayer and ceremony, food and song, that would express the same—or new—deep human needs; that would fulfill the commands inscribed deep within the human spirit by the Root of Being. They knew they were doing much that was new; they felt they were hearing commands and ideas that were old. They felt that level after level of Torah was unveiled when they studied Torah—when they unveiled the hidden truths.

In some ways we are like the ancient rabbis. We, after the Holocaust and the invention of thermonuclear weapons, feel our lives deeply threatened—as they did after the Destruction of the Temple and the decimation of the Jewish community in the Land of Israel. We have been deeply influenced by Modernism, as the rabbis were by Greek culture, Hellenism. As modernized Jews, we have begun to renew Judaism by wrestling with its sources—just as they did.

How are we different from the ancient rabbis? We are women and men together, equal. We live in both the land of Israel and the far-flung Diaspora, as a people and even as individuals. We may care more about our bodies and about the body of the earth. We may care more about our separate selves, our individualities, than they did. We may be more conscious of the process of our own change than they were. We may especially be more conscious that not only our own study of Torah, but also the changed historical conditions of our lives help us to unveil the hidden truths of Torah. We may care more about *why* some practice or idea gives us vitality—instead of doing it because the text, the book, says to do it.

For example: readers will note in Chapters X and XI that I take a lot of time and space to work out *why* the ancient rabbis were so concerned with the dates when the Counting of the *omer* began and when it ended, just before the festival of Shavuot. Why do I bother? Why not just accept what they decided?

For three reasons. First, because in order to wrestle with the past and present we must be clear about exactly what they are. Secondly, because such a detective story need not be dull and boring: it can be fun. The rabbis, too, had a sense of humor. Sometimes when they haggled over a detail they were poking fun at their own habits. And finally, because it is our own habit to search for inner meaning. If the rabbis argued so hard about the issue, perhaps there was some inner meaning to it. And if we read and think about the text, perhaps we will uncover that meaning—or create it for ourselves in a way that helps us live and grow.

In this particular case, for instance, I conclude that the debate over the date of Shavuot was about something extraordinarily important: was there a festival to celebrate God's Giving of the Torah at Mount Sinai? Was there any time when every Jew could feel he, she, was standing at Sinai *now*, ready to hear God's Voice *now*? Is Shavuot that date?

The Torah does not seem to say so, does not explicitly name Shavuot as the anniversary of Sinai. So the only way the rabbis could find a time for every Jew to hear the Torah anew was for themselves to hear the Torah anew.

To understand how they did this, we need to trace the process. For us, the historical process bears a crucial spiritual meaning. It means we too, facing great earthquakes in our world, can remake Jewish life while remaining serious Jews devoted to the Torah. That is what the Jewish renewal movement seeks to do.

Some Jews may believe that there is no historical process in Torah—that Torah does not change. They may be committed to Torah as it was. And others may believe in the historical changes, but have given up on Torah. They may believe that once we see that Torah changes, we must accept that it was temporary. They may become secularists who believe the Jewish people are simply those people who see themselves as Jews; God and Torah have nothing to do with it.

The movement for Jewish renewal is, rather, centered on the notion that the historical process of Torah *is* Torah. It is the unfolding of Torah; it is veil after veil after veil coming off the Torah, where the veils themselves were Torah and what was beneath them was also Torah.

This book is written *from* the standpoint of Jewish renewal. But it is written *toward* a much wider audience . . . for if there is to be a real Jewish renewal, the whole Jewish people—with all our quirks and quibbles—will contribute to it. All the sparks must be regathered in order to repair the holy vessel. So this book was written in the hope that all Jews—and also non-Jews who are curious about the festivals and think there is something to be learned from the Jewish path of life—may find it useful. The book was written for those who are simply interested in how the holidays developed, and for those who want to observe them today. It was written for those who are drawn to the traditional patterns and those who would like to work out new approaches. It was written for those who are synagogue members, and those who will do their celebrating alone or with a cluster of friends. It was written for those who know very little but want to learn; for those who know a good deal but would like to have a handbook handy; and for those who are already scholars, but want to hear some new ideas about the meaning of the yearly cycle.

And most of all, it was written for those who would like to argue, question, suggest, invent, who would like to join the process. There is an ancient tradition of *shylah* and *tshuvah*, question and response, among those in a Jewish community who are trying to learn together. As the ancient rabbis said, "Who are wise? Those who learn from every human being." So let us join together to learn . . . not symbolically, but for real. At the end of this book there is an explanation of how we can do this—how you and I can learn together. Please join in.

Shalom!
Arthur Waskow

◆»» A WORD ON HEBREW «« ◆

When there are translations from Hebrew in this book, the renderings are the author's unless another source is indicated. There is a glossary of Hebrew and Yiddish words in Appendix III.

When there are transliterations of Hebrew, the rendering is the simplest possible: an apostrophe where a *shva* or silent vowel in Hebrew requires a slight silent pause; and ch for the throat-clearing sound that is the nearest English equivalent of the Hebrew letters *chet* and *chaf*. (Where the name of a person or festival is known some other way in English—like Honi or Hanukkah—we will use that form.) The Sephardic (Mediterranean) pronunciation of Hebrew words is the one used in transliterations.

When the book refers to the Sabbath, however, we use Shabbos in the Ashkenazic/Yiddish style, because neither the Sephardic Shabbat nor Sabbath conveys the joyful familiarity and love with which Jews greet the seventh day, the day of rest and contemplation.

In most cases we have translated *rachum* and *rachamim* as 'motherly' when they refer to God, rather than with the conventional 'compassionate.' *Rechem* means womb, and *Av Ha-Rachamim* can therefore be understood as Motherly Father. In a tradition that is often accused of a male bias, it seems valuable to be fully conscious that God's attributes include, and transcend, maleness and femaleness.

◀>>> PREFACE: ‹‹‹▶
SEASONS OF THE SUN, SEASONS OF THE MOON

What does it mean to think of *seasons* of our joy, of a yearly *cycle*, a *round* of Jewish festivals? Most of us do not think of the Jewish holidays this way. Instead, most of us remember them as separate little bubbles of experience, each with its own shape and color, each popping up at us without a rhythm:

Passover . . . matzah, wine, the bitter herb, liberation from slavery.

Rosh Hashanah . . . the ram's horn blasting out its eerie sound, crowds of people in the synagogue, old friends in the community suddenly reappearing from a summer's absence.

Yom Kippur . . . fasting, crying, trying to reckon up our misdeeds, feeling a great sense of release at day's end.

Hanukkah . . . the candles, the *dreidl*, the Maccabees fighting for our freedom.

Purim . . . the noise-makers drowning out the sound of wicked Haman's name, hilarious laughter.

And that's all.

For more and more of us, this is either too much—or not enough.

The holidays have become a kind of ghetto in time—a little enclave in our everyday world where we can withdraw into our Jewishness.

But ghettoes in time are no more comfortable than the ghettoes in space used to be. If the holidays are only ghettoes, we tend to forget them. We forget how to do them, we depend on the rabbis and professional Jews to do them for us, we even forget some of them exist, we let them be *bubbles*—and even less and less of that. The ghettoes in space vanished—and for many of us the ghettoes in time are vanishing too. And as they vanish, so do the things that make Jewish life in America distinctive and attractive.

But at the same time, more and more of us are experiencing a thirst for the water of our spiritual wellsprings, or hunger for the roots of our Jewish ethnic origins—or both. This book addresses that thirst and that hunger. To fill that thirst and feed that hunger means that we must open up to what the holidays can be . . . much more than bubbles.

First of all, *each one* of them is richer in its meanings than we are liable to remember. Most of them relate to nature, to history, and to our inner spiritual lives—and sometimes the same symbol can call forth all those levels of response.

And secondly, *all* of them are richer than we are liable to remember, because *they fit together* into a coherent whole. As the seasons follow each other in a profound pattern, as a human life grows and falls in a profound pattern, as a whole society grows and changes in a profound pattern—so do the Jewish holidays.

Indeed, they were intended to teach us how to experience more fully the profound patterns of the world—how to enrich them, nurture them, learn from them. So if we can learn how the cycle of the festivals works *as a cycle,* we can learn how to live better with the earth and air and water; how to live better with each other; and how to live better inside our selves. Chapter by chapter, we will deal with each holiday as itself and as part of the cycle. Now, at the beginning of our search, we will look at the cycle as a whole.

The Jewish holidays began with those described in the Torah—the Five Books of Moses. At later times—even up to our own generation—new holidays were added, greatly enriching our experience of the year. But the basic pattern was set 3,000 years ago and more.

The first thing to notice in that basic pattern is that there are two cycles: one based on the sun and one on the moon.

In part, the two cycles are *like* each other; in part, they *merge* with each other. They are intended to reinforce each other, to teach the same lessons in two different ways. They are an oval with a circle set inside it:

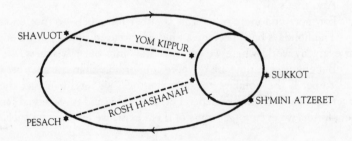

Let us look first at the oval cycle, the one based on the sun. There are four festivals, recognizing the four seasons of the year, four moments of history, four stages of human life, four states of spiritual consciousness:

1. Pesach (Passover), in the spring—the moment of birth and newness; the birth of the Jewish people, of freedom. The flowers rise up against winter; the Israelites rise up against Pharaoh; our creativity first rises up against dullness and routine. The great twentieth-century Jewish thinker Franz Rosenzweig called Pesach the Festival of Creation.

2. Shavuot (the Feast of Weeks, Pentecost), seven weeks and a day after Pesach—at the onset of summer, the peak of nature's glory. It reminds us of the moment at the peak of Sinai when the Jewish people met God face to face in what Jewish tradition called a great wedding ceremony, to receive the Ten Commandments and the Torah. In a human's life it represents the peak of early maturity, the onset of adulthood, the moment when a human being's own identity is clear enough that s/he is first able to reach out from one self to another. In a spiritual process it is when the glimmering potential becomes a shining actuality. Rosenzweig called it the Festival of Revelation.

3. Sukkot (the Feast of Huts), after harvest in the fall—a festival of ingathering, of reaping the benefits of all our work, of fulfillment, of rejoicing. It reminds us of the era of sojourning in the wilderness, gathering in the lessons of the Teaching at Sinai; the era of dwelling safe in fragile huts, dwelling safe with God's Presence in the very midst of Israel. And so it is also the moment of history that has not yet happened, the moment of fulfillment when all our work is done and Messiah comes. In a human life it represents the fullness of a full life: the children grown, the task accomplished. In the human spirit it represents the harvest of creativity—the creative work fully achieved. Rosenzweig called it Redemption, but Fulfillment may be a better word.

4. Sh'mini Atzeret (the Eighth Day of Assembly and Completion)—This is the festival we must explain here at greatest length, because this is the one that is least known, that is least visible. It is the barely visible festival, tacked on to the end of Sukkot—a signal of the onset of the rainy winter. It is the festival of inwardness, contraction, starting over again. It echoes the moment of Jewish history when the sojourn in the wilderness ended and a new task had to be undertaken. For it echoes the moment of the death of Moses: the death that moves at once toward new life, toward the people's crossing of the Jordan into the Land of Israel. When we read the Five Books of Moses in the synagogue, week by week, it is at Sh'mini Atzeret time that the reading ends with Moses' death—and begins again at once with Genesis, creation.

Thus Sh'mini Atzeret completes the cycle: it is the seed gone underground in seeming death—but only in order to be ready for the spring to give it new life. It is the moment when we pray for the chilly rains of winter—because we know those rains will grow new food to nourish new life. And indeed, the festival itself is small and hardly visible, just as the seed gone underground is hardly visible. In our own lives, Sh'mini Atzeret represents the time of inwardness, rethinking, summing up, that infuses a healthy death. In the cycle of creativity, it is the moment when the burst of creativity is exhausted and what is needed is rethinking and review—so that a kernel of new understanding can be passed on to the next stage. For of course the cycle of the festivals begins again—with Pesach.

So goes the year, the circle-dance of life in tune with the music of the sun. There is also, as always in Jewish life, another voice, another dance—for Jewish life is always the conversation, the wrestle, between two partners. The second dance is done to the rhythm of the moon. The Jewish months are truly "moonths," beginning with the new moon and cycling through its phases. The month of spring, according to the Torah, is the first of months— and according to this counting, the seventh month is Tishri—in the fall. Just as Judaism makes holy the seventh day and the seventh year, so it makes holy the seventh month. In that month, alone in all the year, there come four festivals:

1. At the new moon, Rosh Hashanah (Top of the Year). Like Pesach in the sun cycle, it is a feast of beginning. According to tradition, it is the anniversary of the creation of Adam—the birthday of the human race. It is the moment for us to begin renewing our spiritual lives, our sense of decency and holiness. It is the moment of the rebirth of the moon.

2. At the phase of the swelling moon, the tenth of Tishri, Yom Kippur (Day of Atonement). This is the day of intense relationship with God, the one moment when the high priest would enter the Holy of Holies in the ancient Temple in Jerusalem. For us it is the moment of deepest, highest striving. As Sinai was the moment when the whole Jewish people felt closest to God, so Yom Kippur is the moment when each Jewish individual does. So it parallels Shavuot in the cycle of the sun. Indeed, according to tradition, Yom Kippur is the day when God forgave the sin of the Golden Calf and gave the Israelites the second set of Tablets, the second copy of the Ten Commandments. So in this sense also it is a second Shavuot, a second giving of the Torah.

3. Sukkot comes at the full moon, the fulfillment of the moon, on the fifteenth of Tishri. It thus plays in the moon cycle the same role it does in the sun cycle, when it comes at harvest time in the fulfillment of the sun's work of growing food. Here the two cycles touch and for a moment merge, as Sukkot stands with Sukkot. Indeed, this moment is itself one of fulfillment— the merger of the two great cycles of the Jewish sense of time. In a sense, Sukkot is itself that Messianic moment when, as Isaiah prophesies, "the light of the moon will be like the light of the sun."

4. And finally, Sh'mini Atzeret comes on the twenty-second of Tishri,

when the moon is fast diminishing. So here also the festival of approaching winter and the disappearing sun merges with the festival of disappearing moon. And here the two cycles begin to diverge again, as the oval and the circle move apart. Here both move, in their different speeds, toward darkness—and rebirth.

These are the festivals the Torah teaches. Later in Jewish history, the yearly cycle was enriched with holidays that fit into the cycle of the year—Tu B'Shvat or the new year of trees, when there is the first glimmer of light at the end of the tunnel of winter; Purim in the early feverish spring; Lag B'Omer, in the sweet and gentle moment between spring and summer; Tisha B'Av, in memory of the burning of the Temple, at the hottest, driest moment of mid-summer; Simchat Torah, enriching the second day of Sh'mini Atzeret as the time to complete and restart the cycle of Torah reading; Hanukkah, close to the winter solstice, the darkest moment of the year. These holy days were also, with something like spiritual genius, so crafted as to fuse the mood of the nature cycle of the sun with the meaning of the historical moments they recalled. And they thus provided ceremonies to renew the human spirit in its moments of faint hope, crazy hilarity, sunny pleasure, bitter grief, deep despair.

The tradition also provided introductions and departures—a kind of connective tissue—for several of the major holy seasons. The Torah itself provided that from Pesach to Shavuot there should be a counting, day by day, of the *omer*—a sheaf of barley from the spring crop, ripening day by day in different fields in the Land of Israel. Before Tisha B'Av there arrives the shadow of our mourning, and afterward there are the seven Sabbaths of Consolation; and in Elul, a month of study and preparation just before Rosh Hashanah.

And finally, in our own day there has been the effort to proclaim two (and among some groups three) new holy days commemorating the earthquakes of this past generation: Yom Hashoah, Holocaust Remembrance Day, and Yom Ha-atzma-ut, the anniversary of Israeli independence. * The date of Yom Ha-atzma-ut was a given; the date of Yom Hashoah was set ten days before it, as an arbitrary choice. Both of them fall in the period of *omer*, the time between Pesach and Shavuot. It is interesting to note that the one whose history more accords with the sense of spring and celebration—Yom Ha-atzma-ut—has become a mass event in America in the form of rallies and parades for Israel Independence Day. The other, with its historical freight of utter destruction and disaster, has been much harder for large numbers of

*Some groups have urged the celebration of Yom Yerushalayim, commemorating the day in 1967 when Israel and the Jewish people once more gained access to the Wailing Wall, the Temple Mount, and the rest of the Old City of Jerusalem. But this has been much less widely accepted.

Diaspora Jews to observe in any fashion. This may be a result of its intrinsic difficulty, or of the jarring juxtaposition between the lively spring and deadly memories.

So this is a music of theme with variations. Looking at it from the years we live in, with the versions of the holidays we have, this is how the cycle appears:

ROSH HASHANAH

YOM KIPPUR

SUKKOT

SH'MINI ATZERET

SIMCHAT TORAH—The joyful moment when the Torah reading ends and begins, and when we realize that Moses' death leads straight to the Creation of the World.

HANUKKAH—Dark of the moon (the twenty-fifth of Kislev) closest to the dark of the sun (winter solstice). Therefore, the darkest moment of the year—at which we light a growing number of candles to herald the return of light. We commemorate one of the darkest times of Jewish history—when not only was Antiochus, the Hellenistic king, defiling the Temple and insisting on our assimilation, but many Jews had joined the Hellenistic side; and then, at this dark point, the Maccabees turned the tide. We especially focus on the moment when, *after* political and military victory, came a moment of spiritual despair—when it seemed impossible to rededicate the Temple with but one bottle of sacred oil. At that moment, again, the Jews acted—used the oil against all reason—and were redeemed by a miracle. So Hanukkah at every level is about moving from dark despair to sowing seeds of light and hope.

TU B'SHVAT—At the "new year of trees," when the sap begins to rise in the trees of the Land of Israel, the seeds of light sown at Hanukkah show a glimmer of growth. We plant trees and hold a mystical Seder in which we eat four kinds of fruit and drink four kinds of wine, to renew the Tree of Life that sustains all life.

PURIM—The holiday of spring fever. We read in a bawdy, hilarious way the bawdy, hilarious story of Vashti and Esther, Haman and Mordechai. We read how the pompous fool, King Ahasuerus, decides that no woman will ever give him orders—and ends up taking orders from Queen Esther; how Haman decides to wipe out all the Jews—and thereby brings on the wipe-out of his family and his faction. We ridicule their efforts to be tyrants. We wear costumes, get drunk, make carnival—almost as if to get out of our systems the riotous emotions of early spring, in order to address the themes of liberation more profoundly in the Pesach Seder.

PESACH

COUNTING THE OMER—Climbing the 49 steps up from *Mitzrayim* (Egypt, but in Hebrew the root means narrow place or tight spot) to the height of Sinai (Shavuot, on the fiftieth day). During the *omer* we mourn the Holocaust, celebrate Israeli independence, and take a spiritual as well as material picnic for Lag B'Omer.

SHAVUOT

TISHA B'AV—Close to the summer solstice, feeling overwhelmed by the fire of the sun, we remember the burning of the First Temple by the Babylonians and of the second by the Roman legions. We fast so as to let ourselves feel the heat and thirst of the refugee, and we let ourselves feel the exhaustion and dryness that can follow any burst of creativity.

And then we move to Rosh Hashanah. The sun cools down, the breezes help refresh us, we drink to ease the thirst that has dried us since mid-summer. We read of Abraham's renewal from the wellspring of Beersheba, and we take ourselves to a nearby river on Rosh Hashanah afternoon. And so we enter the moon cycle that brings us out on Sh'mini Atzeret—on the verge of winter, ready to move into it more fully. Ready to experience the darkness fully, and to light the lights of Hanukkah. Ready to come full circle.

This is the round of the year, the cycle all life lives through. What do we accomplish by acting out the cycle, using the symbols, telling the stories?

Long ago our people believed that if we celebrated the cycle, the cycle was more likely to continue. The rains would come when they were due, the sun would shine more warmly in its season, the crops would grow—and die, and grow again.

And if we celebrated the cycle, we believed, our deliverance from slavery would come again. The spiral of history would keep on circling upward if we lived through the spirals of our past. Someday the spiral would free us fully—with Messiah.

And the cycle would also help us as individuals. It is intended to help us feel more deeply, more intensely, the cycle of feelings that make us fully human. We learn from these holy days that when it is time to grieve, we are to grieve deeply. When it is time to be angry, we should be furious. If it is time for happiness, we dance with joy.

Jewish tradition does not encourage what is wishy-washy. It does encourage us to know that all these emotions are part of human life—and that specific actions can make them clearer to ourselves. What we sing, what we eat, what we read, what we wear, how we move, what houses we live in—all can be channeled, focused, to clarify the whole range of our feelings. If we are able to feel these feelings deeply enough, we can "use them up." Through walking the path of the year, we can renew in ourselves a sense of deep calm, internal harmony, the peaceful sense of *shalom*.

And there is one reason more to observe the cycle: from the beginning, the Jewish people have celebrated the festivals in order to honor the Unity that underlies all life.

The very interweaving of the themes of history and nature, the human life cycle and moments of spiritual experience—remind us that in some sense all the realms of life are dancing with each other. The circles of the sun, and of the moon; of a single human life between the generations, and an entire people's history of renewal; of every quiet act of newness, birth, creation—all are echoes of One Circle.

Let us then join the circle and begin the dance.

SEASONS OF OUR JOY

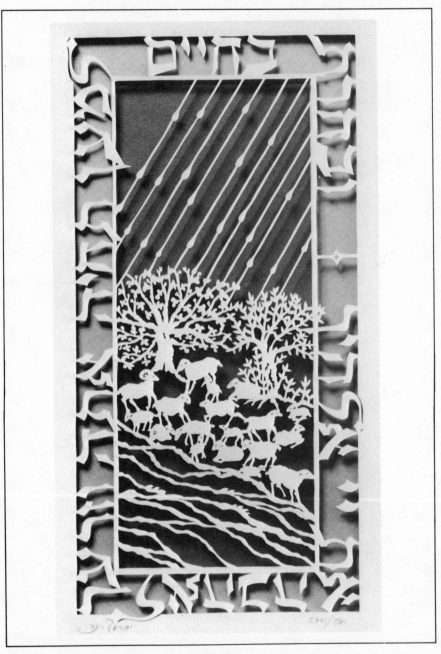

CHAIM

The Shabbos before Rosh Hashanah, in final preparation for the New Year,
we read in the Torah, *"therefore choose life, that both you and your seed may
live: that you may love the Lord your God."* (Deut. 30:19) Life's continuity is
represented by the eighteen sheep.

◄⋙► CHAPTER ONE ⋘►
HEADING UP
THE YEAR—
ROSH HASHANAH

Where does the circle start? When does the year begin?

As with many Jewish questions, there are at least two answers—and both of them are right. The year starts twice.

One beginning is at Rosh Hashanah, which literally means head of the year. But Rosh Hashanah does not occur in what the Bible calls the first month. *That* month is Nisan, the month of spring—the month of Pesach, Passover. That is the month of which God spoke to Moses and Aaron: "This month shall be for you the head of months; it shall be for you the first of the months of the year" (Ex. 18:2). What is more, the spring month of Nisan is when the families of Jewish slaves in Egypt first saw themselves as the united Jewish people. It is the month of the beginning of their freedom, the month when God enters history and reshapes our tangible political and social life. So it is the new year for learning how the Jewish people can reach toward freedom in the world.

And yet for 2,000 years and more, the Jewish people have celebrated the new year half a year after the month of Nisan. Rosh Hashanah comes in the month of Tishri, which the Bible calls the seventh month. It is the month of early fall, of catching our breath after the dry hot winds of summer. Because it is the seventh month, it echoes the seventh day, the Shabbos of rest and contemplation, of catching our breath after six days of hard work.

So perhaps Rosh Hashanah is the new year for renewal. Like Shabbos it is the time to focus our attention on ultimate spiritual truth. This is then the new year for learning how a human being can turn toward God. Perhaps it is the head of the year because the head is raised toward heaven, away from the earth—while Pesach celebrates a more earthy liberation, the freedom of our bodies. Perhaps it is the new year because according to tradition it is the birthday of Adam, the celebration of the beginning of the whole human race—while Pesach celebrates the beginning of the Jewish people.

So the year begins twice—perhaps to teach us that we can never get started with a single, separated part of ourselves, with politics alone or spirit alone, with the Jewish people alone or the universal human being alone, the body alone or the head alone. We need both—always both—to begin.

◆⟩⟩⟩ ORIGINS ⟨⟨⟨◆

Like all the holidays, Rosh Hashanah began with a fairly simple purpose and description in the Bible. From there, the Jewish people developed it, unfolded it, into a many-layered festival for meeting both spiritual and communal needs. The Book of Leviticus proclaims: "In the seventh month, in the first day of the month, there shall be a solemn rest for you, a sacred convocation commemorated with the blast of the ram's horn. You shall not work at any of your ordinary labor, and you shall bring a fire-offering to the Lord" (Lev. 23:23–25). Here the important note seems to be that the seventh month (like the seventh day) is to have sabbatical overtones of solemn rest and ceasing work, with the shofar blast a special calling to this special Shabbos. The overtones are of renewal, not of newness; of refreshing the year, not of beginning it. The phrase "Rosh Hashanah" does not appear.

By the time the Jews had suffered the destruction of the First Temple and had wept and sung their songs in Babylon, the first of Tishri took on a new meaning. The simple thread was woven, twirled, embroidered into a richer fabric of renewal.

After their captivity in Babylon, part of the Jewish people returned to the Land of Israel under the leadership of the politician Nehemiah and the high priest Ezra. It was the first day of the seventh month (about 485 B.C.E.) that Ezra chose as the date on which to convoke the people to hear and understand the Torah, the core of Biblical teaching which many had forgotten. At "the broad space in front of the Water Gate," they gathered to hear the priests and Levites read the scroll and explain the meaning of the more obscure passages. The people began to cry as they realized how far they were from living a life according to the Torah. But Ezra and the Levites told them to celebrate instead, "to eat rich food and drink sweet wine and share with whoever had none." For the day was a holiday, and their rediscovery of Torah should be a joy to them. It was a day to change their lives and turn toward God—but not to mourn their past misdeeds. So the people celebrated "because they had understood the words that were declared to them" (Nehemiah 7–8).

Some scholars believe that deep in the background of this celebration at the Water Gate, this renewal of Israel's knowledge of the covenant with God, stood a Babylonian holiday. Every year, according to this theory, the successful conclusion of the Babylonian harvest was an occasion for pledging renewed obedience to the Babylonian throne. Learning of this custom of the Babylonians either before the Exile or during it, the Jews both borrowed and transformed this coronation—lifted it on high to assert that only God is the true King, and that every year we recognize and celebrate God's power. During the next several centuries—through the great upheavals of Hellenistic rule and Maccabean rebellion, Roman overlordship and the Destruction of the Second Temple, the Bar Kochba rebellion and the decimation of the Jewish population of Palestine—the Jewish community worked out what it meant to enthrone the King of Kings.

By the time the existing practices of the Jewish people were organized and written down in the law-code of the Mishnah (about 200 .C.E.), the rabbis had concluded that if the new moon of Tishri is when God again is crowned the King, then the new moon of Tishri is also when the King passes judgment upon the world, through either renewing life or passing sentence of death on human beings. There are other days of judgment as well: at Passover, the rabbis said, judgment is executed through plenty or scarcity of grain; at Shavuot, through plenty or scarcity of fruit; at Sukkot, through plenty or scarcity of rain. Each of these days of judgment is in some sense the beginning of the year. But the day of judgment for humans came to be understood not as a new year, but the new year: Rosh Hashanah.

Once the rabbis had decided that the first of Tishri was the head of the year, they saw it as the key moment to establish the orderly procession of time and the orderly process of a decent human community. On the one hand, they worked out the rules of evidence for the sighting of a new moon and thus how to decide when a new month begins. On the other hand, they worked out the rules of order in the relationship among all those human beings who must obey God's royal will toward justice. And linking these two—order in God's time and order in our communities—the rabbis heard the call of the ram's horn, the shofar. So the rabbis worked out in careful detail the order of blowing the horn that calls from God to humankind, from humankind to God.

About 300 years after the law-code of the Mishnah had been written down, the rabbis brought together their own commentaries on the Mishnah into what then became known as the Talmud. By that time, the idea of obedience to God the King had been shaped into a powerful metaphor of the decent relationships that human beings owe each other. If all of us are subjects of the one transcendent King, then no earthly king or boss or overseer, no president or premier, can truly rule us. Then each of us owes the others the respect due to an equal—and the redress due to an equal whom we damage. Thus the rabbis wrote, "One is judged on Rosh Hashanah and one's doom is sealed on Yom Kippur . . . Four things cross out the doom of a

person: righteousness expressed through gifts of charity; prayerful supplica-
tion; change of name; and change of conduct."

Three of these actions—righteousness in giving; prayer; and decent
conduct—are mentioned in the Rosh Hashanah prayers themselves, and
have become the keys to our experience of Rosh Hashanah. The Talmud
reminds us that the fourth one, change of name, goes back all the way to
Sarah, foremother of all the Jews, whose name was changed by God. This
method of averting doom was dropped out of the Rosh Hashanah prayers—
perhaps because the rabbis came to feel it was too easy to change one's name
rather than one's life path. Or perhaps they felt it was God's prerogative to
change a person's name—or essence. But a few traditionally minded modern
Jews who see their names as an index to their deepest identities have been
encouraged by this passage to reconsider their names on the occasion of Rosh
Hashanah—and indeed sometimes to rename themselves that day, by asking
to be called up to the Torah by a new name.

For a much larger section of the Jewish community, the Rosh Hashanah
period provides a strong stimulus for undertaking the other three transforma-
tions—remaking their lives, refreshing their charity, and reconnecting with
their spiritual roots.

It is the Talmud that gives the metaphor of the Book of Life to Jewish
tradition: "Three books are opened on Rosh Hashanah: one for the thorough-
ly wicked, one for the thoroughly righteous, and one for those in-between.
The thoroughly righteous are immediately inscribed definitively in the Book
of Life; the thoroughly wicked are immediately inscribed definitively in the
Book of Death; the destiny of those in-between is suspended from Rosh
Hashanah till Yom Kippur. If they do well, they are inscribed in the Book of
Life; if they do not do well, they are inscribed in the Book of Death."

And thus the Talmud makes an unbreakable bridge of the Ten Days
from Rosh Hashanah to Yom Kippur; the *Yamim Nora-im* or Days of Awe, the
Aseret Y'mai Tshuvah or Ten Days of Return and Repentance. The bridge
goes upward toward God and outward toward each other. From the time of
the Talmud on, Jewish communities have celebrated Rosh Hashanah according to the Talmud's pattern. We have addressed our misdeeds, changed our
ways of living, and lifted our eyes to the King. During the intervening
centuries, the service has been enriched by many *piyyutim* (poems), and one
entirely new ceremony, *Tashlich*, has been added on the afternoon of Rosh
Hashanah. (We shall discuss it later.) But the basic mood and intention have
not changed.

◆»» ELUL: MAKING READY «««◆

Rosh Hashanah does not burst in upon us. From ancient tradition, the
entire month of Elul, the month before Tishri, is a time of rethinking, study,

and self-examination leading toward the Rosh Hashanah–Yom Kippur period. Elul became a special time in the ancient Jewish community of Babylonia after the destruction of the Second Temple, during the period of the writing of the Talmud (100–500 C.E.). The custom grew up that during Elul, ordinary Jews—not just the scholars and rabbis—would take time out from their work to join in study groups to read the Bible and rethink their lives. As an explanation for this custom, the Jewish communities looked back to the earliest of all the reconciliations between God and the Jewish people.

Elul is thirty days long, and Yom Kippur is the tenth day of Tishri. So there are forty days from the first day of Elul to Yom Kippur. These forty days became identified with the forty days of repentance Moses spent on Mount Sinai. Moses had come down from Sinai with the Ten Commandments only to find the people worshipping the golden calf. He destroyed the calf and punished the people, and then returned to Sinai to fast and pray for forty days. These ended—presumably on Yom Kippur—with God's act of forgiveness and reconciliation in handing down the second set of tablets with the Ten Commandments. And so Israel's first collective sin was covered over by the first atonement. By identifying this period of Moses' forty days on the mountain with the period before Yom Kippur, the community encouraged itself to spend these forty days as Moses did—in prayerful study and in trying to hear God's word and turn their lives around, so that God could again extend a full forgiveness.

How to mark these forty days? The Jews of Babylonia created two main customs. One was that the shofar would be blown every morning of Elul, except Shabbos and the last day of the month. This horn blast was a spiritual alarm in itself, reminding people to bestir their souls. It was also a way of pointing toward the shofar-blowing on Rosh Hashanah.

On Shabbos it was omitted for reasons on two levels: first, it was feared that the desire to blow the shofar would be so intense, so consuming, that people would forget or ignore the prohibition against carrying an object from a private to a public domain during Shabbos and would carry the shofar from home to shul; secondly, translating this legal caution into its spiritual analogue, blowing the shofar, even on Rosh Hashanah itself, was felt to be the kind of disturbance of the order of the universe that ought not to be done on the contemplative day of Shabbos. And the last day of Elul was omitted to leave a space between the reminder and the reality.

The second custom was that at every service during Elul, Psalm 27 would be read. It is a plea to God for help when we are beset by enemies around us. But reading it before and after Rosh Hashanah, we may well understand it as a plea for help in dealing with the enemies within us— enemies of our own true selves who seek to frighten or seduce us away from our own true paths:

FOR DAVID:

The Lord is my light and my salvation; whom shall I fear?
The Lord is the stronghold of my life; of whom shall I be terrified?
In my very guts came evil to gnaw and consume me,
But these my troubles, my enemies, stumbled and fell.

Though an army encamp against me, my heart will not fear;
Though war rise up against me, even then I will keep faith.

One thing only have I asked the Lord; one thing only will I seek—
That I may dwell in the house of the Lord all the days of my life,
To see the Lord's pleasantness and to visit in His temple.

For He hides me in His sukkah on the day of evil,
He conceals me in the concealment of His tent.
He lifts me up upon a rock.
And now my head will be uplifted—above my enemies all around about
    me,
And in His tent I will offer offerings with a shofar-blast;
I will sing and chant praise to the Lord.

Hear my voice, O Lord, when I call!
Give me grace and answer me!

It was on Your behalf that my heart said, "Seek My face!"
It is Your face, O Lord, that I will seek.
Do not conceal Your face from me,
Do not, in your anger set Your servant aside.
You have been my help before;
Do not now cast me off—do not desert me!—
O God of my salvation.

Even if my father and mother desert me,
The Lord will gather me together.
Teach me your path, O Lord;
And lead me on a smooth and well-kept road—
Because there are those who lie in ambush for me.
Do not hand me over to the will of my adversaries,
For lying witnesses have arisen against me—whose every breath does
    violence.

If I had not kept trusting that I would see the Lord's goodness,
While I was still in the land of the living! . . .
Wait for the Lord;
Be strong, and let your heart take courage;
Wait for the Lord.

The passage that begins "One thing only" has become, in Hebrew, a song to a tune that catches the spirit of Elul:

Achat sha-alti mey-eyt Adonai o-tah ah-va-keysh
Shivti b'veyt Adonai kol y'mei chayai
Lachazot b'no-am, b'no-am Adonai u'l'vakeyr b'haychalo

As Elul draws toward its close, we take the final steps in preparing for Rosh Hashanah. Beginning on the Sunday before Rosh Hashanah (or if Rosh Hashanah begins on Monday or Tuesday, on the second Sunday before the holiday), special prayers for forgiveness—Slichot—are recited for the morning service. Since according to tradition the heavens are most open to prayer at midnight, the custom has arisen to gather at midnight on the Saturday night before Rosh Hashanah, to begin this period of Slichot, which then pauses for Rosh Hashanah and continues in the week between Rosh Hashanah and Yom Kippur.

The Slichot service is built upon an ancient invocation of God's grace and a recitation of the thirteen merciful attributes that God revealed (Ex. 33:21–34:7) in the cleft of the rock to Moses—both of these specified as early as the Talmud—and the chanting of a number of psalms and prayerful poems (piyyutim) composed through the course of Jewish history.

The invocation reminds God (and ourselves) of God's past acts of loving-kindness in response to human prayer and need:

The One Who answered Abraham on Mount Moriah—He will answer us,
The One Who answered his son Isaac, bound upon the altar—He will answer us.
The One Who answered Jacob, at Beth El—
The One Who answered Joseph, bound in prison—
The One Who answered our forebears at the Sea of Reeds—
The One Who answered Moses when Sinai rose up like a sword—
The One Who answered Aaron when he brought sin-offering—
The One Who answered Pinchas in the midst of the congregation—
The One Who answered Joshua at Gilgal—
The One Who answered Samuel at Mitzpah—
The One Who answered David and Solomon in Jerusalem—
The One Who answered Elijah on Mount Carmel—
The One Who answered Elisha at Jericho—
The One Who answered Jonah in the belly of the fish—
The One Who answered Hezekiah in his sickness—
The One Who answered Hananiah, Mishael, and Azariah in the fiery furnace—
The One Who answered Daniel in the lions' den—

The One Who answered Mordechai and Esther in Shushan—
The One Who answered Ezra in the Exile—
The One Who answered all the righteous and the merciful, the whole-
hearted and the upright—He will answer us.

The congregation calls back to God the Merciful Name that God called
out to Moses:

Adonai, Adonai, el rachum v'chanun, erech apayim v'rav chesed
v'emet, notzayr chesed l'alafim, nosey avon vafeshah v'chatah-ah
v'nakey.

The Lord, the Lord, God of motherly compassion Who offers grace and
is slow to anger, Who is full of loving-kindness and trustworthiness,
Who assures love for a thousand generations, Who forgives iniquity,
transgression, and misdeed, and Who grants pardon.

And the congregation reminds God of His response when Moses begged,
"Forgive—please! the people for their sin" . . . And the Lord said, "I have
forgiven—in accordance with your plea" (Num. 14:19–20).

The tone of the whole service is set in Psalm 130: "Out of the depths I
call to You; O Lord, hear my cry, heed my plea . . . Who could endure it, O
Lord, if you kept count of every sin? But forgiveness is Yours; therefore we
revere You."

In this way, throughout the *Slichot* period, the congregation recognizes
that the root of all reconciliation is in the Root of Being. But the tradition
teaches that remorse toward God can bring forgiveness only for those hurts
that we have done toward God alone. Wherever we have hurt another
human being, we must try to make some redress for the harm we have done.
And we must seek forgiveness from the people we have hurt. So among many
chavurot and an increasing number of synagogues, the first midnight of *Slichot*
has become a time for friends, neighbors, and members of the community to
come together to face what harms they have done to each other, to apologize
and try to make redress for those hurts, and to seek each others' forgiveness.
Some congregations have prayed and sung together, and then sat in serious
silence while they collected their thoughts about their misdeeds and quietly
sought each other out. Then they have tried to straighten out in private
conversation what had gone wrong between them in the previous year.

Finally, it is during Elul—and especially the day before Rosh Hashanah—that many Jews visit family graves and give *tzedakah* (righteousness
toward those in need—therefore, contributions to charity). Thus by remembering the dead and facing death, the community acknowledges the
death of its old self so that a new self can be born; makes more intense its
experience of the sweetness of life; and renews its commitment to bring even
the dead into the bond of life—through memory.

THE ROSH HASHANAH SERVICES

Rosh Hashanah comes on the first two days of Tishri, the month connected with the fall equinox. It may fall in the Western months of September or early October. The calendar is so arranged that the first day of Rosh Hashanah is never allowed to fall on a Sunday, Wednesday, or Friday. This is done so that Yom Kippur, ten days later, will never come on a Friday or Sunday—that is, immediately before or immediately after Shabbos. Many Reform Jews celebrate Rosh Hashanah for one day only, the first day of Tishri. In Israel, however, it is the only holiday that Israeli Jews celebrate for two days. *

Rosh Hashanah, like all Jewish days and thus all holy days, begins at sunset. So at dusk of the first evening of the festival, the families and friendship groups of the community gather in their homes, in an atmosphere of joyful awe and expectation, to light the candles that begin each festival and to say *Sheh-hechianu,* the blessing that is always recited when we do something new or something we have not done for a long time, praising God for filling us with life to bring us to this moment of renewal:

Baruch atah Adonai elohenu melech ha-olam asher kid'shanu b'mitz-votav vitzivanu l'hadlik ner shel yomtov . . . Baruch attah Adonai elohenu melech ha-olam sheh-hechianu v'ki-imanu v'higianu lazman hazeh.

Blessed be You, Lord Our God, Ruler of all space-time, who made us holy by your commandments and commanded us to light a candle for the holy day. Blessed be You, Lord Our God, Ruler of all space-time, who has given us life, has lifted us up, and has brought us to this season.

And then, in their millions, the many different kinds of Jews go trooping off to their many different versions of the House of Prayer. To cathedral-like synagogues with formally dressed Western men and women going together to their pews. To storefront *shtiebels* of Chassidim with furry *shtreimels* on their heads, nodding goodbye as their wives climb up to rickety balconies. To Sephardic mosque-like buildings colored in pastels and scattered up and down the hills of S'fad in Israel. To living rooms in rented houses and apartments where intimate participatory congregations or *chavurot,* fellowships as they call themselves, encourage women and men to take off their shoes, find a cushion on the floor, and even to watch a baby crawl between the prayerbooks.

So the myriads of Jews—most of them dressed in some specially fine or

---

*For a discussion of the reasons for celebration of one day or two days of holiday by different Jews, see Appendix I.

joyful clothing, some of them in white for Rosh Hashanah, flock to their prayers, come to see the Torah and the Holy Ark themselves draped in white covers that will stay till Yom Kippur. "Though your sins be as scarlet, they shall be as white as snow."

And in all these Houses of Prayer, there is some version of the *Machzor*, a special prayerbook for the festivals and especially for Rosh Hashanah and Yom Kippur. Where the ordinary daily prayerbook is called a *Siddur*, an order of service, *Machzor* means cycle. Today the Jews are concerned not with what is ordinary but with what is extraordinary, with the first curve of the year that will curve from festival to festival through differences—and only after a year's time will bring them back around the cycle to where they began.

And so they begin the first service of the holy day—the evening service. It is fairly brief, not much different from the regular evening service except that the melody of the Hebrew chanting is extraordinary—filled with awe, celebration, and triumph. In a number of the prayers, praise of the holy God is replaced by praise of the holy King. There is a Royal musical motif:

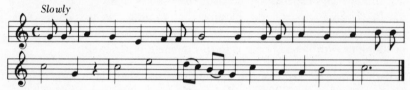

The Rosh Hashanah liturgy varies in several other ways from the regular evening service. Just after the prayer *Hashkiveynu*, Lay us down in peace, the congregation proclaims: "Tiku bachodesh shofar bakeseh l'yom chageynu; ki chok l'yisrael hu, mishpat l'eylohai yaakov. Sound the shofar on the new moon, at the time appointed for our feast day; for it is a statute for Israel, a judgment for the God of Jacob." Then in the *amidah* (the standing, murmured prayer), we add the paragraph that greets all the festivals with a plea for God to remember our past efforts and our future hopes, our holy city Jerusalem and our whole widespread people, so as to stir in us and toward us new life, loving-kindness and fulfillment—even Messianic fulfillment. On this particular festival, our plea for remembrance is underlined by our naming the day *Yom Hazikkaron*, the Day of Remembrance. We add to several of the *amidah* prayers the reminder that God should remember to write us into the Book of Life: "Zachreynu l'chaim melech chafeytz bachaim; v'chatveynu basefer hachaim l'ma-ancha elohim chaim. Remember us for life, O King who delights in life. Write us in the Book of Life—for your own sake, God of life."

And in the *amidah* we meet for the first time a refrain that will recur throughout Rosh Hashanah and Yom Kippur: the three paragraphs "Uv'chen, And therefore," which ask God's help in evoking from us a response to Rosh Hashanah that is three-fold—universally human, communally Jewish, and individually personal:

And therefore, Lord our God, cause all that You created to remember fully all that You have done; cause all Your creatures to revere Your doings and to tremble in Your presence; cause them all to act as one to do Your will wholeheartedly. For we know, Lord our God, that the strength of Your hand, the power of Your right arm, and the awesomeness of Your Name rule over all creation.

And therefore, Lord, give honor to Your people, praise to those who revere You, hope to those who seek You, confidence to those who await You, joy to Your land and gladness to Your city, triumph to the horn of David Your servant and light to the lamp of Messiah, child of Jesse—speedily and in our own day.

And, therefore, the righteous will see and be glad, the upright rejoice, and the faithfully loving celebrate in song while evil is silenced and all wickedness vanishes like smoke—for You will erase the tyranny of arrogance from the earth.

These three paragraphs were written by Rabbi Yochanan ben Nuri during the worst Roman repression of the Jewish people and of Torah. The tyranny of arrogance whose removal from the earth they prophesy was indeed the Roman Empire. But in a broader sense, the prayer rejects the false unity that could be imposed upon the human race by any tyranny, and celebrates instead the unity of a free humankind in which every people and each person is ready to follow only God as King.

With these special Rosh Hashanah interpolations, especially those invoking a Royal God, the evening service leads us through the front door of a royal palace that is built of ceremony and prayer, approaching closer and closer to the Royal Throne. As soon as the service is over, the congregation pauses in its progress toward the Throne room; pauses to celebrate the Coronation in more earthy fashion, with some food and drink. The congregants make the festival *kiddush* over wine, followed by *Sheh-hechianu*, the blessing "Who has given us life," in order again to honor the newness of the year. They dip slices of bread from a round challah into honey and recite the blessings over bread. They dip a slice of apple into honey, recite the blessing over fruit, and add: "Y'hi ratzon milfanechah Adonai elohenu v'elohai avotenu (*or* horenu) shet-chadesh alenu shanah tovah oomtukah. May it be Your will, our God and God of our fathers (*or* forebears), to renew for us a good, sweet year." The round challah and the round apple represent the roundness and fullness of the year—or perhaps the Crown of God the King. (Or perhaps the roundness of the year and the roundness of the Crown are the same thing. Perhaps God's very Crown is the cycle of the year.)

Then people go home to have Rosh Hashanah dinner in families or small groups. Many of them invite guests to join them, so as to fulfill anew what our people did in the days of Ezra, 2,500 years ago, on the first Rosh

Hashanah that we have a description of: "Eat rich food and drink sweet wine, and share with whoever has none." (Some special Rosh Hashanah recipes are given at the end of this chapter.)

As the community gathers again in the morning at synagogue and *shtiebel, chavurah* and temple, we are face to face with solemn joy. A strange and special mood that is at once profound and exalted, deep and high, takes over. As the service begins, the sense of expectancy grows. Suddenly there is a triumphant shout of *Hamelech!*—"O King!" and *Avinu Malkenu,* "Our Parent, Our King," becomes a vigorous imploring prayer: "Our Parent, Our King, reach out to us with grace even though we have not done enough to deserve grace; act toward us with gentle righteousness and with loving-kindness—so as to save us."

> Avinu malkenu choneinu va-aneinu, ki ein banu ma:asim.
> Asei imanu tzedakah vachesed. Asei imanu tzedakah vachesed, v'hoshi-einu.

The sense of sorrow, fear, and awe become mixed with joy. Even as we face our own transgressions, we can feel joy; joy in knowing there is a Judge who cares about transgressions, a Justice to which we are responsible in the first place. And joy in knowing that the Judge is full of motherly and fatherly compassion. What would our world be like if there were no justice in it? And what would our world be like if there were *only* strict justice in it, no forebearance, mercy, or compassion?

BIBLE READINGS

On every Rosh Hashanah morning in every House of Prayer, there comes a moment to pause from calling out to God, and hear some of God's most troubling words to us—by reading Torah. In every House of Prayer the reading is the same, though the ways of reading and understanding it are different. In some, the rabbi will expound upon the reading in a sermon. In some, the chant of reading is itself enough. In some *chavurot* the community may break up for half an hour or so into clusters of three or four people, who talk about how the readings can be understood and their teachings applied in daily life.

Whichever form of Torah-reading a particular congregation uses, it will have to deal with two hard stories. In the first day's reading, Abraham sends his son Ishmael out of the family into the desert, almost to die; in the second day's reading, Abraham carries off his other son, Isaac, almost to kill him. (Reform congregations, since they celebrate only one day of Rosh Hashanah, have chosen the Isaac story as the Torah reading.) These stories begin at the intimate level of the family, but raise the most basic issues of the universe.

Let us hear them first as family tales. Abraham's first wife Sarah has been barren till she conceived in her old age. His second wife, Hagar, has already borne him a son named Ishmael. And now the Rosh Hashanah readings begin . . .

On the first day, the Torah reading is Genesis 21. Isaac, whose name means Laughing Boy, is born to the tune of Abraham's and Sarah's joyful laughter. But the displaced son Ishmael upsets Sarah by mockingly laughing at Isaac, so Sarah demands that Hagar and Ishmael be sent away, and God tells Abraham to agree. Hagar and Ishmael are expelled into the desert at Beersheba, and cry out to God when they are about to die of thirst. God hears them and reveals a well that saves their lives. Abraham and a neighboring king fall into conflict over possession of some wells and finally settle it by assigning Abraham a well at Beersheba. The readings also include Numbers 29:1–6 (the description of what special sacrifices to offer at the Temple on Rosh Hashanah) and I Samuel 1:1–2:10 (the birth of the Prophet Samuel).

On the second day of Rosh Hashanah, the Biblical readings begin with Genesis 22, in which God calls upon Abraham to sacrifice the very son Isaac for whose sake he has sent Ishmael and Hagar away. Abraham prepares to do so and has reached the point of binding Isaac and raising the knife when God intervenes to stop him and rescue Isaac. Abraham then sacrifices a ram as a substitute for Isaac. (According to a tradition of the ancient rabbis, one horn of this ram became the shofar God blew at Mount Sinai to introduce the giving of the Ten Commandments, and the other horn will be used to announce the coming of Messiah.) The other Bible readings for the second day are the passage from Numbers that describes the Rosh Hashanah sacrifice, and Jeremiah 31:1–20, which tells how the people of Israel will be saved from disaster and exile, like a suffering child saved by his mother's tears.

These are not abstract statements of theology and theory, these tales. They are heart-rending, painful stories of a family—stories that tear at the hearts of children and of grown-ups who remember being children, tear at the hearts of husbands and wives, mothers and fathers, and of all who imagine that they may be. Thousands of powerful sermons have over thousands of years, in thousands of Jewish communities and congregations, been preached upon them. Hundreds of congregations have grappled with them. Some have even tried to enter the stories not only in their minds but also in their bodies. In one such effort, pairs of congregants acted out the roles—one of Abraham raising the knife, the other of Isaac watching it flash above him. The congregants flinched, shuddered, and then tried to share their feelings. Another *chavurah* passed out dozens of small mirrors and asked everyone to puff a breath onto the mirror till it turned cloudy—then watch the mirror clear and the faces return, puff again and watch themselves become distorted. Was that what Ishmael did to Isaac—reflect his identity in a clouded mirror?

These two sets of readings are rich with associations for Rosh Hashanah. One is that together they tell the story of the birth, binding, and redemption of Isaac—the prototype of Jewish suffering and readiness to die for the sake of

God. "For the sake of Isaac's suffering, forgive our misdeeds!" say the Rosh Hashanah prayers.

But the rabbis who chose what passages to read on Rosh Hashanah did not need to include the story of Ishmael. That they did may suggest to us another theme: that Abraham was ready to obey God's command to send both his sons to death—and only God's intervention at the last moment saved them. Since the Rosh Hashanah season is concerned with *tshuvah*, repenting and turning our lives back to the path of decency, we may wonder whether these two stories are about God's *tshuvah* in regard to Ishmael and Isaac. Ten days later we will read how God turned back from the brink of destroying the city of Nineveh when Nineveh turned away from its corruption; but in these Rosh Hashanah readings, the question of God's change of mind is even more profound because Ishmael and Isaac are not described as seriously corrupt.

The stories raise so many questions about the nature of good and evil, power and love, stubbornness and change, that any celebration of Rosh Hashanah would gain from reading the stories aloud and examining these questions:

· Did Ishmael have to leave because in laughing at Laughing Boy he became too much *like* Isaac—imitating and clouding his very identity so that for each of them to grow up on his own they had to grow up separate?

· According to tradition Ishmael was the forebear of the Arab peoples and Isaac of the Jews. What does this teach us about the identities of the Arabs and the Jews? Of other peoples, of siblings, of every human being within his/her own self?

· Does the older brother, the more powerful partner, have to be defeated if the younger, the weaker, is to become free? How can there be a reconciliation later?

· Why did Abraham accept in silence the command to sacrifice Isaac? Because he felt utter faith in God, was ready to give up all he owned and believed for the sake of his relationship with God? Or because he decided to test once and for all whether this God that he had followed was a murderer or not? Or because the command accorded with his own deep desire to kill Isaac? Was Abraham a virtuoso of faith, or was he walking the knife-edge of despair?

· What does it mean that Hagar, the banished wife, has a much fuller relationship with God than Sarah does? Can we pierce the veil upon the text to learn the histories, the feelings, the teachings of these women in these stories?

· Why is Abraham in conflict with his neighbors over water until Ishmael and Hagar are sent their well of water? Why are both their well and Abraham's well in Beersheba?

In connection with these two readings from the Five Books of Moses, the rabbis assigned two readings from the Prophets. One of them (I Samuel

1–2:10) parallels the story of the birth of Isaac with the story of the birth of the prophet Samuel. It describes the poignant prayer of the barren Hannah that she become pregnant, and her joyful prayer when Samuel is born. In that prayer and in Hannah's willingness to offer Samuel to God's special service in the Sanctuary, the Prophetic passage may be seen as providing an answer to the dilemma of the sacrifice of Isaac: how can I make an offering to God, even of my son, without killing him? On the second day, the Prophetic reading (Jeremiah 31:1–20) places God in the situation of a loving parent trying to correct and restore a beloved wayward child—the people Israel. With the help of Mother Rachel, God comes to understand the need of reconciliation between the parent and the child. Thus both passages teach about the process of a change of heart, on earth as well as Heaven.

After we return the Torah to the Ark, as morning wanes and we are about to shift from the end of the regular morning service into the *musaf* or additional service, two members of the congregation come forward to carry out the Biblical command of blowing the ram's horn. One of them will call out the notes in a low tone, to free the other—who will actually blow the shofar—from dividing his/her attention between the horn and the prayer-book. The caller may well cover his/her head with a prayer shawl in order to concentrate his own attention, and then calls the three names of the three different tones that evoke a cry of alarm, a wail of sorrow, and the sobs of contrition. (If the first day of Rosh Hashanah falls on a Shabbos, we wait till the second day to blow the shofar.) As we move from awe toward joy, three special sections are added to the murmured standing prayer that is at the heart of the regular service. These are about Kingship, Remembrance, and Shofar notes. They represent God's power in the present, past, and future:

The power God gives us to make fresh every living present moment;
The power God gives us to remember, sorrow over, and forgive
 ourselves and others the mistakes we have made in the past;
And the power God gives us to imagine and transform the future.

For each of these sections, ten verses from different parts of the Bible are read out—three from the Five Books of Moses, three from the Prophets, three from the Holy Writings, and one from the Five Books again. Thus for Kingship, for Remembrance, and for Shofar notes, a *minyan* of verses comes together, as if this quorum is necessary for the three aspects of God's power to be present. And for each of these three the shofar is sounded.

THE SHOFAR

The soundings of the shofar fulfill the special command of the Torah to make the new moon of Tishri into a day of sounding the horn. The shofar is, indeed, the special symbol of Rosh Hashanah.

It is blown in three separate ways:

Tekiah, one long blast of alarm.
Shevarim, three medium blasts like wailing—so the length of one whole
   shevarim is the same as the length of one whole *tekiah.*
Teruah, nine short blasts like broken sobs—altogether, the length of
   shevarim.

The sound of the shofar is so wild, so eerie, so untuned, that over the
millennia it has inspired hundreds of explanations. Here are several that may
lead our ears and minds in various directions:

· The three equal but different sounds may be seen as the surfaces of a
mystical cube in time rather than space. Since the Holy of Holies in the
ancient Temple in Jerusalem was a cube, perhaps the shofar sounds are a
translation of it into the medium of time.

· A ninth-century Babylonian teacher, Saadia Gaon, taught that there
were ten reasons that the Holy One commanded us to blow the shofar on
Rosh Hashanah:

1) Just as earthly kings have horns and trumpets blown to celebrate the
anniversary of their coronation, so God wants the shofar blown on the
anniversary of the Creation—when there came to be a world that God could
rule over.

2) Just as earthly kings have horns and trumpets blown to announce
their decrees—and only after this warning actually enforce the decree—so
God wants the shofar blown to announce the beginning of the Ten Days of
Return, when all are commanded to turn their lives around.

3) Just as the shofar blew when God gave the Torah at Mount Sinai, so
it blows to remind us each year to do as our forebears said at Sinai: "We will
act and we will hearken."

4) Just as Ezekiel compared the words of the Prophets, calling for the
people to change their ways, to a shofar—so we must know that those who
hear the shofar and do not take warning and change their lives will be
responsible for their own destruction.

5) Because the shofar was blown as a war-alarm when the Temple was
destroyed, it should remind us of the destruction of the Temple—the disaster
that we brought upon ourselves—and thus should warn us to abandon our
misdeeds in order to avert disaster.

6) Because God used a ram as a substitute sacrifice for Isaac, the ram's
horn should remind us how Isaac and Abraham were prepared to give up all
their hopes and dreams for God's sake.

7) Since the blowing of a horn causes cities to tremble, so the shofar
will make us tremble and fear our Creator.

8) Since the shofar will be blown on the great day of judgment, blowing
it now reminds us that every day is a day of judgment.

9) Since the shofar will be blown when the tempest-tossed of the Jewish people are gathered in harmony to the Land of Israel, we should hear the shofar to stir our longings for that day.

10) Since the shofar will be blown when Messiah revives the dead, we hear the shofar in order to revive our faith in that supernal transformation, the final victory of life and freedom over death, the ultimate oppressor.

· Along with Saadia's teaching, based on a deep knowledge of tradition, there is another that teaches an emotional truth beyond tradition: Once the great Chassidic rebbe, the Baal Shem Tov, instructed a shofar blower in the mystical meanings of the shofar blasts. But the blower forgot them on Rosh Hashanah and broke down in tears. The Baal Shem Tov told him that the mystical meanings were like keys to the many doors of Heaven. But if the keys are lost, all the doors can be broken open by an axe. And so the heart-broken burst of tears can break down all the barriers between ourselves and God. The shofar's untuned wail, its sobbing, is that burst of human tears.

· When the caller stands beside the shofar blower on Rosh Hashanah and in a low voice calls out the notes the blower is to sound, it is easy to hear the human voice say "Tekiah—Alarm note!" and to hear the reply of shofar blast as the eerie voice of God. Coming not from a man-made silver trumpet, but from the unplanned twists and turns of the ram's horn. Sounding not a tuneful melody, but the unmusical outburst of alarm and grief from Heaven. If we cry out, the Holy One will answer; but the answer is a crying-out toward us.

And the outcry comes full circle. As the Machzor says, "The great shofar is sounded—and a still small voice is heard." Ours. And God's. For an instant fused into a single silence.

MUSAF

In many congregations, the musaf or additional service on Rosh Hashanah and Yom Kippur begins with an extraordinary personal prayer called "Hineni, Here I am"—the answer that Abraham gives when summoned by God and that Isaac gives when summoned by Abraham. The prayer was composed by an unknown East European cantor, who as he began to chant aloud the repetition of the amidah paused to plead in moving tones and language that God overlook his own failings of conduct and of voice, of memory, and of devotion—and respond with forgiveness to the needs and failings of the whole congregation. "Blessed are You, Who hears prayer," the cantor ends, with a simplicity that goes beyond the usual laudatory names applied to God. And thus the cantor—who is presumed to be as nearly unblemished in ethical and ritual sensitivity as anyone could be, the better to be a channel for the congregation's highest yearnings—becomes in this very imperfection a representative of the imperfect congregation, and in this very pleading, a representative of their own hopes.

As the congregation moves deeper into the *amidah*, the imagery of the Books of Life and Death becomes overwhelming in the *Un'taneh tokef*: *On Rosh Hashanah it is written and on Yom Kippur it is sealed:*

> How many shall be crossed out
> And how many shall be created;
> Who shall live and who shall die. . .
> Who by fire and who by water,
> Who by sword and who by beast. . .
> Who shall be rested in his home (yanu-ach) and
> Who shall be wrested from his home (yanu-ah). . .

BUT REPENTANCE, PRAYER, AND ACTS OF GENTLE RIGH-TEOUSNESS CAN CROSS OUT THE SEVERITY OF THE DE-CREE.

B'Rosh Hashanah yika-teyvun
U'v yom Tzom Kippur yey-cha-teymun
Kama ya-avurun v'Kama yibarey-un
Mi yichiyeh u'mi yamut . . .
U'tshuvah u'tfilah u'tzedakah
Ma-avirin et ro-a hag'zerah.

And as the chanting continues, poem after poem celebrates the King Whose triumph will someday encompass all the earth:

> All the world shall serve You, and praise Your glorious name
> And Your righteousness triumphant all humankind acclaim
> And all their congregations so loud Your praise shall sing
> That the uttermost peoples, hearing, shall hail You crowned King.

In the Rosh Hashanah *amidah*, we recite one of the most well-known prayers of the daily service, *Alenu*. Indeed, Rosh Hashanah is the time for which it was originally created. It was intended by one of the great rabbis of the Talmud, Rav, to introduce the Kingship section of the Rosh Hashanah *amidah*. That is why the *Alenu* refers again and again to God as triumphant ruler, to Whom we owe our loyalty beyond all earthly kings and institutions. Indeed, on Rosh Hashanah, as the congregation says, "To You we bend the knee," the leader—and in some synagogues and *chavurot*, the whole con-gregation—actually kneels and bows their heads toward the ground. This act—in a community which otherwise never kneels, proudly asserting that its devotion to the God of freedom is too deep to permit servility toward Him—is a powerful way to embody the Rosh Hashanah theme of God's Kingship.

Uniting the sense of Coronation with the sense of Creation—for the Ruler of all space-time becomes King at the moment the kingdom comes into being—the *amidah* continues, "Hayom harat olam. Today the world was conceived, today there stand in judgment all the creatures of the universe." Thus the service echoes the traditional assertion that the human race—the original Adam—was created on the first of Tishri, so that Rosh Hashanah is the day of God's Kingship because it is the day on which the Image of God was first stamped upon the coins of the realm: the varied human beings. And so, the *Machzor* points out:

> Hayom ta-amtzeynu . . . Today You strengthen us.
> Hayom t'varcheynu . . . Today You bless us.
> Hayom t'gadleynu . . . Today You magnify us.

And so the *musaf* service draws to a close, repeating the *Alenu*. The community retreats home to rest and eat, so as to return late in the afternoon for *Tashlich*.

TASHLICH

The theme of water that appears in the Bible readings for the first morning of Rosh Hashanah is strengthened through action later in the day. For centuries, traditional Jews have gone that afternoon to the nearest body of free-flowing water—a river, lake, or ocean. (If the first day of Rosh Hashanah is a Shabbos, the ceremony is postponed till the next day.) There they have recited several Psalms and a line from the prophet Micah: "And You will cast all their sins into the depths of the sea." And they have shaken out their pockets of lint and bread crumbs, symbolically shaking loose their sins of the past year so that they could be swept downstream—"into the depths of the sea." Since the word for "You will cast" in Hebrew is *tashlich*, the ceremony has become known as *Tashlich*.

Among some Jewish communities, there have been special versions of *Tashlich*. Kurdish Jews actually leaped into the water and swam like fish to cleanse themselves of sin. Chassidim in Galicia sent little floats of straw out upon the water, set them afire with candles, and rejoiced that their sins were either burned up or washed away. In Jerusalem, where even brooks are hard to find, *Tashlich* is done at a well.

Tashlich began after the Talmudic period. Indeed, no direct mention of it has been found in any manuscript until a thousand years later. Scholars think it took root first among the Jews of Europe in about the thirteenth century, and spread among Sephardic and Oriental Jews in the sixteenth century through the influence of the Kabbalists who lived in the mystical town of Safed in Northern Palestine.

It spread despite the opposition of the rabbis. They feared that Jews who took part would rely on the magical powers of emptying their pockets to achieve the clearing of their sins—instead of changing their conduct, turning their lives around, and returning to God's path. But *amcha*, the ordinary people of the Jewish community, insisted on continuing.

The rabbis tried to instill ethical content in the ceremony. One of them connected it with the story of the Binding of Isaac through a legend that Satan tried to deter Abraham by appearing as a rushing river in his path—and so we celebrate Abraham's determination by seeking out a river. Others suggested that the ceremony used water so that fish could be its witnesses—since the eyes of fish never close, symbolizing the unblinking eye of God reviewing our behavior. But despite these explanations, the rabbis preserved their distaste—so much so that many editions of the *Machzor* do not include a *Tashlich* service.

Why have the people insisted on preserving *Tashlich* despite rabbinical disapproval? It may be simply that it felt like a pleasant outdoor break from the solemnity of Rosh Hashanah—especially on the afternoon of the first day, moving toward a second full day of prayer and penitence, inside the synagoguge. Children find *Tashlich* especially delightful, and parents may be relieved to offer them a refreshing respite to run and jump in the open air, to clamber on the rocks along a river, to empty out their pockets above the rushing stream.

Or there may also be a reason that, despite the rabbis, is rooted in the most profound meanings of Rosh Hashanah. In the passage about Ishmael that we read on the morning of the first day, we see that Hagar, in thirst and despair, having used up the bottle of water that Abraham gave her, *casts* her son Ishmael beneath a bush so that she will not have to see him die: *"Vatashlaych et-hayeled."* It is her act of *tashlich* that brings God to show her a well of water.

Yet surely Hagar does not want to get rid of Ishmael. She wants him to live. It is her casting him that brings them both to the life-giving water, that transforms him from dying to living, transforms him from her burden to her fruitful offspring. Perhaps the passage is telling us that when we do *Tashlich* at the water's edge we are not trying to get rid of our misdeeds but to transform them. We are trying to seek out and renew the life-giving energy that is concealed within a sin, and turn it into an energy for good. We are trying to give that energy new life, so that it can give new life to us.

Such a view of *Tashlich* is borne out by the fact that on the culminating day of the Ten Days of Turning—on Yom Kippur—we read both the passage of *Tashlich* from the prophet Micah—"You will cast all their sins into the depths of the sea"—and from the Book of Jonah, where this line appears as Jonah cries out to God from the belly of the great fish: "You cast me (*vatashlichayni*) into the depths, into the heart of the sea." Here again God did not intend to get rid of Jonah, but to transform him. Here again the water gives life—transforms and renews.

That the Ten Days are bracketed by these versions of *Tashlich*—in word and ceremony—may provide us with an approach to the refreshing well of water that Hagar and Abraham experienced. After the dry and thirsty summer, after the spiritual thirst of remembering on Tisha B'Av the destruction of the Temple and the brokenness of the world, we drink on Rosh Hashanah from the Well of our salvation—and we renew ourselves, turning even the death-energy of our sins toward life.

SECOND DAY

After *Tashlich* we repeat the evening service, now for the second day of Rosh Hashanah—and then return to light the festival candles and to share again a pleasant meal. Over the centuries, many celebrants have wanted to say the *Sheh-hechianu* blessing once again on the second night, but have felt constrained—since that blessing is reserved for new experiences, and to greet the new year all over again does not seem quite new. So the custom arose of eating a fruit we have not had for months, or wearing new clothes we have saved for the second night. Then *Sheh-hechianu* becomes proper for their newness. The second day of Rosh Hashanah proceeds much like the first— with changes in some of the poems inserted in the liturgy and with *Tashlich* omitted.

GREETINGS

Most of the festivals have their own special greetings. As befits the festival in which we greet a new year, there is a special sense of wanting to greet our friends when Rosh Hashanah comes. Long ago those who wrote letters during Elul (or during the days between Rosh Hashanah and Yom Kippur) would be sure to add: "L'shanah tovah tikkateyvu v'tichatemu. May you be written and sealed for a good year." More recently, greeting cards have been printed with that message or one similar, and still more recently some Jews have taken to drawing or painting their own colorful Rosh Hashanah greetings for their friends.

In face to face meetings, many simply say in Yiddish: "Goot yuntoff, goot yohr! Have a good holiday, have a good year," or in Hebrew, "Shanah tovah! Good year!" There is a delicate distinction to be preserved regarding whether one wishes that another be written or sealed for a good year. The Talmud says that on Rosh Hashanah itself those who are wholly good are at once written into the Book of Life, and those who are wholly bad are at once written off as dead. Only for those in-between is the decision delayed until Yom Kippur. So once Rosh Hashanah is past, to wish that one's friends be written into the Book of Life is to express our doubts about their status. If we wish to avoid this, from the end of Rosh Hashanah until Yom Kippur we can wish our friends that the Holy One *seal* them for a good year—that on Yom

Kippur God will affix the Royal Seal to their names where they have already been written, in the Book of Life. Thus, "L'shanah tovah tichatemu."

◆»» NEW APPROACHES «««◆

In some small and intimate *chavurah* congregations, there have been long and sometimes painful discussions of how—in a modern, intensely active, hurried society—it is possible to achieve the profound contact between people that is necessary for *tshuvah* and *slichah*, turning or repentance and forgiveness, to occur. If people will not ask for forgiveness, is it possible to forgive them? Is it necessary to confront them first?

Such questions led people in one *chavurah*, Fabrangen in Washington, DC, to develop and successfully use an experiential approach to the *Slichot* process. Fabrangeners then shared this approach with members of synagogues of more traditional kinds, and several synagogues used this *Slichot* exercise with great success.

Members of the community sat in a circle with separate bowls of salty water and fresh, sweet water scattered around the circle. They sang *"V'taheyr libeynu l'avdecha b'emet.* Purify our hearts to serve You in truth." Using pens of water-soluble ink, each of them wrote on a slip of paper the words, thoughts, actions that were their worst misdeeds of the previous year. They took time to think this through, each addressing his or her own misdeeds.

Whenever they were ready, each one said or chanted, "V'tashlich bimtzulot yam chol chatotam. You shall cast all their sins into the depths of the sea," and plunged the papers into the bowls of water. They sat, watching the words dissolve.

After they had fully experienced the dissolution of their misdeeds, they turned to the bowls of fresh water. As a way of showing that each one accepted that all the others had confronted themselves and taken responsibility to change their lives, each person used a cup to pour water from this bowl over the hands of the next person in the circle. Then each one lovingly dried that person's hands. Together all sang "Oseh shalom bimromav hu ya-aseh shalom aleynu v'al kol Yisrael. May the One Who makes ultimate harmony in the universe make harmony among us and among all Israel." And thus the community felt that it had taken a long step toward both repentance and forgiveness.

◆»» FOODS «««◆

Since at-least as long ago as the Jews ate matzah in their headlong exodus from Egypt—which predated even the command of kosher food—the Jewish people have believed that how we eat has much to do with what we become. Not only at Passover but at every festival, Jews have assigned special foods as part of the celebration. (For all except Passover and the fast days, these special foods are customary rather than part of the required path of holy life.)

For Rosh Hashanah, the main qualities of the special foods are sweetness (for a sweet year); roundness (for the cycle of the year); and abundance (for fruitfulness and prosperity). Among some major special foods and recipes for Rosh Hashanah are these:*

TEIGLACH
(Honey Confections)

SYRUP:

1¼ cup honey

1 cup sugar

2 teaspoons ginger

DOUGH:

3 eggs

¼ teaspoon baking powder

2 cups flour

2 teaspoons sugar

2 tablespoons oil

½ teaspoon lemon rind

¼ teaspoon ginger

1 teaspoon vanilla

½ cup raisins (chopped)

½ cup finely cut nuts

FOR DOUGH: Mix flour, baking powder, sugar, ginger. Beat eggs, add oil and rind, then flour mixture to make soft dough that can be handled. Divide dough in two parts. Roll each part into a long narrow strip ⅛ inch thick and 5 inches wide. Spread with raisins and nuts, press into dough lightly with rolling pin. Roll up strip, pinch open edge firmly closed. Flour knife and slice into ½ inch pieces. If preferred the filling may be mixed into the dough then hand rolled into strips about 1 inch thick and cut into pieces.

COOKING: Bring honey and sugar to boil in deep kettle. Turn flame low but keep boiling slowly. Carefully drop dough, one at a time, into boiling honey. When all are in, cover and cook on low flame. DO NOT UNCOVER for ½ hour or the dough will not rise. Then raise cover only high enough to peek in. When top layer of teiglach has become golden brown, turn the mixture very carefully with a wooden spoon, bringing the bottom ones up. Cook until all are golden brown and sound hollow when stirred with spoon. Test by breaking one open—should be crisp and dry inside. Sprinkle 2 teaspoons ginger into mixture and stir carefully. Turn off light, add 2 tablespoons boiling water and stir again. Quickly remove teiglach from honey with slotted spoon and spread on board or platter which has been rinsed with cold water. Keep pieces separated. Roll in coconut or sugar and finely cut nut mixture. Keeps very well.

---

*These recipes, like most of the others in the book, have been used by Hannah Waskow and Rose Gertz.

MOCK CHOPPED HERRING

1 lb. can herring
3 medium onions
8 hard boiled eggs
salt, pepper, sugar
vinegar

8–10 slices white bread
2 peeled apples (tart)
2 tablespoons oil
dash of garlic powder

This makes enough for a buffet serving, but may be halved for 4 to 5 portions.

Skin, gut, remove dark meat from herring. Trim crusts from bread and soak bread in vinegar. Grind fish, bread, onions, apples and 6 of the eggs. (Use the 2 extra eggs as decoration either by slicing or separating the yolks and whites and forcing through a sieve or ricer and sprinkling over herring before serving. They may be used in the herring and radishes and parsley used for decoration.) Season to taste with salt, pepper, garlic powder, and sugar. Add oil and additional vinegar as needed for taste and consistency. Let stand overnight and check for taste and texture. Keeps well.

FRUIT CAKE

1 cup sugar
½ cup shortening
1 egg
2 cups flour
1 teaspoon baking soda
1 cup tomato juice
1 teaspoon juice
1 teaspoon vanilla
¾ cup of mixture of dates, candied
    fruit, & coconut

1 teaspoon cinnamon
½ teaspoon cloves
½ teaspoon nutmeg
dash of ginger
dash of allspice
lemon rind
1 cup raisins
½ cup nuts

Cream shortening and sugar. Add egg. Sift flour, soda, spices and add alternately with tomato juice. Add lemon rind and vanilla. Fold in raisins, nuts, and fruit mixture. Pour into prepared pan. Grease pan, line with waxed paper, and grease again. Use 9 or 10 inch tube. Bake at 350° for 10 minutes and then at 325° for about 45–50 minutes. Check with cake tester or straw. Tester should be clean. Cool in pan on rack for 20 minutes before removing. Bourbon or other liquor may be poured over the cake when cold. (About 2 or 3 ounces.) Keeps well.

KREPLACH

1 egg, slightly beaten
¼ teaspoon salt
1 cup sifted flour (about)
1 cup cooked beef, chopped
2 tablespoons onion, minced

2 tablespoons chicken fat (or vege-
    table fat)
1 egg
½ teaspoon salt

Make a noodle dough of the egg, salt, and flour, mixing together in the order named, to make a stiff dough that can be handled with fair ease. Knead on a lightly floured board until smooth and elastic. Roll out to paper thinness; cut into 2 to 3 inch squares.

Mix together the remaining ingredients and use as filling. Place a spoonful of filling on half of each square of dough, folding remaining half over top, point to point, to make triangles. Press edges together and secure with a fork dipped in flour. Drop into boiling, salted water, cover tightly, and cook for 20 minutes. Serve in the soup. They may be fried or baked and served as a side dish with meat. Makes about 2 dozen.

HONEY CAKE

½ cup fat
1 cup sugar
1 cup honey (may be mixed with white syrup)
3 eggs
1 cup warm black strong coffee
½ cup raisins

½ cup nuts
3 teaspoons baking powder
1 teaspoon baking soda
2 teaspoons cinnamon
2 teaspoons ginger
½ teaspoon each nutmeg, cloves, allspice
3 cups flour

Cream fat and sugar. Add honey and eggs. Sift all dry ingredients and add alternately with coffee. Fold in raisins and nuts. Pour into greased 10 inch tube pan or several bread pans. Bake at 325–350° 50–60 minutes.

◆»» GO AND STUDY ««◆

Shmuel Yosef Agnon, *Days of Awe* (Schocken Books), is a classic and wonderful collection of brief stories, Biblical excerpts, descriptions of communal practices, etc., in regard to the whole period of repentance and return. See also Max Arzt, *Justice and Mercy* (Holt, Rinehart & Winston), for a commentary on the Rosh Hoshanah liturgy; Philip Goodman, *The Rosh Hashanah Anthology* (Jewish Publication Society of America); and Irving Greenberg, *Guide to High Holy Days* (National Jewish Resource Center, NYC).

There is a wide variety of *Machzors*, of which the one edited by Jules Harlow for the (Conservative) Rabbinical Assembly has been most useful to me. It does not include a *Tashlich* service; that can be found in Philip Birnbaum's *Daily Prayer Book (Ha-Siddur Ha-Shalem)* (Hebrew Publishing Company). *Selihot* is a booklet published by the Rabbinical Assembly for use in *Slichot* services. For an excellent description of how to make and sound your own shofar, see *The First Jewish Catalog* (Jewish Publication Society).

YONAH

From Yonah, read on Yom Kippur, "*And Yonah prayed to the Lord his God out of the fish's belly . . .* " (Yonah 2:2-2:8) Yonah the prophet and the dove (*yonah*) from Noah's Ark were both endangered by water, sent on two missions, failed the first, and eventually wound up on the dry land (*yabasha*).

CHAPTER TWO
FACE TO FACE—
YOM KIPPUR

The moon of Tishri swells into an oval. If the barely visible new moon at Rosh Hashanah is the moment of birth, then the oval moon is the moment of developed identity. It is when we are grown up enough to face God.

In the moon cycle of the seventh month, the month of Tishri, Rosh Hashanah has the place analogous to that of Pesach in the solar cycle—the place of spring, of birthing, of newness. In the lunar cycle of Tishri, Yom Kippur has the place analogous to that of Shavuot in the solar cycle. At Shavuot, God and the Jewish people stand face to face at Sinai. We receive the Torah, and we enter the Covenant. At Yom Kippur, God and the Jewish people stand face to face at an inward, not an outward mountain. It is the mountain of our misdeeds and our sorrows.

So Yom Kippur has become the moment when most Jews individually and the Jewish people collectively experience the strongest sense of partnership and covenant with God—the strongest sense that if the people have striven with all their energy to redress the wrongs they have done, God will forgive them and give them a sense of harmony and wholeness. In this way, Yom Kippur fills in emotional fact the place it represents in the time sequence of the lunar cycle as an analogue to Shavuot, the moment of the Covenant at Sinai.

This moment of most intense spiritual experience is the moment of atonement—the moment when all misdeeds are covered over. Yom Kippur becomes a kind of *tallis* in time—a prayer shawl to cover the confusions of the year. As worshippers walk into shul and pick up the *tallis*, they cover their heads for a moment so as to wipe away the pointless, pathless wanderings of the world. Under the *tallis*, with the world invisible, it is possible for a moment to look toward God. So we could look at Yom Kippur as the prayer shawl that God spreads over all the people Israel, if we will take the trouble to pick the *tallis* up. Under this *tallis* we can stand face to face with God.

◆≫≫ ORIGINS ≪≪◆

In the Torah, the Five Books of Moses, there are four different recountings of the festivals. Two of these address the cycle of the solar year alone, and ignore the Tishri lunar cycle of the seventh month. In these two, Rosh Hashanah and Yom Kippur do not even appear. But the Books of Leviticus and Numbers describe both the solar and the lunar cycles, and it is in Leviticus that Yom Kippur takes on its special significance:

Mark, the tenth day of this seventh month is the day of atonement. It shall be a sacred occasion for you: you shall practice self-denial [or: you shall afflict your souls; or: you shall press down your egos], and you shall bring an offering by fire to the Lord; you shall do no work throughout that day. For it is a day of atonement, on which atonement is made on your behalf before Adonai your God. Indeed, any person that will not be pressed down throughout that day shall be cut off from his people. And any person who does any work throughout that day, that person I will destroy from amidst his people. . . . A Sabbath of complete rest [or, a fully shabbosdik Shabbos] shall be for you, and you shall press down your egos (Lev. 23:26–32).

It is also Leviticus (Chapter 16) that specifies the tenth of Tishri as the date on which the high priest shall conduct a special ceremony to purge defilement from the Shrine and from the people. The heart of the ritual is that the high priest shall bring a bull and two goats as a special offering.

· First, the bull is sacrificed so as to purge the Shrine from any defilements, what might now be called uncanny vibrations, caused by misdeeds of the priest himself and of his household.

· Secondly, one of the goats is chosen by lot to be sacrificed so as to purge the Shrine of any similar defilement stimulated by misdeeds of the whole Israelite people.

· Finally, the second goat is sent away—not sacrificed—so as to cleanse the people themselves. The goat is marked "for Azazel" and sent away to wander in the wilderness. (This word is not fully understood; Azazel may have meant an inaccessible place of rocks and cliffs, or a demonic power that dwelt in the wilderness; or it may simply have meant an escape goat—what came into English as scapegoat.) Before this goat is sent out, the high priest lays both his hands upon its head and "confesses over it all the iniquities and transgressions of the Israelites, whatever their misdeeds, putting them on the head of the goat." Thus, the Torah adds, "the goat shall carry on it all their iniquities to an inaccessible region."

By the time of the Second Temple, this ritual had been somewhat elaborated, and one crucial element had been added to it. That element was that on three separate occasions, in a grand crescendo, the high priest appeared before the people, and three times he recited a formula of confession in their hearing. The first confession was on the account of his own sins and those of his household; the second, on the account of the priestly tribe of Levi; the third, on the account of the whole people.

On this occasion only, in the entire year, the confession included the priest's saying aloud the Name of God embodied in the letters YHVH. This was the Name that God gave and explained to Moses at the burning bush, the Name that was a kind of distillation of "I Am Becoming Who I Am Becoming," the Name that was not a name in the sense of a label by which God could be called and controlled, and therefore the Name which could not be said aloud. It was, therefore, all year long euphemized by saying, whenever YHVH appeared in a text or invocation, Adonai, The Lord. Only on Yom Kippur was the Name said, aloud, in all its original awesomeness. (How the Name was pronounced on this occasion was so thoroughly protected from record-keeping that might profane it that we no longer know how it was done.)

In each confession, when the high priest reached the recitation of the Name, the whole people would prostrate themselves and say aloud, "Baruch shem K'vod malchuto l'olam va-ed. Blessed be the Name of the radiance of His Kingship, forever and beyond." On the third recitation, the one for their own sins, they knew that the high priest had just before—on this one occasion in all the year—entered the Holy of Holies, the inmost room of the Temple where God's Presence was most fully felt. He had entered it three times, and only then come out to confess on behalf of all the people and put their sins upon the head of the goat for Azazel.

The result of this triple entry into the Holy of Holies, this triple recitation of God's most holy Name, and this triple prostration by the entire people, was an utterly awesome sense of God's Presence making atonement for the people, cleansing them of all their sins, permitting them to begin the year afresh, renewing their lives. So total was this sense of transformation that after it, the mood of the people shifted from solemn awe to joyful celebration. The young, unmarried men and women went to dance in the fields and to choose spouses for themselves. Yom Kippur and the fifteenth of Av were the only days in the year when this kind of mass public espousal would take place.

Theodore Gaster, a historian of Jewish ceremonies and rituals, points out that a public purgation of the accumulated communal sinfulness is to be found in many cultures. In ancient Babylonia, the rite of *kuppuru*, purgation, came in the midst of the ten-day coronation festival. It involved the sacrifice of a ram in order to eliminate impurity in the holy places, and the public confession of sins by the King. A human scapegoat—a condemned criminal—was then beaten in the public streets.

We can only, each of us, draw on our own sensibilities to understand the differences between this ritual and that of the Israelites. The key difference is that where the Babylonians used a ram and a human being, the Torah uses two goats—one to purify the shrine, the other to purify the people. To me it seems that this makes a big difference. The Babylonians seem to be saying that the impurities of the two realms are quite different. Those of the sacrificial realm can only be focused by a sacrificial beast; those of the people, by a person. In the Israelite ceremony, the very similarity of the goats underlines the close relationship between God's world of holy ceremony and God's world of holy human interaction. The Shrine, God's house, is defiled not by sacrificial errors that are different from those errors that disfigure God's people—but by the very same misdeeds that the people must expel from their own midst. Moreover, the fact that the scapegoat is, indeed, a goat—not a human being, even a criminal—underlines the possibility of *tshuvah*, repentant return, for *all* human beings. No human is to be expelled from the community.

The ritual of the goats echoes the stories that we read ten days before, on Rosh Hashanah, of the ordeals of Ishmael (sent into the desert) and Isaac (bound for sacrifice). Thus the Yom Kippur ritual gives further emphasis that human beings are precious: offer up goats, not people! Perhaps there is even a hint that God might by Yom Kippur want, as it were, to do *tshuvah* for His threat, which we recall on Rosh Hashanah, to the lives of Ishmael and Isaac. Indeed, rabbinic tradition claimed it was on Yom Kippur that God's command to bind Isaac was fulfilled and God's order to release Isaac came. So the patterns of God's own *tshuvah* may have been evoked in this ten-day period as a lesson to the people: "If even God can turn from a stern decree to loving-kindness, then so can you . . . and if you do, you can expect forgiveness."

The fact that the goats are chosen by lot reminds us, says Rav Joseph Soloveitchik, that chance and fate, though they do not rule the universe, play a part in it. Since we cannot really establish utter control over our own lives, we owe forgiveness to each other, and God to us, for our failings.

If these are reasonable ways to sense the impact on the people of the Yom Kippur ritual while the Temple stood, then the evolution of Yom Kippur since the destruction of the Temple strengthens this basic approach. How people act toward each other is not simply important, but *vital* to the

God Who extends universal forgiveness—on condition of a universal commitment to turn human behavior around.

Once the Temple, and with it the sacrificial system, had been shattered, the rabbis concluded that Yom Kippur itself—the very fact of the day's arrival in the cycle of the calendar—brought about God's forgiveness . . . on condition:

> If someone said, "I will sin and repent, and sin again and repent," he will be given no chance to repent. If he said, "I will sin and Yom Kippur will effect atonement," then the Day of Atonement effects no atonement. For transgressions between human beings and God, Yom Kippur effects atonement; but for transgressions between a person and his fellow, Yom Kippur effects atonement only if he has made peace with his fellow.

With the Temple and the scapegoat gone, what remained from the Torah's commands as a form of life-practice and ritual that could focus consciousness on the day? There remained only two factors: the command to the people that they press down the self, or soul, or personality; and prayer.

As to self-denial or self-abnegation, the rabbis concluded that it must be carried out in five ways: fasting from food, from drinking water, from washing or anointing the body, from wearing leather shoes, and from sexual intercourse. How did these practices accord with the sense that Yom Kippur was a day of transcendent joy, the day of restoration of harmony with God? Some commentators on the Fast—writing much later—explain how these observances may be joyful rather than ascetic:

> And they fast on this day to approach a resemblance to the angels, in as much as the fast is consummated by humbling themselves, lowering their heads, standing, bending their knees, and singing hymns of praise. Then all the physical powers abandon their natural functions and engage in spiritual functions, as though having no animal nature (Yehuda Halevi).

> If it was in my power, I would do away with all the afflictions—except for the afflictions on the bitter day of the destruction of our Temple, Tisha B'Av, for who could *bear* to eat on that day!—and the afflictions on the holy and awesome day, Yom Kippur, for who *needs* to eat on that day? (Abraham Joshua Heschel, The Apter Rebbe, as quoted in Agnon's *Days of Awe*).

Closely entwined with self-abnegation was the second remaining element of Yom Kippur, prayer. The mouths not used for food were used for chanting praise to God. So powerful was the sense of a full day of prayer that Philo of Alexandria explained Yom Kippur as one long blessing before one enormous meal. Yom Kippur, he pointed out, came just before the harvest . . . the meal that lasted all the year. So, just as Jews paused before a meal to say the *motzi* over bread, they paused before the harvest to thank and praise the God Who gave the harvest. But for the meal that would last all year, the blessing must last all day. So the Jews would pause from eating for one full day, and use the time to pray.

✦➤➤ MAKING READY ◄◄◄✦

Out of these overlapping senses of Yom Kippur as a time of solemnity and joy, purification and atonement, pressing down of the self and giving away of the self, came a pattern of observance that lasted with little change into our own day. To begin with, the tradition built a conscious bridge from Rosh Hashanah to Yom Kippur.

The ten days from Rosh Hashanah through Yom Kippur are known as the Days of Awe or the Days of *tshuvah* (repentance, turn-about). The traditional metaphor was that during this time God might rewrite a name, taking it from the ledger of death into the Book of Life, depending on how we act—whether we return to the path of decency, or not. So the seven days that lie between the two holy days are turned into a spiritual bridge from one to the other by several special practices in ceremony as well as in daily life.

One is that in the standing silent prayer, the *amidah*, on each of these days there are inserted several passages:

Remember us for life, King Who delights in life, and inscribe us in the Book of Life for Your own sake, Living God.

Who is like You, compassionate (or Motherly) Father, compassionately remembering Your creatures toward life?

Inscribe all the children of Your covenant for a good life.

In the Book of Life, Blessing, Peace, and an honorable sustenance may be remembered and written before your very eyes—we and the whole of your people, the house of Israel—for a good life and for peace. Blessed are You, Who makes peace.

And two blessings in the *amidah* are changed during the Ten Days: "Blessed be You, Adonai, the Holy God" becomes ". . . the Holy King," and "Blessed be You, Adonai, King Who loves righteousness and judgment" becomes "Blessed be You, Adonai, the King of judgment."

During these days (except for Shabbos), the *Slichot* prayers for forgiveness are recited early in the morning, and *Avinu Malkenu* is recited every morning and afternoon.

Meanwhile, these days are an especially important time for acts of *tzedakah* (charitable righteousness), for study of the Prophets and the later books of the Bible, and for re-examination and correction of one's own behavior.

As a time of introspection and repair, it is unsuitable for starting new relationships, whether conflictful or harmonious—and so it is not a time for either lawsuits or weddings. But it is especially suitable for restoring old relationships—making apologies and offering forgiveness.

The day immediately after Rosh Hashanah is a traditional day of limited fasting—Yom Tzom Gedaliah, the Day of the Fast of Gedaliah, commemorating the assassination of Gedaliah ben Achikam shortly after the Destruction of the First Temple. Gedaliah was a member of a leading Jewish family, friend of the prophet Jeremiah, and supporter of Jeremiah's policy of non-resistance to the Babylonian conquest. The Babylonians appointed Gedaliah provincial governor of Judah after they captured Jerusalem, and shortly afterward he was killed by a zealous patriot who evidently hoped to overthrow the Babylonian rule. The later prophet Zechariah mentions the observance of a fast day in his memory. It could be argued that the fast fits well into the Days of *tshuvah*, since the murder of Gedaliah out of patriotic motives in a sense represents, at the political level, the human proclivity for turning the desire for selfhood into the behavior of selfishness. The fast (from food and water only) lasts from dawn to sundown on the third day of Tishri. Reform Judaism does not view the Fast of Gedaliah as mandatory, and many Conservative and modern Orthodox Jews do not observe it. Moving to the other pole, some traditional Jews observe a limited fast during *all* the Days of *tshuvah* except Shabbos and the day just before Yom Kippur.

The Shabbos between Rosh Hashanah and Yom Kippur is known as Shabbos Shuvah, the Shabbos of Return. It is named after the prophetic portion that is read—made up of passages from Hosea (14:2–10), Micah (7:18–20), and Joel (2:15–27). The Hosea passage begins, "Return, O Israel, to Adonai your God; for you have stumbled in your iniquity." The passage from Micah includes the line that is used in *Tashlich*, "You will cast all their sins into the depths of the sea," and the passage from Joel begins, "Sound the shofar in Zion, hallow a fast, call an assembly." So the readings for Shabbos Shuvah bring together the sense of human repair and Divine response that are intended to suffuse the whole of the Ten Days. Shabbos Shuvah was also one of only two in all the year (the other was Shabbos Hagadol, just before Pesach) when the leading rabbi of the city would give a sermon in its leading synagogue. His topic would be *tshuvah*, and usually he would urge and encourage, rather than attack or disparage.

According to the reckoning that Yom Kippur was the day of the Binding of Isaac, the eighth of Tishri was the day on which Abraham rose early to take Isaac on his sacrificial journey. It is also the day on which Solomon's dedication of the First Temple began. So the eighth of Tishri was traditionally given a special place among the Ten Days. The congregation rose even earlier than usual to pray, chanted a poem called "Thirteen Qualities" in praise of God's thirteen attributes of loving-kindness (Exodus 34:6–7), and in parts of central Europe on that day the women would make candles by measuring a graveyard with string, then dipping the string into wax so as to become a wick. Meanwhile they would recite the names of the dead, invoking the merit of their piety in the seeking of God's forgiveness.

On the day before Yom Kippur, the preparations reached an even higher pitch. In most traditional Jewish communities the ceremony of *Kapparot* was performed. For centuries some great rabbinical scholars opposed it, and in Reform and Conservative congregations almost everyone has abandoned it. Yet in many Orthodox shuls it continues, and in the *chavurah* communities, some have argued that we could learn from its physicality how to embody and act out our hope of forgiveness, and might try to work out a variant that feels fulfilling.

The most usual custom was that at dawn of the day before Yom Kippur, each man took a rooster and each woman, a hen. Each held the fowl in the left hand, laid the right hand on its head, and swung it three times around one's own head, three times saying, "This is my substitute, this is my exchange, this is my atonement. This fowl will go to death, and I will enter upon a good, long life and peace." Then at once the fowl was slaughtered by the traditional ritual. Its liver, kidneys, and guts were put outside for the birds—to show compassion for all God's creatures. In some places the rest of the meat was given to the poor; in others, the family kept the meat and gave the cost of the chicken in money to the poor. In some places long ago, *Kapparot* was done with food plants instead of animals. Children would take baskets early in Elul, fill them with dirt, and plant seeds of wheat, barley, peas, and beans in them. By the eve of Yom Kippur, the plants were a few inches tall—ready to be swung about the head with the same invocation and thrown into a stream.

Some of the rabbis urged that giving *tzedakah* money to the poor be substituted for the whole *Kapparot* ceremony. One custom that fused these two approaches was that 18 coins would be held in a fist over the head of each child, whirled as *Kapparot,* and then given to the poor. (The number 18 was used because in the Jewish number system the letters of the alphabet are used to represent numbers—*aleph* as 1, *beit* as 2, etc. The letters for the word *chai,* life, add up to the number 18.)

On the day before Yom Kippur, the rabbis said, eating and drinking well was of as deep importance as fasting was on Yom Kippur itself. For eating is a way of taking the physical and transforming it into the spiritual: using the body energy of food for the conscious service of God. Since on Yom Kippur we devote ourselves utterly to the spiritual, all the more important that we be conscious of where that energy comes from. Some bake loaves of challah in the shape of wings, since on Yom Kippur all Israel is like angels. Others decorate the challah with a ladder, echoing the prayer "Let our entreaties climb to You."

The afternoon before Yom Kippur was traditionally a time to visit the mikveh, the ritual bathhouse, for an immersion that would symbolize the oceanic experience of atonement and purification. Then the Separation Meal would be eaten, and in some communities after dinner the table would be covered with a fine tablecloth and books of Torah be spread upon it—to show that for Yom Kippur the words of prayer and study were replacing food.

Finally, the family would remove their leather shoes and put on cloth ones instead—since leather was seen as a luxury, too fancy for this solemn day—and perhaps also to avoid using the skin of animals on a day of innocence, a day when we refrain from using their meat. The family would dress in white clothes to resemble angels, and would cover these clothes with a plain white kittel—a simple robe worn for one's own wedding, at the Passover Seder, on Yom Kippur, and as a shroud for the dead. For "in these garments we shall go to the world above, to give a reckoning before the King of Kings. Therefore let us imagine that we are already standing in these garments before the Throne of Glory to give our reckoning. Let us wholly regret our sins, for in that hour one really does regret them. No regretting helps after death—but it does help now."

Then the family gathered round, and the parents blessed their children:

May God make you as Ephraim and Menashe. May it be the will of our Father who is in heaven to place his love and fear in your heart. May the fear of God be before you all the days of your life, so that you will not sin; and may your delight be in the Torah and in the commandments. May your eyes look straight ahead. May your mouth speak wisdom, and your heart contemplate fear. May your hands be engaged in keeping the commandments, and your legs run to do the will of your Father who is in heaven. May He give you sons and daughters who are righteous and engage in the study of the Torah and in keeping the commandments all their days. May your spring be blessed; and may God allow you to find your rightful sustenance in ease and with plenty, beneath His own broad hand, and not through the gifts of flesh and blood. May your livelihood be one which will set you free for the service of God; and may you be inscribed and sealed for a good and long life in the midst of all the righteous of Israel. Amen.

And then the holy day candles were lit and the family left for shul.

◆>>> YOM KIPPUR ITSELF <<<◆

Traditionally, the actual doing of Yom Kippur (aside from the non-doing involved in the five forms of fasting) is participation in five separate services during the 25 hours of the day—separate in the sense that each includes the quiet standing prayer, the *amidah*. These five—the largest number of services on any day in the Jewish year—preserve an ancient Jewish tradition of five services on all days, a tradition that entered Moslem practice where five services a day became standard throughout the year. The five are *Maariv*, evening; *Shacharit*, morning; *Musaf*, additional; *Minchah*, afternoon; and only on Yom Kippur, late afternoon *Neilah*—the service of the closing of the gates of Heaven. In traditional practice, the four daytime services take the entire day, with little or no pause between them.

KOL NIDRE NIGHT

Before the regular evening service, chanted to the same melodies as the evening of Rosh Hoshanah, comes a unique ritual of Yom Kippur—the chanting of Kol Nidre. For this evening service, unlike any other in the whole year, the congregants wear the *tallis*. They put it on just before sundown, so that by natural light they can still see the *tzitzit*, fringes. One member of the congregation who will lead the chanting stands flanked by two others, the three representing a court of justice. They must also begin just before sundown, for the court is about to do a legal action—and a Jewish court cannot make decisions at night. Together they say:

> In a session of the Court on high and in a session of this court below, based on the consent of that Place Which is beyond all places and on the consent of the community that sits in this place, we declare it permitted to plead together with all who are transgressors.

And then three times, the first in a whisper like someone who is overwhelmed at newly entering the palace of the King and the third time aloud like one who feels at home as a member of the king's household, the three members of the court and the whole congregation recite:

> All vows and oaths, all promises and obligations, all renunciations and responses, that we shall make from this Yom Kippur till the next—may it come to us in peace—all of them we retract. May we be absolved of them all, may we be released from them all, may they all be null and

void, may they all be of no effect. May these vows not be vows, may these oaths not be oaths, may these responses not be responses.

Then all the people remind God of the promise of forgiveness:

And the whole congregation of the children of Israel shall be forgiven as well as the sojourner who sojourns among them, for all the people acted in error (Numbers 15:26).

The leader of the service repeats the words of Moses after the sin of the Golden Calf:

Please forgive the sin of this people, out of your great loving-kindness. Forgive us as you have forgiven this people, from Egypt until here and now.

And the congregation answers with God's words:

I have forgiven—as you asked. (Num. 14:19–20.)

There are several puzzling aspects of Kol Nidre.

Why this permission to plead with God along with transgressors? It is said to have been instituted in the thirteenth century so that those who had violated communal regulations and come under the ban could return to the community on the Day of Atonement. But there is a broader sense in which all the worshippers are transgressors; they both recognize their failings and agree to pray with each other nevertheless—or indeed, all the more.

Why this annulment of vows? And why does it look forward to the *coming* year, instead of annulling vows from the year just past? Some of the greatest of the rabbis objected to the whole business, warning that the seriousness of vows would be undermined. A century ago some Reform Jews tried to eliminate it—but after several decades took Kol Nidre back. In the earliest version of the text and among the Sephardic communities still, the annulment looks back to vows made between the last Yom Kippur and the present one—which may seem more rational.

Some believe that the transgressors being mentioned were likely to keep sinning in the future, since they were loyal secret Jews who were posing as Christians or Muslims in fear for their lives, who had taken their lives in their hands to come to synagogue on Yom Kippur, but who would keep on posing. Thus the plea for their release from false vows of apostasy.

Yet even today there is a teaching in the forward-looking annulment that may best be understood visually. Imagine standing in a great steamship, looking forward into unknown, turbulent waters. *Ahead* of the ship there is a cleavage of the sea; the waters are affected even before the ship can reach them. Yom Kippur acts like such a ship—casting its influence ahead, healing the spiritual disturbance that will arise from a troubled vow, even before it can be uttered.

And why annul vows? To free us from the imprisonment of acting only out of a promise—rather than out of a free and serious choice of what is good. Is it good to honor our parents, be faithful to our friends, love and teach our children? Then let us do these things *because* they are acts of goodness, not because we have bound ourselves by a vow to do them. Kol Nidre cancels every guilt trip.

With the special Kol Nidre passage completed, the congregation recites *Sheh-hechianu*, blessing the One Who keeps us alive to reach this moment, and then it enters into the evening service.

The service introduces several special elements of Yom Kippur: the *Ashamnu* and *Al Chet* versions of a confession of misdeeds, and one of the most powerful poetic songs of the day—an imploring of God, "Ki anu amecha, v'atah eloheynu." The two confessions are in the plural—"*We* have sinned"—and the misdeeds are listed in alphabetical order. In this way the congregation takes collective responsibility for undoing all the misdeeds of its members, all the sins "from A to Z"—even those it does not think to mention.

The song "Ki anu amecha" is sung:

> Ki anu amecha, v'atah eloheynu;
> Anu vanecha, v'atah avinu.
> Anu avadecha, v'atah adoneynu;
> Anu k'halecha, v'atah chelkeynu.
> Anu nachalatecha v'atah goraleynu;
> Anu tzonecha v'atah ro-eynu.
> Anu charmecha v'atah notreynu;
> Anu f'oolatecha v'atah yotzreynu.
> Anu rah-yah-techa v'atah dodeynu;
> Anu s'gulatecha v'atah kroveynu.
> Anu amecha v'atah malkenu;
> Anu mamirechah v'atah mamireynu.

Its successive verses go through a series of complementary pairs, "We are Your people, You are our God; we are Your children, You are our Parent; we are Your flock, You are our Shepherd . . ." and end with a triumphant equality, "We are Your bespoken, and You are our Bespoken." In a sense, this song is a miniature of the whole process of Yom Kippur: first it plunges the Jewish people into humble submission, a cleansing affirmation of their dependence on God—and then, as a paradoxical result of this very submission, lifts them up to be able to see God face to face. For a moment, the people become as glorious in possibility and as clear in purpose as God's own Self.

There is a tradition that the Yom Kippur evening service never ends—that there is a continuing bond through the night from that service to the morning one. Some Jews sleep overnight in the synagogue, or stand watch through the night. In some *chavurah* congregations, this continuity has been expressed by ending the evening service with an open-ended meditation. Drawing on a prayer of the Chassidic rebbe Levi Yitzchak of Berditschev, they say, individually:

> Lord of the World, I stand before You and before my neighbors—pardoning, forgiving, struggling to be open to all who have hurt and angered me. Be this hurt of body or soul, of honor or property, whether they were forced to hurt me or did so willingly, whether by accident or intent, whether by word or deed—I forgive them because we are human. May no one feel guilty on my account. I am ready to take upon myself the commandment, 'Love your neighbor as yourself.'

and remain in the prayer room, meditating, until each feels satisfied, having fully forgiven those who have harmed him/her. One by one the congregants quietly leave as they reach this point. Since the congregation as a whole never formally closes the service, the atmosphere of prayer and reconciliation continues, hovering in mid-air even after the last member leaves.

THE MORNING SERVICE

In the morning, the service is much like that for Rosh Hashanah. One moment is unique: after the *Sh'ma* (Hear O Israel, the Lord our God—the Lord is One), on this day alone in all the year the traditional response, "Baruch shem k'vod malchuto l'olam va-ed. Blessed is the name of the radiance of His Kingship, for ever and beyond" is said aloud—instead of murmured. The distinction was based on the tradition that the response was forbidden by a ruling empire, which thought it was subversive of the Jews to be celebrating any other King than the Emperor—even an invisible King in Heaven. So the Jews acquiesced in murmuring it all year. But defiantly, on Yom Kippur—on the day that when the Temple stood, the people had shouted out "Baruch shem k'vod" as the high priest called out the Holy Name—on that one day, they insisted on saying it aloud. (Reform synagogues now say the response aloud all year, on the ground that in a free society there is no reason to keep acting like victims. Others continue as they were—for the sake of tradition, or for the sake of remembering oppression even when not experiencing it, or for the sake of enhancing the triumphant shout on Yom Kippur.)

On Yom Kippur, unlike most holidays, there are two full Torah services, with two different readings and two different Prophetic passages. In the morning, the Torah passage is Leviticus 16, the description of the high priest's special sacrifice on Yom Kippur. It is followed by a reading from Isaiah (57:14–58:16) that forces everyone to confront the full meaning of Yom Kippur. The inner experience of Yom Kippur, says Isaiah, is the empty belly of the one who fasts; but this is not the real inner meaning. It is the *outer* experience—making sure that the hungry have food to eat, that the naked have clothes to wear—it is this outward help to others that God demands and recognizes as the deed that brings atonement.

Thus the rabbis placed this powerful lesson just at the point in mid-morning when the fast is beginning to bite at the innards of the congregation. Just at that moment, when all might be feeling sorry for themselves or triumphant in their sacrifice, God and the prophet challenge them to a deeper feeling. The Torah reading affirms the cleansing importance of a powerful ritual; the Prophetic reading insists that it be acted out in social justice.

Among Ashkenazic Jews, the morning service includes *yizkor*, the memorial prayer for the dead. In some congregations, those who have no close relatives to mourn leave the prayer room during *yizkor*. In others, all remain, in recognition and memorial of those in the wider *mishpacha* or family who have died, especially those martyrs who died for *kiddush hashem*—in affirming the holiness of God's Name against oppressive mobs or rulers.

MUSAF

The *musaf* or additional service on Yom Kippur serves to re-enact the special *Avodah* or service brought by the high priest at noon this day when the Temple stood. The heart of the *musaf* is a reading of the Talmudic passage describing in detail exactly what the priest and the people did, rising in pitch three times to the tempo of the three prostrations of the entire people. In many congregations, the entire body of congregants prostrates itself on the floor at those three moments in the recitation, calling out as our forebears did, "Baruch shem kavod malchuto l'olam va-ed." To a modern eye, this prostration looks like a little death. Perhaps we accept the posture of death in order to embody—literally to act out in our bodies—our acceptance of the death of pride and self as well as selfishness. When the Temple stood, it was the moment of most intense encounter with God; for many Jews today, it still is.

When we rise from the *Avodah*, it is at once to hear of the deaths of the ten great rabbis whom the Emperor Hadrian condemned for teaching Torah. It is as if this *minyan*—representing our whole people—fell in death so that Torah might rise, teaching us that our small death in the *Avodah* is to bear witness to our individual and collective will to renew a holy life.

In many congregations, this martyrology section of the *musaf* service has been reworked to include the martyrdom of the Six Million who died in the Holocaust and of other, smaller martyrdoms of many kinds. In the Fabrangen, an independent *chavurah* in Washington, DC, it has on occasion included a reading of parts of *Kaddish*, Allen Ginsberg's agonized memory of the madness and death of his mother; a memory of the Jewish women who died in the Triangle Shirtwaist Factory fire; a memory of Schwerner, Chaney, and Goodman, who were murdered in 1964 in Mississippi—Black and Jew together—for their devotion to racial justice; a memory of Orlando Letelier and Ronni Karpen Moffit, South American Christian and North American Jew, who were murdered nearby in Washington for seeking to build a free society in Chile.

In the Fabrangen it has also included, year after year since 1973, a stark memory of the moment during Yom Kippur that year when word reached the congregation of the outbreak of renewed war between Israel and her neighbors. When that word came in 1973, the congregation stood, paralyzed and silent, until it was able to sing, to a melody composed by one of its members for a peace vigil years before:

Eytz cha-im hi, l'machizikim bah; eytz chaim hi, l'machizikim bah; eytz cha-im hi, l'shalom. Eytz cha-im hi, l'shalom.

"She (the Torah) is a Tree of Life, for those who hold her close. A Tree of Life—for peace." And each year since, the congregation has done the same, yearning for and affirming the peace ordained by the Torah.

MINCHAH

The afternoon service focuses around the reading of another Torah portion and of the Book of Jonah as the Prophetic passage. The usual Torah portion is Leviticus 18, the chapter that catalogs forbidden kinds of sexual relationships. Some scholars believe that this passage was chosen to check any tendency to license and abandon that might have followed and sprung from the spiritual intensity and release of Yom Kippur. In Temple days, that afternoon was the moment of dancing and betrothals. So the passage might have been intended either to prevent this celebration from descending into an orgy, or to remind the men and women of what marriages were forbidden by the Torah. There is a minority suggestion in the Talmud that Leviticus 19, the holiness code of decent behavior and social justice, be read instead; and some congregations do so now. A widely used Conservative *Machzor*, edited by Jules Harlow, includes it.

The reading of the Book of Jonah—and in some congregations, an open discussion of its meaning—is one of the richest experiences of Yom Kippur. The book can be read on many levels. It is an allegory of the individual soul, struggling between hunger for death and oblivion, and the readiness for rebirth and new responsibility. It is a teaching about the obligations of the people Israel in regard to all the nations. It is a theme and variations on *tshuvah*—repentance—in the prophet, the city Nineveh, and God's own Self. It is a meditation on one of the themes of Tishri, water as death and as life. Immediately after Jonah, the brief *Tashlich* passage from Micah is read, underlining the moment when Jonah himself cries out to God, "You have cast me into the depths, into the heart of the sea." And thus as the daylight of Yom Kippur dims in later afternoon, there is an echo of the Rosh Hashanah afternoon ten days before, when the congregation did *Tashlich*, casting, at the stream.

NEILAH

Finally, there comes the fifth service: the closing of the gates. The gates of the Temple; the gates of Heaven; the gates of the human heart and human possibility—all are said to be about to shut. "Open the gate for us at the time the gate is closing. The day is done, the sun is setting, soon to be gone. Let us enter Your gates."

Some congregations keep the Ark open and stand for all of *Neilah*. Although the *Ashamnu* confession of sins is recited for the fifth time, the *Al Chet* is not—and instead the prayers shift toward a consciousness of God's forgiveness. The prayer "Write us in the Book of Life" is replaced by "Seal us in the Book of Life." One last time the congregation sings *Avinu Malkenu*, and then proclaims God to itself and to the world:

Sh'ma Israel Adonai Eloheynu adonai echad!
Baruch shem k'vod malchuto l'olam va-ed! (Three times.)
Adonai hu ha-elohim! (Seven times.)

The Lord—that is who God is! joyously affirming that "The Liberator—that is the Creator!" or perhaps, "The still small Voice within is also the Ultimate and Infinite!"

This last outcry comes from the mouths of the Israelites at Mount Carmel, when the prophet Elijah called them to choose between Adonai and Baal as the fructifier of the earth—between the faith that the God Who liberated them from slavery, gave them the Torah, and spoke as an intimate, was *also* the wellspring of nature—and on the other hand the belief that the God of history and human contact had no connection with a god who sent the rain and shaped the fertile earth.

It is no accident that affirming the Unity behind nature and history is the final word of Yom Kippur—when the human body has paused from its natural acts of life, and history has stopped from its normal ups and downs, so that the spirit can be utterly reborn.

These outcries by the people are sealed by the eerie voice of the shofar, in the long blast that ends Yom Kippur. The congregation calls out, "L'shana ha-ba-ah b'Yirushalayim! Next year in Jerusalem!"

AFTERMATH

In many congregations the evening service is said at once. Then, still in shul together or going home in clusters of family and friends, people make *havdalah*, the ceremony that separates a holy time from an ordinary time. (This havdalah does not include the first paragraph, "Hiney eyl y'shuati," from the havdalah after Shabbos. It does include the blessings over wine and fire. For the fire, many traditional households use a long-burning candle lit before Yom Kippur to light a new candle.) Then people break their fast.

Looking forward four days to the celebration of Sukkot, the harvest Festival of Huts, some Jews nail one board to another as a symbolic head start in building the sukkah. One way to see this symbolic act is that it carries out the tradition that the completion of one commanded act helps us move directly to the doing of another. Another way to see this first nailing in the sukkah is that it embodies the shift from the inward rebuilding that goes on during Yom Kippur to the outward rebuilding of the world that we are now obligated to begin.

Finally, many communities use the night after Yom Kippur as the time to bless the swelling moon of Tishri. The ceremony of *Kiddush Levana*— hallowing the pale-white moon—is done each month on a night between the crescent and the not-quite-full moon. Its joyful shouts of "Shalom aleichem! Aleichem shalom!" and its dancing gestures toward the moon make a fitting connection with the joyful celebration of the full moon at Sukkot.

◆»» NEW APPROACHES «« ◆

According to Philo of Alexandria, a learned Jew who was strongly influenced by Hellenistic philosophy, the fast of Yom Kippur comes when it does because it is like a pause to say a blessing over a meal. The meal is the harvest—the meal of the entire year—so the pause is long.

On the basis of this thought, the Fabrangen—a *chavurah*-style congregation in Washington, DC—has used these poems/blessings as part of its Yom Kippur service.

Blessed are You, O Lord,
Who gives us this day of atonement;
Who asks us to pause from our mouthing of food
In order to speak of You and only You;
Who asks us to pause from our drinking of water

In order to fill ourselves with You;
Who asks us to pause from making love with each other
In order to focus on our love of You;
Who asks us to pause from the cleansing of our bodies
In order to address the cleansing of our selves;
Who asks us to pause from anointing our heads
In order to bring nearer the Anointing of Mashiach;
Who asks us to pause from wearing shoes of skin
In order to bare our skins to holy ground;
Who chooses that for Your day of fasting
We share our food with the hungry;
Who chooses that for Your day to press down our selves
We let the oppressed go free.

Baruch attah Adonai, elohenu melech
   ha-olam, asher kid'shanu
   b'mitzvotav v'tzivanu la'anot et-
   nafsh'taynu.

Blessed are You, Adonai, our God,
   ruler of all space-time, who
   makes us holy through Your
   commandments and commands us
   to press down our selves.

Blessed are You,
Adonai our God,
Seed of seeds,
Root of roots,
Life of all living,
Who brings the ear of corn to fulness
And ripens the fruit.

Today Your food is spread
On one great earthly table,
So we pause before we eat:
Pause to make the brocha.

Tomorrow we will eat of the harvest;
All year we will eat of the harvest.

This fall we will munch fresh nuts and apples,
This winter we will eat what we have stored while the land turns
   barren,

Next spring we will sow from the seed we are harvesting now,
Next summer we will eat for the strength to turn the soil.
But today we fast while Your meal lies ripe before us.

We feast our eyes on the red of Your apples,
We feast our ears on the rustle of Your cornstalks,
We feast our hands on the prickle of Your berries,
We feast our noses on the musk of Your melons,
We feast our souls on the fulness of Your mercy,
And today we will use our mouths to sing Your praises.

Today we bring You that food which alone You have asked of us:

Our love.

Blessed are You,
Adonai our God,
Seed of seeds,
Root of roots,
Life of all living,
Whose food we will eat—
Tomorrow.
(Amen.)

◆≫≫ GO AND STUDY ≪≪◆

Philip Goodman's *The Yom Kippur Anthology* (Jewish Publication Society) should be consulted, in addition to the books suggested at the end of Chapter I, especially Agnon's *Day of Awe*. See also Irving Greenberg's *Guide to the High Holy Days* (National Jewish Resource Center, NYC). For the *Kapparot* ceremony see Philip Birnbaum's *Daily Prayer Book* (Hebrew Publishing Co.).

YOSEF

". . . *and lo, my sheaf arose and also stood upright.*" (Gen. 37:7). Yosef, the foundation, is one of the seven "guests" we invite into the *sukkah* during the seven days of the harvest festival.

CHAPTER THREE
HARVEST MOON—
FULFILLMENT
AT SUKKOT

Full moon, full harvest, full hearts. As the moon of Tishri draws to fullness, we are ready to celebrate Sukkot—the Festival of Huts. We have experienced the moment of rebirth, the rediscovery of our true identity, the re-examination of our selves, the return to our true path—at Rosh Hashanah, the moment of new moon. We have experienced the moment of intense contact and reconciliation with God at Yom Kippur, in the swelling of the moon. And now at the full moon we celebrate Sukkot—the festival of fulfillment, of gathering in the benefits that flow from repentance and forgiveness. The harvest that takes the form of joy and *shalom*, harmony, in the world.

But Sukkot is not only the fulfillment of the moon of Tishri. It is also the fulfillment of the yearly cycle of the sun. All the sun's work upon the earth comes to fullness as the harvest ripens and is gathered in. Six months from the Pesach festival of spring comes the Sukkot festival of fall. As we have shown in the Preface, Pesach has celebrated the earth's rebirth and Shavuot, the peak of earthly power as spring moves into summer; so Sukkot celebrates the glory of the earth fulfilled. As the moon has rewarded our celebration of her birth and growth by bursting into a glowing perfect circle, so the earth rewards our care of seed and stalk by bursting into ripened fruit and grain.

And just as Sukkot is the fulfillment of the moon and of the sun, the fulfillment of both nature cycles, so also in the aspect of the year as a lesson plan in history, Sukkot represents fulfillment: Pesach and Shavuot symbolize not only phases of the solar cycle, but also phases of the people's history.

Pesach reminds us of the moment of liberation from slavery in *Mitzrayim;* Shavuot reminds us of the moment of transcendent contact with God at Sinai. In this pattern, too, Sukkot is the reminder of the fulfillment of this work of liberation and encounter; for Sukkot reminds us of the time of traveling in the wilderness under God's close protection, making camp in temporary huts.

Just as we ourselves grow from our first spiritual awakening—an awakening to the possibility of freedom, creativity—into the passionate, awe-filled reality of contact with God, so we are now rewarded in our spiritual lives with the ingathering of spiritual riches. Our relationship with God bears psychic fruit.

We walk into the sukkah—the fragile field hut, open to the light of moon and stars, that our forebears lived in while they gathered in the grain. We dangle apples and onions, oranges and peppers, from its leafy roof. And we feel the joy that for a moment life is so safe, the world so loving, that we can live in these open-ended huts without fear.

So in both the lunar and the solar cycles, Sukkot comes as the time of redemption or fulfillment. Indeed, this special double role is in a way a higher affirmation of its redemptive quality—for it is Sukkot that unifies the sun and moon, brings the two cycles into harmony, fulfills both cycles by joining in one festival the moment of fulfillment in each one.

◆>>> ORIGINS <<<◆

Practically all societies and cultures celebrate the harvest—the gathering in of the food that will keep the people alive all year. This is how the Torah commands that Sukkot be done:

> Three times a year you shall hold a festival for Me . . . the Feast of Ingathering at the end of the year, when you gather in the results of your work from the field (Ex. 23:14–16).

> On the fifteenth day of this seventh month is the Feast of Huts [Sukkot], seven days for the Lord. On the first day is a holy convocation; you shall not do any menial work. Seven days you shall bring a fire-offering to the Lord . . . When you have gathered in the income of the land, you shall take for yourselves on the first day the fruit of goodly trees, branches of palm trees, boughs of thick trees, and willows of the brook, and you shall rejoice before the Lord your God seven days. For seven days you shall dwell in huts; every citizen in Israel shall dwell in huts, so that your generations know that I made the children of Israel dwell in huts when I brought them out from the Land of Mitzrayim (Lev. 23:33–44).

After the ingathering from your threshing floor and your vat, you shall hold the Feast of Huts for seven days. You shall rejoice in your festival, with your son and daughter, your male and female slave, the Levite, the stranger, the orphan, and the widow in your communities. You shall hold festival for the Lord your God seven days, in the place that the Lord will choose; for the Lord your God will bless you in all your income and all your handiwork, and you shall be fully joyful. Three times a year shall all your males let themselves be seen by the face of the Lord your God in the place that He will choose . . . and they shall not let themselves be seen empty-handed, but each shall come with a gift in his hand—depending on the blessing that the Lord your God has given you (Deut. 16:13–17).

While the Israelites had a traveling Shrine and then afterwards while the Temple in Jerusalem still stood, Sukkot (like all the other festivals) was celebrated partly by the offering-up to God of sacrificial animals. For each of the holy days there was a special pattern. Sukkot was unique, even compared with Pesach which was also a week long, in the sheer number of animals that were sacrificed. The fullness of number was probably felt as a symbol of gratitude for this moment of full harvest, the fulfillment of the year. Numbers 29:12–34 prescribed this pattern: on the first day of Sukkot, 13 young bulls, 2 rams, and 14 lambs; on the second day, 12 young bulls, 2 rams, and 14 lambs; and so on through the seven days, with the number of bulls dropping by one each day until on the seventh day there were 7 bulls, 2 rams, and 14 lambs. The total of the bulls, therefore, was 70. As we will see below, the rabbinic tradition found an ethical meaning in this number.

When King Solomon built the Temple in Jerusalem, he decided to dedicate it at the season of Sukkot. On the eighth of Tishri—to allow seven days for the dedication and seven for Sukkot—he assembled all the elders and leaders of the people. They brought the tent of meeting, which still survived from the days of trekking in the wilderness, holding the Ark with the two stone tablets at Sinai—from the place on Mount Zion where his father David had set them down. And every Israelite assembled to celebrate the dedication of the Temple and to hear Solomon say "But is it true that God will dwell on earth?—Here, the most heavenly of heavens cannot contain You; far less this house that I have built! Still, Lord my God, turn your face to hear the prayer of entreaty, the prayer of praise that your servant prays to You today—so that Your eyes may be open toward this house day and night" (I Kings 8).

We can only speculate why Solomon chose Sukkot as the time to dedicate the Temple. Perhaps it was simply the first pilgrim festival (when all Israel would come up to Jerusalem) after the builders had completed it. But perhaps he saw some analogy between the fragile sukkah—open to sky, to wind, to wanderers—and the house that he knew could not contain the God of earth and heaven. Indeed, the Book of Kings reports that God responded

to Solomon's prayer by warning that if Israel turned away from the commandments, a stormy-tempered God would smash "this House, be it ever so high."
So perhaps Solomon was saying that the Temple too in all its grandeur, was
but a fragile sukkah.

Whether Sukkot was regularly celebrated during the period of the First
Temple is not clear. After the return from Babylon, Nehemiah (8:17) wrote
that from the days of Joshua's crossing into the land of Israel until his own
day, the children of Israel had not built the huts of Sukkot. But from
Nehemiah's day on, the festival was celebrated at the Second Temple. Each
celebrant brought an *etrog* or citron—the yellow citrus fruit that is about
the same size as a lemon but sweeter and spicier—to serve as the "fruit of the
goodly tree" that is mentioned by Leviticus. Each brought as well the
branches of a palm, of a myrtle, and of a willow. The three branches were
held in the right hand and the *etrog* in the left—and they were brought
together to be waved east, south, west, north, up, and down. Since the palm
branch of *lulav* was the stiffest, most prominent element of the four species,
the whole ceremony was called waving the *lulav*. (We will return to this
waving as it is done in the modern congregation.) The *Mishnah* (Sukkah
4:4–5) describes the use of the four species in an exuberant ceremony that
even—in its homage to the Altar—echoes pagan customs:

How was the rite of the *lulav* fulfilled [on the Sabbath]? If the first
festival day of the Feast fell on a Sabbath, they brought their *lulavs* to
the Temple Mount and the ministers took them and set them in order
on the roof of the portico, but the elders set theirs in a [special]
chamber. The people were taught to say, "Whosoever gets possession of
my *lulav*, let it be his as a gift." The next day they came early and the
ministers threw the *lulavs* down before them and the people snatched at
them and beat each other. And when the Court saw that they incurred
danger, they ordained that every one could carry his *lulav* in his own
home.

How was the rite of the willow branch fulfilled? There was a place
below Jerusalem called Motza. Thither they went and cut themselves
young willow branches. They came and set these up at the sides of the
Altar so that their tops were bent over the Altar. They then blew [on
the shofar] a sustained, a quavering, and another sustained blast. Each
day they went in procession a single time around the Altar, saying,
"Save now, we beseech thee, O Lord! We beseech thee, O Lord, send
now prosperity." R. Judah says: "Ani waho! save us we pray! Ani waho!
save us we pray!" But on that day they went in procession seven times
around the Altar. When they departed what did they say? "Homage to
thee, O Altar! Homage to thee, O Altar!" R. Eliezer says: "To the Lord
and to thee, O Altar! To the Lord and to thee, O Altar!"

The Temple ceremonies included a ritual that is not mentioned in the Torah: the water pouring, which became the focus of the joy that the Torah commands for Sukkot. (On no other festival are we commanded to be joyful, and as a result Sukkot becomes known as the season of our joy, as Passover is the season of our freedom and Shavuot the season of giving Torah.) Says the *Mishnah*:

"The water-libation, seven days"—what was the manner of this? They used to fill a golden flagon holding three *logs* [measures] with water from Siloam. When they reached the Water Gate they blew [on the shofar] a sustained, a quavering, and another sustained blast. [The priest whose turn of duty it was] went up the [Altar-] Ramp and turned to the right where were two silver bowls. R. Judah says: "They were of plaster, but their appearance was darkened because of the wine." They had each a hole like to a narrow snout, one wide and the other narrow, so that both bowls emptied themselves together. [Thick wine poured more slowly than water; so the drain-hole for wine was wider.] The bowl to the west was for water and that to the east was for wine. But if the flagon of water was emptied into the bowl for wine, or the flagon of wine into the bowl for water, that sufficed. R. Judah says: "With one *log* they could perform the libations throughout eight days." To the priest who performed the libation they used to say, "Lift up thine hand!" for once a certain one poured the libation over his feet, and all the people threw their citrons at him.

This last incident was no minor matter. The high priest of the day was also the king—Alexander Yannai. His double role was itself a violation of the ancient constitution of the Israelites, which separated royal and priestly powers as a check on each other. His dumping the water on his feet showed his contempt for the common people in both their daily life and their religious outlook. At one level, he scorned the offering that every Israelite, no matter how poor, could bring—the water—while treating the wine offering of the rich with respect. At another level, he scorned the orally transmitted tradition of the water pouring which the priestly caste of Sadducees did not endorse because it was not explicitly mentioned in the written Torah. The folk tradition that it should be done, passed on by word of mouth, was honored as oral Torah by the Pharisees who had wide support among the people—and whose ideas were later gathered and elaborated by the rabbis of the Talmudic period into what we know as Judaism. The common folk responded to Alexander Yannai's contempt with an outraged protest that was more than symbolic—pelting him with *etrogs* even though (or because) he was the king.

The water pouring became the occasion for an outpouring of intense joy:

1. "The flute playing, sometimes five and sometimes six days"—
this is the flute playing at the Beth ha-Sho-evah. They have said: "He
that never has seen the joy of the Beth ha-Sho-evah has never in his
life seen joy."

2. At the close of the first festival day of the feast they went down
to the court of the women where they had made a huge additional
structure. There were golden candlesticks there with four golden bowls
on the top of them and four ladders to each candlestick; four youths of
the priestly stock and in their hands jars of oil holding a hundred and
twenty *logs*, which they poured into all the bowls.

3. They made wicks from the worn-out underclothes of the priests
and with them they set the candlesticks alight, and there was not a
courtyard in Jerusalem that did not reflect the light of the Beth
ha-Sho-evah.

4. Men of piety and good works used to dance before them with
burning torches in their hands, singing songs and praises. And count-
less Levites (played) on harps, lyres, cymbals and trumpets and instruments of music, on the fifteen steps leading down from the court of the
Israelites to the court of the women, corresponding to the fifteen songs
of ascents in the Psalms; upon them the Levites used to stand with
instruments of music and make melody. Two priests stood at the upper
gate which leads down from the court of the Israelites to the court of
the women, with two trumpets in their hands. At cockcrow they blew a
sustained, a quavering, and another sustained blast. When they
reached the tenth step they again blew a sustained, a quavering, and
another sustained blast. When they reached the court (of the women)
they again blew a sustained, a quavering, and another sustained blast.
They went on until they reached the gate that leads out to the east.
When they reached the gate that leads out to the east, they turned
their faces to the west and said, "Our fathers when they were in this
place turned with their backs toward the Temple of the Lord and their
faces toward the east, and they worshipped the sun toward the east; but
as for us, our eyes are turned toward the Lord." R. Judah says: They
used to repeat the words, "We are the Lord's, and our eyes are turned to
the Lord" (Tishby, *The Mishnah*).

So in the days of the Second Temple, Sukkot was a time of intense,
ecstatic celebration. Dancing, torches, juggling, flutes, the burning of the
priests' old underclothes—all contributed to the ecstasy. The description is
climaxed with the report that earlier all this was part of a sun-worshipping
ceremony. This report is one of the few explicit memories in the rabbinical
tradition of a pagan past in the heart of Jewish celebration. Since in the solar
cycle, Sukkot stands close to the autumn equinox, it is no surprise that an

element of sun-worship had entered the Temple celebration. It is no surprise that the celebration had come to include gigantic candlesticks and dancers juggling torches—human evocations of the sun's light and heat. It is more surprising that the rabbis chose to keep alive the memory of the facts. Perhaps their very choice—their readiness to break their usual restrictions on themselves—was a testimony to the overflowing joy, the sense of fallen boundaries and wild abandon, that marked Sukkot in the Second Temple period.

There are also echoes of the pagan past in the water pouring itself. It was intended, according to Rabbi Akiba, to remind the King of time and space to send the rain in its correct season. If we pour water in a seasonal rhythm, that will help God remember to pour water—when we need it. For in the Land of Israel, six months of dry weather come to an end—usually—around the time of Sukkot. If the drought lasts longer, it can bring disaster. So the water pouring, with its hint of sympathetic magic, may seem somewhat like the outlook of those who worshipped Baal, the Canaanite weather god. But there was a crucial difference. For the Baalists, there was no connection between the processes of history and those of nature. Each land had its own local gods of sun and rain, fertility; history was only the endless circle of the fruitful year. For the Jews, the same God Who inspired liberation and revealed the Torah is responsible for nature and for rain. History moves through the circles of the years into a spiral, reaching toward the days of peace and justice; and the One who brings the work of sowing to its harvest brings also every people's reach for freedom to fulfillment.

Indeed, the inclusion of this water pouring rite in the Sukkot celebration of the Second Temple, along with the exclusion of the Baalist sexual orgies that had been intended to provoke the land's fertility by imitation, may represent the defeat of Baalism among the Israelites in the course of the exile in Babylon. The prophetic attacks upon Baalist fertility orgies and upon the Baalist separation of the weather god's sphere of power from that of God won out in the crucible of exile. So when the Temple was rebuilt, the moral and ethical demands of Torah—prohibiting sexual license—were joined to the other kinds of ceremonies that had celebrated Baal and the Sun. Both were incorporated in the celebrations of Sukkot—thus firmly asserting that the God of Torah is also the God of rain.

This may be another way in which the tradition was asserting that Sukkot is fulfilling, redemptive, messianic: for what could be more messianic than the moment in which the formerly separate, partial, and amoral gods of the various nations find their truthful transmutation into the Universal Lord and Judge of all the earth? To celebrate this triumph properly it is necessary to be conscious that it has happened—and so the Mishnah reminds us of the pagan roots of the Temple celebration.

Indeed, this sense of the coming unification of all the different worships of the world is embodied in the water itself. As Eliyahu Kitov says:

At that hour, all rises with them; not only their Jewish brethren but every living being and all existence as well . . . Water remains eternally pure for all Mankind. The waters preceded the Earth, and when the Earth was destroyed, the waters were not—they remained eternally pure. . . . So when the Earth is blessed with water—all the world's inhabitants are blessed.

And in the sacrifice of animals, as well, Sukkot was a reaching-out to universal humankind, in all its differences and similarities. The rabbinic tradition teaches that 70 bulls were sacrificed during Sukkot in order to celebrate the 70 nations of the earth. (This is the way Jewish tradition saw the multiplicity of peoplehoods it discovered in Europe, Asia, and Africa.) Thus during Sukkot the people of Israel became priests on behalf of all the peoples, interceding for them all with the God of all, asserting—even without their consent—that they needed the help of the God of Heaven.

With the destruction of the Holy Temple, there ended not only the sacrifices of the 70 bulls but also the water pouring and the homage to the Altar. But the open-air sukkot themselves remained, as did the waving of the *lulav* and the beating of the willow branches. To meet the needs of worship in the synagogue, Sukkot had to be redefined through prayer and Torah reading. As the mystical aspects of Judaism were developed and encouraged by the Kabbalists from the 13th to the 16th century, the sukkah also became the home of mystical yearnings toward the unfolding aspects of God. How then do we celebrate Sukkot today?

◆❯❯❯ MAKING READY ❮❮❮◆

From the evening after Yom Kippur on, the preparations are mostly physical. They can be felt as an outward, energetic exercise, a reflex from the introspection of the days of *tshuvah*.

· People find a place for the sukkah—the backyard, an apartment house roof, a grassy part of campus, a public park, the synagogue lawn. They choose an open site, not directly under a tree—for then God would have built the sukkah, which the people are supposed to build themselves. They plan a sturdy structure that can withstand the winds.

· People begin to search out concrete blocks, wood, canvas, ropes, hammers, nails, paint, banners that will be needed to build the sukkah. They begin to gather s'chach, the leafy branches which will make the sukkah's roof. They must be green and lively. It is not always easy to find some in a modern metropolis. (In Los Angeles, the municipal park service makes huge amounts of cut or fallen branches available to sukkah-builders. You might try your own local park people.) This s'chach is to be laid in an open latticework on some supporting cords or planks for the roof of the sukkah—open enough to let in starlight but thick enough that there is more shade than sun within.

· The building begins. If there is a Sunday between Yom Kippur and Sukkot, family, friends, neighbors can all join in, make a party of it, finish one sukkah and go on to the next. If not, in a fall evening there is still plenty of good time to build a simple sukkah.

It must be no more than 10 yards high and no less than 10 handbreadths high, must have at least three walls, and should be decorated with fruits and vegetables, drawings and other hand-made decorations—sewn, knitted— that add to its beauty. (These decorations cannot be eaten or used in other ways until after Sukkot.)

· People seek a *lulav* and *etrog* for the waving. This search—which nowadays is carried on at Jewish bookstores or the stalls of Jewish market- places in neighborhoods like the Lower East Side of Manhattan or Borough Park in Brooklyn—can be turned into a joyful exploration. The customer has a chance to compare the shape and color and freshness of a number of *etrogim*, judge how it would feel to throw one at a king, make sure that the *pitom* at its top is intact. (Sniffing its smell waits till Sukkot morning.)

· There are also meditations that are traditional for this period. The 11th, 12th, 13th, and 14th of Tishri were felt by the mystics to be the days of the four-letter Name of God—*yod, hay, vav,* and *hay,* connecting Yom Kippur to the days of Sukkot with their own mystical significance in regard to aspects of God. So each day could be greeted with contemplation on the Name: perhaps seeing the four letters as the elements of the Tree of Life (the small *yod* as seed, the flowing *hay* as the spreading roots, the tall *vav* as a trunk, the flowing *hay* as leaves and branches). Or the Name can be seen as a breath: chest empty, contracted like the *yod;* a breath in, *hay!;* the chest tall and full like a *vav;* and a breath out. . . . *haaaay.* This Breath is the One that when it becomes a word, creates and gives life to all the world; for the word YHVH in Hebrew can be understood as a form of the verb to be that means causes to exist. Thus the word that is itself a breath is the word that means the transformation of God's breath, speech, into physical reality. A breathing exercise in which the meditator holds the Four Letters in consciousness while breathing could be a useful practice during these four days.

◆»» SUKKOT ««◆

Finally, the evening of Sukkot itself arrives. (Sukkot begins the night of the fifteenth of Tishri. In the Diaspora, except among Reform Jews, the second day is also observed as a full holy day; in Israel and in Reform congregations, only the first.) Friends, families, or congregations bless and light the festival candles together, if possible in the sukkah. The evening service changes from an ordinary one only in the standing *amidah*, where there is a special paragraph inserted:

> Our God and God of our forebears, may there arise and come before Your face, to be accepted and seen, to be desired and heard, to be recalled and remembered; the remembrance and recollection of ourselves, and the remembrance of our forebears, the remembrance of Messiah child of David Your servant and the remembrance of Jerusalem Your holy city, and the memory of all Your people, the household of Israel—for deliverance and good, for grace and loving-kindness and compassion, for life and for peace, this day of the Festival of Huts, the season of our joy. Remember us this day, Lord our God, for good; recall us this day for blessing; save us this day for life. With a word of salvation and compassion, spare us and extend grace to us. Mother us and save us—for our eyes look toward You because You are a gracious and motherly King . . . Blessed are You, Lord, Who hallows Israel and the festival seasons.

After the service, everyone goes out to the sukkah to share some wine and food there. But first some guests—both mystical and flesh-and-blood, especially from among the poor—must be invited in. One of the great mystics of the town of Safed in the sixteenth century, Rabbi Isaac Luria (Ha-Ari or The Lion) specified that on each of the seven nights of Sukkot, one of the great Biblical shepherds should be invited to sit in the sukkah. Each of these seven men evoked or represented one of the *S'phirot*, the aspects and emanations of God. For the mystics, the *S'phirot* were the unfolding energy levels of God that acted as a bridge between the Ultimate, Infinite God Who is beyond all understanding, and the created world with all the sparks of Divinity it contains. There are ten *S'phirot* in all, of which seven are in the discussable realm of contact with the created world. These seven—*Chesed* or Loving-kindness, *Gevurah* or Severity, *Tiferet* or Beauty, *Netzach* or Victory, *Hod* or Glory, *Yesod* or Intimacy, and *Malchut* or Majesty—have their analogues in the processes of Jewish history. Their crystallizations, as it were, came about in the seven great shepherds who are invited to be our guests in the sukkah.

So during the seven days of Sukkot, the community could reach through these seven invisible mystical guests, and through the physically palpable guests from among the poor, up to the unfolding levels of God. One of the sukkah-builders says, before eating:

> May it be Your will, Lord my God and God of my forebears, to send Your Presence to dwell in our midst and to spread over us the sukkah of Your peace, to encircle us with the majesty of Your pure and holy

radiance. Give sufficient bread and water to all who are hungry and thirsty. Give us many days to grow old upon the earth, the holy earth, that we may serve you and revere you. Blessed be the Lord forever—Amen, amen.

I invite to my meal the exalted guests—Abraham, Isaac, Jacob, Joseph, Moses, Aaron, and David.

And on each night the reader speaks directly to one of the *ushpizin* or guests:

Abraham, my exalted guest, may it please you to have all the exalted guests join me and you—Isaac, Jacob, Joseph, Moses, Aaron, and David.

And so forth, changing the guest each night.

In recent times, some groups of Jews—especially among the participatory congregations on fellowships of *chavurot*—have invited other guests into the sukkah—particularly Jewish women of the Biblical and modern ages, from Sarah the Matriarch to the poet Muriel Rukeyser. And some groups have arranged for older Jews—living alone or in hotels and nursing homes for the elderly—to visit the sukkah.

After the *ushpizin*, the guests, are invited in, there is a special *kiddush*, a blessing over wine to welcome and hallow the festival:

Baruch atah Adonai eloheynu melech ha-olam boray p'ri hagafen.

Baruch atah Adonai eloheynu melech ha-olam asher bachar-banu mi-kol am (*or* "im kol am), v'romimanu mi-kol lashon (*or* im kol lashon) v'kidshanu b'mitzvotav v'titen-lanu Adonai eloheynu b'ahavah mo-adim l'simcha, chagim uzmanim l'sasson, et yom chag ha-sukkot hazeh, z'man simchateynu, mikra kodesh zeycher l'tziyat mitzrayim. Ki vanu vacharta, v'otanu kidashta mikol (*or* im kol) ha-amim umo-adai kad-shecha b'simcha uv'sasson hinchaltanu. Baruch atah Adonai mikadesh Yisrael v'hazmanim.

Blessed are You, Lord our God, King of the universe, Who creates the fruit of the vine.

Blessed are You, Lord our God, King of the universe, Who has chosen us and lifted us up from among all peoples, has made us holy through Your commandments, and lovingly given us, Lord our God, festivals for joy, celebrations and seasons for gladness—this day of the Festival of

Huts, the season of our joy. It is a holy assembly in memory of the
Exodus from Egypt . . . Blessed are You, Lord, Who makes Israel and
the seasons holy.

Then the group says together the blessing for sitting in the sukkah:

Baruch atah Adonai, eloheynu melech ha-olam asher kid'shanu b'mitzvotav v'tzivanu leysheyv ba-sukkah.

Blessed are You, Lord our God, Who makes us holy through Your
commandments, and commands us to sit in the sukkah.

And on this first night the group adds *Sheh-hechianu*, blessing the One
Who has kept them alive till the return of the Sukkot season. And then all sit
on a seat in the sukkah, to drink the wine and eat the food.

Traditionally, adult Jewish men have tried to sleep in the sukkah and to
eat all their meals there during Sukkot. In the past few generations, many
(women and men) have treated the sukkah as a sort of way station between
camping out and living at home. Children have slept there in sleeping bags;
some people have arranged to have at least one meal a day there; it has
become a place to have a party that is joyful with the deeper undertones of
ancient celebration. In Jerusalem especially, but in other Jewish communities
as well, the Joy of the water pouring (Simchat Beit ha-Sho-evah) is recalled
in song, dance, good food, and festive clothing.

THE MORNING SERVICE

Besides the festival prayer added to the *amidah*, there are four special
aspects of the Sukkot morning service: the waving of the *lulav*, the singing of
the psalms of *Hallel* (Praise), the procession of the congregation carrying
lulavim around the Torah; and the reading of special Torah portions for
Sukkot.

BENSCHING (BLESSING) LULAV

The bundle of the *lulav* is made up of three myrtle twigs, two willow
twigs, and one palm branch. They are all bound with the cut edge down,
with the palm branch in the center. When the worshipper grasps the palm
branch with its back toward the worshipper's face, the myrtle should be on
the right and the willow on the left.

The point of *bensching lulav* is reached in the morning service after the
amidah. Each worshipper then picks up the *lulav* bundle in the right hand and
the *etrog* in the left, with the *pitom* of the *etrog* pointing downward (unlike
the way it grows). They say the blessing of the *lulav*:

Baruch atah Adonai eloheynu melech
ha-olam asher kid'shanu b'mitzvotav vitzivanu al n'tilat lulav.

Blessed are You, Lord our God, King of all space–time, who makes us
holy through his commandments and commands us concerning the
shaking of the *lulav*.

And this is followed by *Sheh-hechianu,* praising God for giving life to
reach this moment. Then the worshippers shift the *etrog* around in their left
hands so that the *pitom* is upward, and bring their left hands close to the
right—so that all four species are close together. Next they stretch their arms
out frontward (facing east) and with a shaking motion pull both hands, held
together, toward themselves—three times reaching out and pulling in. This
is the shaking or waving. Still facing east, the worshippers stretch their arms
out to the right and do the same waving three times; reach over their
shoulders and again wave from outward in toward themselves three times;
and again to the left, and toward the sky, and toward the earth.

If some worshippers did not buy *lulav* and *etrog* before Sukkot, those who
did can make them gifts of their own after waving. The gift can be returned,
but traditionally while you are waving you should be conscious that the *lulav*
is your own. If the congregation as a body buys the *lulav* and *etrog*, every
member owns it.

What is going on in the waving? There are many possibilities of spiritual
approach:

· Close your eyes as you wave. Focus on the rustling sound of the *lulav*
and the smell of the *etrog.* Let them become *your* branches and *your* fruit, so
that *you* are the four-in-one tree whose fruit and branches are waving in the
wind. You. Are. The. Tree. The. Tree. Of. Life, which according to
tradition is what the Torah is. A human being living a decent, holy life
becomes a Torah, a Tree of Life. Such a person becomes an organic part of the
natural world, a microcosm of the universe.

· As you wave, be conscious that you are pulling all six directions of the
universe toward you, for a moment the very center of all the worlds. They *all*
depend on your internal clarity and unity.

· The four species represent the four letters of the Name. The *etrog* looks
like a *yod;* the soft and curving myrtle like a *hay;* the tall and springy palm
branch like a *vav;* the soft and curving willow like a *hay.* The bringing
together of the right and left hands unifies the Name. (It is spelled in the
right order only for someone facing you. God? Your friends and comrades?
Those who are not yet conscious of the Unity, since Sukkot is the moment
when God's Name will become One to all who live on earth?)

· The four species are like four different kinds of Jews; the *etrog,* with
both taste and smell, those who both study Torah and do good deeds; the
palm, with tasty fruit but no smell, those who study Torah but do not act; the

myrtle, with a smell but no taste, those who do good deeds but do not study; the willow, with neither taste nor smell, those who do neither. *All four* are necessary to a community—even those who neither act nor study.

· And each new experience with waving *lulav* may lead to a new sense of what is going on.

The *lulav* is to be waved every morning of Sukkot except on Shabbos. (It could be done communally or individually, with special joy, in the sukkah.) Immediately afterward, on every morning of Sukkot, *Hallel* (Praise) is sung. This is a collection of psalms—from Psalm 113 to 118—which is sung on each of the four Torah-based festivals and on Hanukkah as well (but not on the solemn holy days of Rosh Hashanah and Yom Kippur). For parts of these Psalms there are traditional tunes.

Hallel begins with the leader of congregational prayer reciting a blessing. The individual participants respond "Amen" and then say the blessing themselves.

Baruch atah Adonai eloheynu melech ha-olam
asher kid'shanu b'mitzvotav vitzivanu likro et ha-Hallel.

Blessed are You . . . Who has commanded us to call out the Hallel.

During the "Hodu l'Adonai kitov, ki l'olam chasdo" and "Yomar na Yisrael ki l'olam chasdo" the *lulav* is waved again to the six directions of the world—one direction for each word, pausing for God's name, Adonai.

Close to the end of Psalm 118, the outcry "Please, Lord, save us! Please, Lord, send us prosperity" is chanted responsively:

> Ana Adonai hoshia na
> Ana Adonai hoshia na
> Ana Adonai hatzlicha na
> Ana Adonai hatzlicha na

and during the first two lines (hosannas in English, a word made from *hoshia na*) the *lulav* is shaken again in six directions—two directions for each of the words, again leaving out Adonai.

When the *Hallel* is completed, there is a closing blessing:

Baruch atah Adonai melech
m'hulal batishbachot. Blessed are You, Lord, King who is praised with songs of praise.

After *Hallel* (or in some congregations after the festival *musaf* or additional service), a Torah scroll is taken out of the Ark, and everyone joins in one *hakkafah* or encircling procession around the Torah, chanting *"Hosha-*

not." Most of these prayers for deliverance were written by Eleazar Kalir, who lived in the eighth century. Each *Hoshanah* is arranged in alphabetic phrases running from *aleph* to *tof*. The order in which they are said depends on which day of the week is the first day of Sukkot. On Shabbos the *Hoshanot* are recited, but there is no procession; and on the seventh day of Sukkot there are seven processions and the day is named *Hoshanah Rabbah* (the great *Hoshanah*). It takes on a special character of its own, and will be discussed below.

BIBLICAL READINGS

When Sukkot begins on a weekday, the preparatory service before the Torah reading includes a sublime passage from the Torah on God as Loving-kindness personified. The passage is chanted:

> Adonai adonai eyl rachum v'chanun erech apayim v'rav chesed v'emet, notzeyr chesed l'alafim nosey avon vafesha v'chata-ah v'nakey.

> The Lord, the Lord, God motherly and gracious, slow to anger, bountiful with loving-kindness and truth, Who keeps loving-kindness to the thousandth generation, pardoning iniquity, transgression, and sin, and forgiving.

The passage is chanted three times. In some congregations the custom is to chant it with vigor the first time, gently the second, and in a whisper the third—so that by the end the Loving One is experienced as the still small voice within.

The Prophetic readings for Sukkot point toward the universal messianic transformation of the world, and thus represent in words of Torah the messianic vision that was embodied in the special Sukkot sacrifices while the Temple stood.

On the first (and second) day of Sukkot, the Torah reading is Leviticus 22:26–23:44. Most of this is the recitation of the festival cycle of the year, but it begins a paragraph earlier than it would need to, with the commandment: "When a bullock, a sheep, or a goat is born, for seven days it shall be under its mother; from the eighth day on it may be accepted for a fire-offering to the Lord." Since the reading ends with the provisions for seven days of Sukkot and an eighth-day festival, Sh'mini Atzeret, in its seven days/eighth-day formula there may be an intentional echo, a hint that the seven days of Sukkot are a time especially close to the Motherly One—followed by the wintry eighth day of Sh'mini Atzeret, a day of memorial for the dead.

The *maftir* or concluding Torah portion, from Numbers 19:12–16, prescribes the sacrifices for the first day of Sukkot. The Prophetic reading for the first day is from Zechariah (14:1–21). It includes the passage that is the climax of the *Alenu* prayer in the synagogue service: "On that day the Lord shall be One and His Name One." Zechariah describes a great convulsion, a battle at Jerusalem and an earthquake cleaving the Mount of Olives in two, but ending with Jerusalem safe. Then from all the peoples there shall come pilgrims to Jerusalem, to worship God and to celebrate the festival of Sukkot. Whichever of earth's peoples will not go up to celebrate Sukkot, for them there shall be no rain—as if the relationship between God and Israel would then be broadened on the same terms to all the earth.

On the second day, the *haftarah* is from I Kings 8:2–21. It is the description of Solomon's dedication of the Holy Temple at the time of Sukkot: a house for God's Name. On the Shabbos that comes in the midst of Sukkot, the Torah reading is Exodus 33:12–34:26, in which Moses asks for a direct personal revelation of the essence of God and receives instead a revelation of God's attributes of compassion and loving-kindness, concluding with a brief review of the festivals. The *maftir* is the relevant burnt offering from Numbers 29—that for the second day if Shabbos falls on the second day of Sukkot, etc.

The *haftarah*, from Ezekiel 38:18–39:16, describes the last great battle of the future, the battle of Gog and Magog against Israel. It describes the stunning disaster that God will send upon Gog, so that once and for all the people of Israel shall be safe and God's triumph shall be recognized throughout the earth.

On most of the festivals there is traditionally assigned for reading one or another book from the *K'tuvim* (Writings or Literature) section of the Bible—the section made up of poems like the Psalms, novellas like the Books of Ruth and Esther, histories, and tragedies. At the Sukkot season, the book traditionally assigned is *Kohelet* (or Ecclesiastes), to be read either on the Shabbos in the middle of Sukkot or on Sh'mini Atzeret. The content of *Kohelet* feels more appropriate to the wintry, contracting atmosphere of Sh'mini Atzeret than to the fulfilling and expansive atmosphere of Sukkot; so we will examine *Kohelet* in the next chapter.

HOSHANAH RABBAH

When the Temple stood, on the seventh day of Sukkot the priests marched seven times around the Altar, waving the *lulav*, beating its leaves against the ground, and standing specially new-cut willow branches around the Altar. The historian Theodore Gaster suggests that the beating of the willows was a widespread custom in many cultures, where the willow symbolized fertility and the beating was intended to increase potency and procreation. In any case, the beating of the willows and the seven processions survive in traditional synagogues today.

Through the centuries, the belief grew that *Hoshanah Rabbah* was a special day of completion of the High Holy Days, the very last moment when human life or death might be decreed by Heaven. The leader of congregational prayer often wears a white *kittel* as a reminder of the wearing of the *kittel* on Yom Kippur, and uses the melodies of Yom Kippur. A number of the special prayers for the Days of Tshuvah and Yom Kippur are added to the service (*Avinu Malkenu* and *Un'taneh Tokef,* and the sentences in the *amidah* focusing on the God of life). Some people stay awake through the night of *Hoshanah Rabbah* reading all five of the Books of Moses or the Books of Deuteronomy and Psalms, and immerse themselves in the *mikveh* before dawn.

When the *Hallel* has been sung and the seven processions of *Hoshanot* have been completed, the celebrants take five willow branches, bound together. They chant together a number of prayerful poems, and then beat the willow branch five times on the ground. As the leaves fall off the willow, they can be seen today as a symbol of fading, falling lives, or as a symbol of casting off our old and dying sins.

The willow is then saved, to be used to heat the oven where matzah is baked next Pesach. The *lulav* can also be saved for the same purpose, or used instead of a feather in the hunt for *chametz* (leaven) the night before Passover begins. The *etrog* can be made into preserves for Pesach, or whole cloves can be stuck into its skin so that it becomes a naturally fragrant spicebox to use at the *havdalah* ceremony on Saturday night. All these customs help bind the doing of one *mitzvah* to the doing of another, the celebration of one season to the celebration of another—especially Sukkot to Pesach, exactly six months later.

THE SEVENTH SUKKOT

The Torah commands that in every seventh year, all land shall lie fallow and there shall be a release or anulment (*shmitah*) of all debts. In this way the land and its farmers were to have a long Sabbath, and those who had fallen into debt were to recover their economic equality.

In addition, the Torah proclaims that at the Sukkot connected with this *shmitah* or Sabbatical year, the whole people—men, women, children, even the foreigner sojourning in the land—should assemble to hear the priests read the Torah so as to teach the people their obligations to observe the Teaching.

The *Mishnah* required that this ceremony (called *hak-heyl,* assemble) take place on the first day of Sukkot following the completion of a Sabbatical year. (According to later commentators, this made sure that the people would be honoring God's word after a year in which there had been neither sowing nor organized harvesting, but God's providence had been shown forth without these acts of human planning.) The rabbis, the priests, and the king would all be involved in the reading. The readings were taken from Deuteronomy: 1:1–6:19, 11:13–21, 14:22–27, 26:12–15, 17:14–20, and 27:15–26.

The readings ended with blessings similar to those said by the high priest on Yom Kippur.

The ceremony of *hak-heyl* fell into disuse after the collapse of the Jewish monarchy; but in the past generation, some Israeli settlements that observe the Sabbatical year have revived a symbolic form of it. Among a few American *chavurah* and synagogue congregations, there were some observances of the ceremony in 1973 and 1980, at the ends of the last two Sabbatical years. The next years in which *hak-heyl* might be done are 1987, 1994, 2001, and 2008. In addition to part or all of the traditional readings, the ceremony might include a seven-year review of how the Jewish community and the general society are doing in regard to preservation of the earth-environment and in regard to economic equality and social justice.

◆》》 FOODS * 《《◆

CARROT AND SWEET POTATO TZIMMES

1 lb. carrots
1½ lb. sweet potatoes
1 tart apple
½ cup brown sugar and honey

3 tablespoons chicken fat (or vegetable fat)
salt and pepper
lemon juice and assorted spices

Dice carrots, potatoes, and apple and cook until very tender and very little water left. Add rest of ingredients. Adjust to slightly spicy, tart taste. Heat through watching carefully so it doesn't burn. Will serve 5–6. A white potato may be added.

COOKIE DOUGH STRUDEL

3½ cups sifted flour
¼ teaspoon bicarbonate of soda
¾ teaspoon baking powder
½ cup sugar

1 cup vegetable fat
2 eggs—separated
½ cup orange juice

Cut fat into sifted dry ingredients as for pie dough. Add egg yolks. Gradually add orange juice to make smooth dough. Chill. Roll into three or four leaves about ⅛ inch thick. Whip the whites of the eggs and use to paint the leaves and the tops of the rolls. Paint and then put layers of jam, nuts, coconut, some finely diced apple, a mixture of sugar and cinnamon, and lemon rind, raisins. May be sprinkled with a little lemon juice if more tartness is desired.

---

*Recipes by Hannah Waskow and Rose Gertz.

Roll as for jelly roll being sure to seal the ends and edges to avoid leaking. Paint top with beaten whites and sprinkle with cinnamon and sugar. Bake on *ungreased* sheet at 375° 30–40 minutes or until done. Remove pan and slice quickly. A filling of prepared mohn may also be used.

MONDELBROT

6 cups flour
4 teaspoons baking powder
⅓ cup water
3 eggs
dash salt
grated lemon rind

1 scant cup sugar
½ lb. vegetable fat
⅓ cup oil
1 teaspoon vanilla
1 teaspoon almond extract

Mix flour, baking powder, salt, sugar. Add beaten eggs, fat, oil, rind, extracts and water. May add a little more flour and water if dough is too short to handle. Add ½ cup raisins, ½ cup nuts, cherries (optional) and knead to mix well. Refrigerate for several hours or overnight. Shape into rolls about 2½ inches wide and 1 to 1½ inches thick and 10 inches long. Bake 350° until light brown. Cool slightly, cut into 1–1½ inch slices and dip into mixture of sugar, cinnamon, dash of nutmeg, cloves and return to oven to brown lightly. (Place on side. Turn and repeat.)

CINNAMON COOKIES

4 cups flour
4 teaspoons baking powder
3 eggs
⅛ teaspoon salt
1 scant cup sugar

1 teaspoon vanilla
1 lemon rind
½ lb. vegetable fat
½ cup oil
¼ cup water

Mix for handling, cut into shapes, and sprinkle with mixture of cinnamon, sugar, nutmeg, and cloves. Bake until light brown at 375°.

◆≫≫ GO AND STUDY ≪≪◆

See Philip Goodman, *The Sukkot and Simhat Torah Anthology* (Jewish Publication Society) and Irving Greenberg, *Guide to Sukkot* (National Jewish Resource Center, NYC). For instructions on sukkah-building, see *The First Jewish Catalog* (JPS).

MINTZ-GANIN KETUBAH

The autumn rains, for which we begin to pray at Sh'mini Atzeret, represent
that time of the year when the desert begins to take on the nourishment
which will cause the land to bring forth fruit.

⟨⟫ CHAPTER FOUR ⟪⟩
SEED FOR WINTER— SH'MINI ATZERET

After the moon of Tishri has been celebrated in its birth, its swelling, and its fullness, the moon begins to wane, prophesying its own disappearance. At the same moment, in the solar cycle of the year, the fields stand bare and the seed is stored away. In the land of Israel, farmers begin to sniff the smell of rain. Winter looms, the fourth season of the year. The earth prepares to hibernate, go underground, build up reserves of strength to make new life.

The waning moon and the fourth season need a fourth festival, for we need to welcome winter in the world and in ourselves. Mechanical symmetry might have required that a fourth festival stand on its own at the outset of winter, as Shavuot stands at the outset of summer. But Rabbi Joshua ben Levi explained that when the Temple stood, we could not wait till winter to make the pilgrimage to the Temple in Jerusalem. Torrential rains, muddy roads— these meant that we must stay home. So the winter festival was placed immediately at the end of the fall festival, when the pilgrims were still at the Temple.

Just as the spring festival of new life and liberation was not complete till we had counted seven weeks plus one day to the summer festival of fullness and revelation, so the fall festival of ingathering and redemption was not complete till we had counted seven days plus one day to the winter festival of sleeping and inwardness. When the pilgrims returned home, they needed just behind them not the boisterous joy of the sukkah and the water pouring, but the quiet celebration of a sense of inner peace.

So to meet this need we had Sh'mini Atzeret. Some translate this as the Eighth Day of Completion, others, the Eighth Day of Assembly. For *atzeret* means putting a boundary, restraining, collecting—either the days (and so, completion of the festival) or the people (and so, assembly of the multitude).

We can understand the restraint as inward, too. While the Temple stood, we turned from the expansive week of the multiple sacrifices of Sukkot to the minimum: one bull, one ram. The Talmud teaches that this reduction of the sacrifice from 70 bulls to one represents God's turning from concern with the 70 nations—the whole world—to a quiet tête-à-tête alone with the people of Israel. The approach fits well with seeing Sh'mini Atzeret as the inward, wintry holy day, the festival of self-restraint.

Not only was the explicit message of Sh'mini Atzeret a measure of constriction, retreat, quiet—so was its medium, the implicit message of its form. For by tacking Sh'mini Atzeret right on to Sukkot, the Torah made sure that it would almost disappear from sight—like a seed disappearing into the ground; made sure that the tradition would speak of the *three* pilgrimage festivals—Pesach, Shavuot, and Sukkot—while almost forgetting the fourth. Almost—but never quite.

It is as if this shadowy festival, this miniature celebration, was the *yod*—the tiny letter of the four in God's most holy name. The *yod* is the first letter of the Name, but suppose we see the Name as a continuing process, a spiral in which the end is a new beginning and the beginning stands also at the end. Then the *yod* is a tiny seed at the *end* of the Name, the concentrated lesson of its flowering, the seed that carries meaning forward to begin the next saying of the Name.

◆»» ORIGINS «« ◆

In the four passages where Torah recites the festivals, Sh'mini Atzeret appears only twice. In Exodus 23 and Deuteronomy 16, Sukkot appears as a seven-day holiday, standing alone. But in Leviticus 33:36, God tells Moses to explain to the Israelites:

> On the eighth day you shall observe a sacred assembly and bring a fire-offering to the Lord; it is a solemn gathering; you shall not work at your occupations.

And Numbers 29:35–38 specifies:

> On the eighth day you shall hold a solemn gathering; you shall not work at your occupations. You shall present a burnt-offering, an offering by fire of pleasing odor to the Lord; one bull, one ram, seven yearling lambs, without blemish; the meal offerings and libations for

the bull, the ram, and the lambs, in the quantities prescribed, and one goat for a sin offering—in addition to the regular burnt offering, its meal offering and libation.

During the period of the Second Temple, it became the norm to pray for rain for the first time each year on Sh'mini Atzeret. Thus Sh'mini Atzeret became the specific place among the Tishri festivals to locate that part of the ancient Middle Eastern autumn celebration that looked forward to the winter rain. The *Mishnah* explains that rain during Sukkot would drench the lattice-roofed sukkah, and so would feel to those who were living there like a curse rather than a blessing. So the prayer for rain should wait till the sukkah dwelling was complete. It may also be true that by waiting to pray for rain till Sh'mini Atzeret, separating the water pouring of Sukkot from the rain prayer of Sh'mini Atzeret by one full week, the tradition kept the two from fully combining into one act of sympathetic magic.

With the destruction of the Temple, the rabbis preserved the sense of restraint and retreat that had pervaded Sh'mini Atzeret by seeing it as a faint and final echo of Yom Kippur. It is the day on which the world is rewarded or punished through the giving or withholding of rain, and therefore the last day of the Tishri season on which repentance and prayer before God may bring forgiveness.

◆》》》 PRESENT PRACTICE 《《《◆

Sh'mini Atzeret begins as do other Festival days. The Festival candle is lit and the blessing *Sheh-hechianu* said to praise God for keeping us alive until this moment. *Kiddush* is made over wine, and the evening service follows the usual Festival pattern.

In the morning, the *Hallel* psalms of praise (Psalms 113–118) are sung, the special Festival paragraph is read in the *amidah,* and the *yizkor* memorial service for the dead is read. There are two Torah readings: Deuteronomy 14:22–16:17 describes the tithing process to support the poor, the release of debts in every seventh year, and the liberation of slaves in the seventh year of their service. The brief passage from Numbers 21:35–39 describes the special sacrifices for the day: one bull, one ram, and seven yearling lambs. The Prophetic *haftarah* is I Kings 8:54–66, in which King Solomon and the whole people complete—on Sh'mini Atzeret—their dedication of the Holy Temple, and the people begin their departure to their homes.

After the Torah is read, the recitation of the *Kaddish* that ends the morning service is done with the melody used on Yom Kippur, and the leader of prayer puts on the Yom Kippur white robe or *kittel* in preparation for the rain prayer.

It is in the *musaf* (additional) service that Sh'mini Atzeret has its distinctive moment, different from all the other holy days. Since the previous Passover, through the summer months, the congregation has been praying that God send dew to keep the earth moist—for there is no rain in the Land of Israel during those months. Now, at *musaf* on Sh'mini Atzeret, the prayer changes.

When it is time for the standing *amidah* prayer to be repeated aloud by the person who is leading the congregation in prayer, the Ark is opened. The leader begins the *amidah* and pauses in the midst of the first of its blessings after ". . . O King, Helper, Savior, and Shield!" The reader then chants a brief prayer: "*Af-Bri* is the name of the prince of rain, who gathers the clouds and makes them drop rain, water to adorn the earth with green. Be it not held back because of unpaid debts! Shield your faithful who pray for rain," and completes the blessing, "Blessed are you, the Shield of Abraham. You are mighty forever, Lord; You revive the dead and are great in saving power." The reader then chants a prayerful poem by Eleazar Kalir that is presumably a plea for rain, but in fact asks some thirty times not for rain, *geshem*, but for water, *mayim*. In a way this prayer brings all the water imagery of the Tishri festivals to a flood of meaning, for it reminds us of all the adventures our forebears had with wells and seas and rivers.

The prayer can be sung in English to the tune of "Cool Clear Water" and the translation of David de Sola Pool:

Our God, God of our forebears:

Remember one who followed Thee as to the sea flows water
Thy blessed son, like tree well set where rivers met of water
Where'er he moved, Thou wast his shield; in fire or field or water
And heaven-proved, his seed he sowed, wherever flowed a water.
For Abram's sake send water!

Remember one whose heralds three beneath the tree had water,
Whose sire was won to do Thy will, his blood to spill like water.
Himself as high in faith could soar, his heart to pour like water.
Where earth lay dry, he dug and found deep underground the water.
For Isaac's sake send water!

Remember one, his staff who bore from Jordan's shore o'er water,
And rolled the stone—his love to tell—from off the well of water,
And, wrestling hard, achieved to tire a prince of fire and water.
Hence Thy regard him safe to bear through fire and air and water.
For Jacob's sake send water!

Remember one whose ark 'mid sedge was drawn from edge of water,
Thy shepherd son who could not sleep before his sheep had water.
And when Thy flock did likewise burn with thirst and yearn for water,

He struck the rock, there gushed a rill, to give their fill of water.
For Moses' sake send water!

Remember one, Thy Temple-priest, who hallowed feast with water.
Atonement's sun declined to night with fivefold rite of water.
The Law was read, and then afresh he laved his flesh with water.
Remote, in dread, he served his folk that swiftly broke like water.
For Aaron's sake send water!

Remember last the tribes who fled across the bed of water,
Thy chosen caste for whom turned sweet the bitter sheet of water.
For Thee their race have ever shed their hearts' best red like water.
Without Thy face their spirits whirl as in a swirl of water!
For Israel's sake send water!

And finally, the prayer comes to a climax:

For You are the Lord our God, who makes the wind blow and the rain
fall!—for blessing and not for disaster; for life and not for death; for
plenty and not for famine.

From this point on in every *amidah* until the *musaf* service on the first
day of Pesach, the congregation mentions that God is the One Who makes
the wind blow and the rain fall.

Once we experience the pleading of this prayer, the Sukkot water
pouring takes on a deeper quality. Perhaps it was intended not to coerce
nature, but to free the people from their own dryness so they could one week
later plead with God. It is to be our prayers that water heaven, not the water
poured upon the ground.

Why is the prayer for rain introduced into the blessing that praises God
for reviving the dead? Because rain revives the parched and deadened earth,
gives life to seeds that are buried underground. And so, as Sh'mini Atzeret
ends, we look once more to the great revival.

In the afternoon, although Sukkot is over and it is no longer a *mitzvah* to
eat in the sukkah, the traditional custom was to eat there anyway one last
time, as a gesture of love and respect, and on leaving to say: "Just as I merited
to sit in this sukkah, may it be Your will that next year I merit to sit in that
sukkah made from the skin of Leviathan. Next year in Jerusalem!" For when
Messiah comes, according to folk legend, God will turn leatherworker (as at
the end of Eden when God made leather garments for Eve and Adam). God
will at last slay the primeval sea monster Leviathan, and from its skin will
tailor the great sukkah that enfolds all Israel in peace. Under that sukkah we
will all sit, to dine on Leviathan's meat. No longer will we need to fear a
monster from the deeps—the ocean deep, or the depths of our own souls.

THE READING OF ECCLESIASTES

On Shabbos during Sukkot or on Sh'mini Atzeret, the book of *Kohelet* or Ecclesiastes (Convoker or Assembler) is traditionally read as one of the five scrolls or *megillot* set aside for five of the holy days. (The others are the Book of Esther for Purim, Song of Songs for Pesach, Ruth for Shavuot, and Lamentations for Tisha B'Av.)

The tradition gives two reasons for reading *Kohelet* at this season. One is that its melancholy overtones fit the time of year; the other, that the verse (11:2) "Distribute portions to seven or even to eight . . ." refers to the seven day/eighth-day pattern of Sukkot and Sh'mini Atzeret. On either ground, it would seem especially appropriate to read *Kohelet* during Sh'mini Atzeret.

It is a wintry book, the summing up of a cycle of life that has revolved its way through joy and sorrow, war and peace, merry-making and boredom. Its author has concluded: "Whoever keeps watch on the wild will never sow seed; whoever scans the clouds will never reap . . . Sow your seed in the morning, and don't hold back your hand in the evening, since you don't know which is going to succeed, the one or the other, or if both are equally good." It is the book of detachment, of accepting whatever you get, of learning to enjoy not only the peaks but also the chasms of an involved life—and then learning to float beyond those very hills and valleys. It is the book that says: In the light of my approaching death, how disastrous is this disgrace? How wonderful this triumph?

In traditional congregations, *Kohelet* is read just before the Torah service. Some congregations read it individually, as a kind of introspective meditation. Others read it aloud from a handwritten scroll, like the reading of *Esther* at Purim, and pronounce over it the blessing "Who has commanded us about the reading of the scroll":

Baruch atah Adonai eloheynu melech ha-olam asher kid'shanu b'mitzvotav vitzivanu al mikra megillah.

And then, the blessing *Sheh-hechianu*, in praise of the One Who keeps us alive. In less traditional congregations, the song "Turn Turn Turn" (taken from 3:1–8) may be sung to Pete Seeger's tune, and part or all of *Kohelet* may be read and discussed later in the day.

◆⟩⟩⟩ NEW APPROACHES ⟨⟨⟨◆

On Sh'mini Atzeret we remember the dead in *yizkor* and then pray for water. Is our water prayer a plea for drops of rain alone—or also for tears, the ability to cry? Tears less exalted than those of Yom Kippur, less frightened than those of Tisha B'Av—but tears of memory and compassion?

In the phrase we add to the *amidah*, "Who makes the wind blow and the rain fall," we use *ruach* for wind—the word that means not only the rush of air in the world but also the rush of breath within our bodies and the rushing spirit in our souls. Just so, perhaps, the raindrops that we pray for can be the drops within as well as those without: the tears that fall from our bodies and our spirits when we are most sad and most compassionate, when we are full to overflowing with a sad and plaintive love. Perhaps the real water pouring that evokes God's love is our pouring out of tears.

One spiritual task of Jews at Sh'mini Atzeret may, therefore, be to open the wellsprings of their own compassion. The recitation of *yizkor* may be a time for the congregation not only to remember the family dead and far-off famous martyrs, but the deaths and cripplings that are near at hand. A few participatory *chavurah* congregations have read part of Allen Ginsberg's *Kaddish*—his memorial poem for his mother, one of the greatest crystallizations of the first painful generations of American Jewish life. In its transmutation of that pain into great art, the poem not only helps tears to fall but achieves the same revival of the dead that we celebrate in the prayer for rain.

There was a time one fall when Jews from all across America came together to plant a tree of peace on the grounds of the United States Capitol. It was a dismal rainy day, a dismal dispirited time in the long years of effort to end the Vietnam War. The tens of thousands who had gathered months before to call for peace had vanished, and there were only dozens in their place.

One by one, people vowed to end the destruction of the trees of Vietnam. One by one they placed a shovel-full of earth upon the roots of the tree, and one by one they watered it with tears of sorrow and frustration. Together they sang a new and plaintive tune to an old song, a song long sung about the Torah:

Etz chayim hi l'machizikim bah . . . etz chayim hi l'shalom.
She is a tree of life for those who hold her tight; a tree of life, for peace.

And since then on Sh'mini Atzeret it has been possible to remember and to cry:

Remember those who struggled in the desert, Lord,
And for their sake please give us water.

The trees of life need water, Lord.
In this new desert, napalm-seared,
We till a soil that rots our flesh.
We turn a soil so poison-soaked it turns the rain to poison.
It rains and rains, but our trees die.
Our trees need water.

The tree of peace needs water, Lord.
On this deserted lawn beneath the Capitol
We lift our puny spades against its power.
We turn a soil so power-soaked it turns the rain to poison.
It rains and rains, but our tree dies.
Our tree needs water.

The Tree of Life needs water, Lord.
In this dry city of Your absence, Lord,
We plant old prayers of withered meaning.
We walk a land so soaked with fear it turns Your rain to poison.
It rains and rains, but Torah dies.
The Tree needs water.

We do not pray for rain, O Lord;
We have enough.
We pray to be allowed to cry.
We pray You open dry canals.
We pray for tears: a stream of tears,
Enough to water into strength
The seeds that fall from helpless trees
That we have planted.

Remember us still struggling in the desert, Lord,
And for Your sake please give us water.

 FOODS

ANGEL-WING CHALLAH*

2 envelopes dry yeast	4 tablespoons vegetable oil
½ cup lukewarm water	2 teaspoons salt
2 cups hot water	2 tablespoons sugar
2 eggs, beaten	poppy seeds
7–8 cups flour (about)	

Note: pinch of saffron (brew in a little hot water and strain if you want a
    yellow challah)

Soften the yeast in the lukewarm water. To the boiling hot water, add the
saffron (brew) if wanted, oil, salt, and sugar. Stir until the sugar is dissolved.
Cool and when lukewarm, *not before*, add the softened yeast. Reserve about 2

---

*Recipe by Hannah Waskow and Rose Gertz

tablespoons of the egg for brushing loaves later, and add the remainder to the liquid. Turn into a large mixing bowl, add about three cups of flour. Stir and beat to a smooth, thick batter. Set aside for 10 minutes; add flour to make dough that can be handled. Turn out on a floured board and knead until smooth and elastic. Shape into a ball and grease the entire surface well. Place in well-greased mixing bowl, cover with a clean cloth. Let rise in a warm, never hot, place to double in bulk. (If your oven does not have a pilot light, a warm pan of water in the bottom of the stove will help the dough to rise. It may be necessary to change the water once or twice.) Try to avoid over-rising as it will affect the texture of the challah. Punch down and knead again until dough is fine-grained. Divide dough to make two loaves. Form each portion into a long roll about 2 inches thick. Coil each roll to look like a coiled snake with its head up in the center—which is how people saw angels with their wings raised. (Tuck the end of the coil under the side to hold in place.) Place loaves on greased baking sheet. Using pans of a size that will allow the ends of the challah to climb for support will help. Cover, let rise to double in bulk as before. Add a spoonful of cold water to the reserved egg. Brush the surface of both loaves and sprinkle with poppy seed. Bake in a hot oven (400° F.) for about 15 minutes. Reduce temperature to moderate (350° F.) and bake for 45 minutes. Test for doneness by tapping bottom of challah. They should sound hollow. Cool on racks. May be sliced and frozen. Very good toasted.

◆❯❯ GO AND STUDY ❮❮◆

See Philip Goodman, *The Sukkot and Simhat Torah Anthology* (Jewish Publication Society).

BIRKAT HACHAMAH

A scene from the Garden of Eden on the third day represents the creation story which is read as we complete one cycle of Torah readings and begin another.

CHAPTER FIVE
DANCING WITH TORAH—SIMCHAT TORAH

S h'mini Atzeret teaches us to put seeds of *Yod*, of new life, quietly underground, there to hibernate until the spring. But it is hard to wait. We need some proof of new life now. So Sh'mini Atzeret also carries within itself the proof of the flowering. On the second day of the festival we turn from the natural world to the Torah—and behold, its end leads at once to its beginning!

About ten centuries ago, the second day of Sh'mini Atzeret was turned into Simchat Torah—a special holy day of Joy in the Torah. It celebrates the completion of the annual cycle for reading the Torah—the Five Books of Moses—and it is when we start afresh to read the beginning of the Torah. If this were all there was to it, it would be enough to see Simchat Torah as the festival of end-and-beginning. But there is more: the content of this end and this beginning underscore the lesson. For at the end of the Five Books is the death of Moses our Teacher; and at the beginning is the Creation of the World. So Simchat Torah acts out by public proclamation what Sh'mini Atzeret preaches as an underlying fact of life: that from seeming death comes profound new energy for birth.

There is also a sense in which the emphasis on Torah underscores the Sh'mini Atzeret lesson of the uses of contraction, inwardness. The rabbis saw that the ceremonial expansiveness of Sukkot was suddenly reduced: no sukkah, no *lulav*, no water pouring, no beating of the willows—only students reading the black ink on white parchment. No resplendent Temple, no pomp of sacrifices, no widespread Land of Israel. Only the portable Torah and the tiny territory of self-determination that clings tightly around each observant Jewish body—the four ells of the *halachic* process—remain as God's contact with us. And this is enough—for inwardness can flower.

In mood as well, Simchat Torah is a way of proving what Sh'mini Atzeret preaches: that profound meditation, inwardness, even tears, lead not to depression but to jubilation. We dance with the Torah scrolls, children are called to the Torah and carry flags and banners, there is exalted frenzy in the synagogue.

◆»» ORIGINS «««◆

In Talmudic times, the second day of Sh'mini Atzeret was treated much like the first. The Torah reading for the day, however, was the last two chapters of Deuteronomy—embracing the death of Moses. But this was not because the Torah reading cycle ended then—for at that time a great part of the Jewish people read the Five Books of Moses in a three-year cycle ending in the third year just before the month of spring and Passover. Instead, the passage of Moses' death was evidently chosen because it was felt appropriate to the wintry spirit of Sh'mini Atzeret. There may even have been a hint that if in the history of the first years of freedom for the people of Israel, Pesach represented the Exodus from Egypt, Shavuot the giving of the Torah at Sinai, and Sukkot the period of sojourning in the wilderness, then Sh'mini Atzeret represented the time of Moses' death.

As for the Prophetic *haftarah* assigned by the Talmud for the second day of Sh'mini Atzeret, it was a passage from I Kings 8, close to the passages read on Sukkot and the first day of Sh'mini Atzeret. In it Solomon prays during the dedication of the Temple. Among other prayers, he asks God to forgive the people and send rain even if they should sin and God be inclined to shut up the founts of heaven. It is perhaps this passage that seemed especially appropriate for Sh'mini Atzeret.

But during the next period of Jewish history, the second day of Sh'mini Atzeret became Simchat Torah, a distinctive holy day. That happened while the *geonim*—leading rabbinic scholars of the Babylonian Diaspora, from the 6th to the 11th century—were respected and followed by the whole Jewish world. Under the leadership of the *geonim*, an annual cycle for reading the Torah became the custom of almost all Jews. The *geonim* developed the special celebration of Simchat Torah, defining it as the end of reading the Torah in the new one-year cycle. They also redefined the *haftarah* as the first portion of the Book of Joshua, which in an historical sense continues the story from Moses' death. And later they decided that the cycle should not only end on Simchat Torah but begin there as well, with the reading of Genesis I.

In mood, Simchat Torah has become the modern equivalent of the Joy of the water pouring celebration that in Temple days characterized the first day of Sukkot. The children of Israel dance and sing, and create special ceremonials for honoring and reading the Torah.

◆≫≫ PRESENT PRACTICE ≪≪◆

The special celebration of Torah begins in the evening after the first day of Sh'mini Atzeret. In many congregations there have been celebrations all afternoon, in which the various circles of the burial society, the *tzedakah* collective, the Talmud-study group, etc., have all had meals and parties. Everyone is brimful of good spirits—and many, of real schnapps. So by the time of evening and the *Maariv* service, the congregation is often a little tipsy.

After *Maariv*, the congregation takes all the Torah scrolls it owns out of the Ark, in order to do seven *hakkafot*, or circlings with them. (Some communities then light a candle in the empty Ark so that the light of Torah should not go dark there.) In the *hakkafot*, the scrolls are carried by dancing congregants around the raised pulpit area or around the prayer hall—or even around the building itself, with excursions into the streets.

The actual carrying of the scrolls is shared among all the congregants. Even in synagogues where women are traditionally segregated, on Simchat Torah they are welcomed into the main sanctuary, there to touch and kiss the Torah scrolls. And children join in the processions—often carrying flags with an apple impaled on the flagpole and a candle burning in the apple. (Perhaps this is a displaced version of the burning torches the Levites used to juggle at the water pouring celebrations in Jerusalem?)

The seven *hakkafot* provided Kabbalists with an opportunity to see in Simchat Torah a microcosm and a unification of the seven days of Sukkot. We have described in Chapter III how seven guests came day by day to the Sukkah to represent the seven *S'phirot* or aspects, emanations, of God. On Simchat Torah, these seven turn into the seven circlings of the Torah. And since these circlings take place not on seven different days but within one day, Simchat Torah is the time when the seven *S'phirot* fuse into Unity, show that they are in fact emanations of the Holy One.

For this reason, the seven *hakkafot* have long been associated with the seven lower *S'phirot*, those emanations from God that make tangible contact with the world. In recent years some congregations have been developing a practice whereby the forms and rhythms of the seven dances, the melodies used for each one, the stories to be told, colors of banners—all are differentiated, each tuning in to one of the *S'phirot* so that in the very bones and muscles of the Torah-dancers the various aspects of God are acted out. Thus the gentle and flowing rhythms of *Chesed,* Loving-kindness, are quite different from the strong and stately rhythms of *Gevurah,* Power. (For more details on the *S'phirot,* see Chapters III and XI.) For this to work, grouplets of the congregation have to be asked in advance to wrestle with each of the *S'phirot* and to plan a dance, a melody, a color for each one.

While the differences from *hakkafah* to *hakkafah* are acted out, the *hakkafot* are also tied together with a continuing thread of prayer. As each one is danced, the dancers sing:

Ana Adonai, hoshi-a-na; ana Adonai, hatzlicha-na, ana Adonai, aneynu—b'yom kareynu.

Lord, please save us! Lord, please prosper us! Lord, please answer on the day that we cry out.

Between the repetitions of this pleading chorus there march in alphabetic procession the verses that address God, from *aleph* to *tof,* as Aid of the desperate, Bearer of righteousness, Cleanser of hearts, Defender of the fallen. So not only the Torah as a whole but the letters that comprise her, not only the Holy One as a Unity but the *S'phirot* that emanate from Him—the whole of the Creation and the whole of the Creator—are brought together for redemption.

After the dancing, all but one of the Torah scrolls are returned to the Ark, and the congregation reads the last two chapters of Deuteronomy, dealing with the death of Moses. It is the only Torah passage that is read at night, and the only one never read on Shabbos. Aside from the practicalities, perhaps this has to do with the relationship between night, sleep, and death—and with an unwillingness to recount the death of Moses on Shabbos. Next morning that passage is reread and the first chapter of Genesis, dealing with the seven days of Creation, is added. In many modern American congregations, both passages—the whole end-and-beginning—are read in the evening, probably out of the experience that many fewer congregants will come in the morning if Simchat Torah falls on a workday. The *haftarah* from the Book of Joshua describes Joshua's accession to the leadership of Israel, after Moses' death, and his preparations for crossing over the River Jordan into the Land of Israel.

Thus the readings reassert the cycle of death-into-life at two levels: the cosmic level in which Moses' death leads straight to the creation of the world, and the historical level in which it leads straight to new leadership and the beginning of a new task. We are being taught, as it were: "The building of a new society is like the creation of a new world."

On Simchat Torah, the Torah dancing begins with the physical dance with physical scrolls; but the dancing mood is then extended into the process of reading the Torah. The reading takes a playful turn, one in which the text itself is tossed from reader to reader as ballet dancers might toss one of themselves. The whole congregation—even those usually left on the fringes—gets involved. Not just a few people, as on any normal festival, are called up to read from the Torah—but every eligible adult. This is usually accomplished by having the first two-thirds of the Deuteronomy passage read over and over, as many times as necessary; but in some congregations, all the adults are called up together, as a *kahal,* and in still others, zany subgroups— all firstborns and then all others, for instance—are called up.

The *aliyot* are extended not only to all the adults who might usually be bypassed, but even to all the children—*kol ha-n'arim*—under the age of *bar* and *bat mitzvah.* They are called up with a prayer shawl spread above them so as to encompass all at once, and a token adult with them to represent and fulfill the congregation's formal obligation. Once again part of Deuteronomy is read, and when the children are finished the whole congregation recites Jacob's blessing over Menashe and Ephraim (Gen. 48:16–20): "May the angel who has redeemed me from all evil, bless these children . . ."

When this congregation-wide reaffirmation of the Torah has been ful- filled, the community focuses itself around two highly respected members— one who is called up as *chatan Torah* or *kallat Torah*—bridegroom or bride of the Torah—to complete the reading, from Deuteronomy 33:27 to the end; and the other, as *chatan B'reshit* or *kallat B'reshit,* bridegroom or bride of "In the Beginning," to begin the reading all over again. In some congregations, the Torah scroll is unrolled the whole way and held by the congregants in a huge circle around the room. Thus the end and the beginning stand next to each other, ready to be read from one parchment panel to the next; and the congregation is encircled not only figuratively but literally—letter by letter— by the Torah.

Cecil Roth has pointed out that the *chatan Torah* tradition was built upon the custom of the congregation's rejoicing with every newly married bridegroom on the Shabbos after the first seven days of his marriage—a celebration in which he was called to the Torah with a flowery introduction, showered with candies while he arose, and handed back to his seat with a Torah scroll to hold for the rest of the service. Much of this panoply is or was part of the ceremonial for Simchat Torah in many traditional congregations.

The special formulas for calling up the two special readers on Simchat Torah read like unutterably solemn requests for permission from God to read the Torah. In the celebratory atmosphere of the evening, however, the *Mereshut Ha'eyl* and *Mereshut Haromam* take on a humorous tone as well, as praise after praise is twirled in spiral after spiral upon God and the Torah:

> With the permission of God, the great, powerful and awe-inspiring, and with the permission of the precious Torah which is richer than fine

gold and precious pearls, and with the permission of the holy and pure Sanhedrin, and with the permission of the learned heads and leaders of academies of the Torah, and with the permission of the elders and the young there assembled, I would open my lips in lauding hymn to sing the praise of God who dwells in light. He has given us life and sustained us in purifying reverence of Him, and has brought us to the happiness of this rejoicing in His Torah which gladdens the heart and enlightens the eyes. The Torah gives life with riches, honor, and glory. It makes happy those who walk in its ways of goodness and right. By adding to their strength it lengthens the days of those who love it and keep it with all its guiding commands, who occupying themselves with it cling to it with reverence and love.

May it be Thy will, Almighty God, to give life with Thy loving-kindness and crowning glory to _____ who has been chosen to complete the reading of the Torah. May he be singled out for a life with honor and happy companionship. Guide him in purity as he follows Thy light. Mayest Thou direct him and crown him by teaching him with Thy instruction of right. Keep him from all harm as Thou wilt give him Thy support, clearly sustaining him and bearing him ever forward. Give him delight and maintain him in that which is right among the people Thou hast created. Draw him near to Thee in Thy love and keep him from all trouble and distress. Strengthen him, uphold him and be his support in his humility of spirit.

Arise, arise, _____, *chatan Torah*, and give glory to God the great and awesome. From the God of awe may there come to you the reward of seeing children and children's children occupied with the Torah and carrying out its commandments among their cleansed and purified people. May you be privileged to share in the joy of rebuilding the Holy Temple, and may your countenance reflecting glory shine with righteousness. May we see the realization of the prophecy of Isaiah who was filled with the spirit of counsel and insight and who said "Rejoice with Jerusalem and be glad in her. Rejoice with her in joy all you who are mourning for her" in grief and sorrow.

Arise, arise, _____, *chatan Torah*, with the permission of all this holy congregation, and complete the reading of the Torah. Arise _____, *chatan Torah*.

With the permission of God who is exalted above all blessing and hymns, who is awesome above all praise and song, who is wisdom of the heart and might, power and strength, and who as Lord of all creation rules the world.

And with the permission of the Torah preciously preserved and honored, which is His foremost thousandfold treasured possession, that

Torah which in its perfect purity revives and restores the soul, that Torah which was given to Israel as a heritage to be realized and preserved, that Torah studied by us from beginning to end, that Torah which is the crown of glory of Him who holds back strife and who gives power to those in authority, to the heads of the academies of Torah and the heads of far-flung scattered Israel.

And with the permission of this holy and joyous community, both young and old of every group gathered here this day for the rejoicing of the Torah, closing and then reopening its reading with reverent joy, cherishing it as on the day when it was given in its glory, esteeming it as a new experience and not as something past and finished, thirsting to draw from it radiant glory with rejoicing as it brings happiness to the heart, removes care and gives its comfort to delight the soul of those who glory in it and pore over it in its Scriptural text with interpretations in *Mishnah*, Talmud, and rabbinic story.

And with the permission of those who hasten to bring their children to the house of prayer and who follow its guiding precepts— great be their reward from Him who is the source of all strength and may abiding joy rest on their head—and who are yearning to see the rebuilding of His chosen Temple in the Holy City.

Now by us unitedly the choice has been made, and from this congregation one has been selected to be accorded high honor. He is one who is true-hearted, who walks in the true paths following right and kindness. His heart has uplifted him and his spirit has stirred him to be the first to begin the reading of the Torah. Therefore, arise and gird yourself with strength, _____. Come forward take your stand beside me and read the story glorifying God for His creation of the world. May we all continue to read on daily, steadily, uninterruptedly, from beginning to end so that we may ever remain true to this Torah. You have been chosen for the privilege of publicly beginning the fulfillment of this religious duty. How good is this for you and may your reward be overflowing. May your blessing from your Creator be generous and be bountifully spread, and may all who honor the Torah as a diadem of light be themselves honored and growing in strength and happiness. Arise, arise, _____, *chatan B'reshit*, at the call of all this holy congregation to bless the great and awesome God, and we all will seal your blessing with a fervent Amen. Arise _____, *chatan B'reshit.*

As the reader approaches the last verses of the Torah, the whole congregation stands, and when the last words are completed—"which Moses had done before the eyes of all Israel, asher asah Moshe l'eynai kol Yisrael"— the whole congregation heralds the end of the Book of Deuteronomy and of the Torah by chanting together: "Chazak chazak, v'nitchazeyk. Be strong, be strong; let us strengthen each other."

Then as the reading shifts to the beginning of the Torah and the Seven Days of creation are read, many congregations respond in a good-humored, joyful way: with a "bom-ba-bom, bom bom bom bom bom-bom!" after the completion of "And there was evening and morning . . ." when each day has been created.

When the Torah scrolls are returned to the Ark, several special songs are sung, among them "Sisu v'simchu, Be glad and rejoice in Simchat Torah and give honor to the Torah . . . for she is our strength and our light."

Sisu v'simchoo b'simchat Torah oo-t'nu kavod la Torah. Ki tov sachra mikol s'chora, mi paz oomifninim y'karah. Nagil v'nasis nagil v'nasis b'zot haTorah haTorah. Ki hi lanu oz, ki hi lanu oz, oz, oz v'ora.

Since Simchat Torah is the only second day of a festival that has its own liturgy and practice quite distinct from that of the day before, there are certain peculiarities in its celebration in communities that do not celebrate second days of the holidays. In Reform synagogues and in Israel, Simchat Torah is combined with Sh'mini Atzeret. In Israel, however, it has become the custom to dance hakkafot with the Torah in the public streets on the night after Sh'mini Atzeret, in order to coincide with the public dancing in the Diaspora.

◆>>> NEW APPROACHES <<<◆

Three developments in recent years have given a new dimension to Simchat Torah. One of these is that some congregations have focused on the traditional involvement of children, and have introduced a special ceremony in which all the children who have just begun their Jewish studies rise to affirm their intention to study Torah. They receive the congregation's blessing, perhaps a small prayerbook, and some honey or honeycake.

The second is that during the 1960s, young Jews in the Soviet Union began to use the public hakkafot as an opportunity to affirm and celebrate their Jewishness in public—even if they defined it in secular rather than Torah-centered ways. As the crowds dancing near the Moscow and Leningrad synagogues each Simchat Torah grew into tens of thousands, the Western press and Western Jewish visitors began to attend the celebrations, and they became a symbol of the insistence of Soviet Jews on their desire and right to live Jewishly or to leave the Soviet Union. As a result, the movement in Israel and the West to assert solidarity with Soviet Jews in their pursuit of these rights began to dedicate public hakkafot on Simchat Torah to freedom for Soviet Jewry, or to hold mass rallies on or near Simchat Torah.

Finally, in some *chavurot* during the 1970s there emerged a strong interest in new forms of Jewish dance and body movement as an expression of Jewish spirituality, and because of the traditional dancing orientation of Simchat Torah there began to grow up a custom of celebrating the new dance forms at Simchat Torah time.

◀▶▶▶ GO AND STUDY ◀◀◀▶

See Philip Goodman's *The Sukkot and Simhat Torah Anthology* (Jewish Publication Society).

CHANNUKAT HABAYIT

"a psalm for the dedication of the house . . ." In many homes Psalm 30 is sung
after *Ma–oz Tzur* during the week of Hanukkah.

CHAPTER SIX

DARK OF THE SUN, DARK OF THE MOON—HANUKKAH

After the explosion of holy days in Tishri, there is no festival for two full months. From Sh'mini Atzeret on the 22nd and 23rd of Tishri through the whole month of Cheshvan and on till the twenty-fifth of Kislev, there are only the new moons and Shabbos to celebrate. The Jewish people rest from the seventh month, the sabbatical month that is full of holy rest days—which is to say, we work full-time at our ordinary work.

By the twenty-fifth of Kislev, we are ready to experience the moment of winter that was foreshadowed by Sh'mini Atzeret. By the twenty-fifth of every lunar month, the moon has gone into exile. The nights are dark, and getting darker. And late in Kislev, we are close to the moment of the winter solstice—when the sun is also in exile. The day is at its shortest and the night at its longest, before the sunlight begins to return. It is the darkest moment of the year, the moment when it is easiest to believe that the light will never return, the moment it is easiest to feel despair.

At this dark moment, we celebrate Hanukkah—the Feast of Dedication—by lighting candles for eight nights. Night after night, the candle-light increases. And night after night, we make our way into, through, and out of the darkness of the sun and moon. We experience and feel the turn toward light from the moment of darkness, the turn toward salvation from the moment of despair.

◆⟩⟩⟩ ORIGINS ⟨⟨⟨◆

Hanukkah is the only one of the traditional Jewish festivals for which we have a clear, nearly contemporaneous historical statement about how and why it started, on whose initiative. And yet . . . there remain some mysteries about its origins.

To everyone it is clear that in its present form, Hanukkah dates back to the struggle led by the Maccabees—a family from the priestly tribe—against the Hellenistic overseers of the Land of Israel and against Hellenized Jews, from 169 to 166 B.C.E.

The Maccabean war was a fusion of anti-colonial and civil war. Antiochus Epiphanes, the Hellenistic King of the Syrian branch of Alexander's empire, had decreed that local religions, including Judaism, be rooted out. Circumcision, kosher food, and Shabbos were outlawed on pain of death. Pagan rituals and sacrifices were instituted at the Holy Temple in Jerusalem and at shrines throughout the land. Many Jews, filled with admiration for the worldly wisdom and power of Hellenistic culture, followed the direction and obeyed the decrees of Antiochus.

But others, deeply committed to Torah, were filled with fury at the oppressive decrees and with revulsion at the cooperation of their compatriots. They rallied under the leadership of Mattathias the priest, a Hasmonean who lived in Modin, and of his five sons—who came to be called the Maccabees. After three years of guerrilla warfare in the hills and forests against the regular armies of Antiochus and his collaborators in the Jewish community, the Maccabean forces won. They recaptured Jerusalem in 166 B.C.E., and set out to rededicate the Holy Temple.

During the next century, the deeds of the Maccabees were recorded and celebrated:

> But Judah and his brothers said: "Now that our enemies have been crushed, let us go up to Jerusalem to cleanse the temple and rededicate it." So the whole army was assembled and went up to Mount Zion. There they found the temple laid waste, the altar profaned, the gates burnt down, the courts overgrown like a thicket or wooded hillside, and the priests' rooms in ruin. They tore their garments, wailed loudly, put ashes on their heads, and fell on their faces to the ground. They sounded the ceremonial trumpets, and cried aloud to Heaven.
>
> Then Judah detailed troops to engage the garrison of the citadel while he cleansed the temple. He selected priests without blemish, devoted to the law, and they purified the temple, removing to an unclean place the stones which defiled it. They discussed what to do with the altar of burnt-offering which was profaned, and rightly decided to demolish it, for fear it might become a standing reproach to them

because it had been defiled by the Gentiles. They therefore pulled down the altar, and stored away the stones in a fitting place on the temple hill, until a prophet should arise who could be consulted about them. They took unhewn stones, as the law commands, and built a new altar on the model of the previous one. They rebuilt the temple and restored its interior, and consecrated the temple courts. They renewed the sacred vessels and the lamp-stand, and brought the altar of incense and the table into the temple. They burnt incense on the altar and lit the lamps on the lamp-stand to shine within the temple. When they had put the Bread of the Presence on the table and hung the curtains, all their work was completed.

Then, early on the twenty-fifth day of the ninth month, the month Kislev, in the year [164 B.C.E.] sacrifice was offered as the law commands on the newly made altar of burnt-offering. On the anniversary of the day when the Gentiles had profaned it, on that very day, it was rededicated, with hymns of thanksgiving, to the music of harps and lutes and cymbals. All the people prostrated themselves, worshipping and praising Heaven that their cause had prospered.

They celebrated the rededication of the altar for eight days. There was great rejoicing as they brought burnt-offerings and sacrificed peace-offerings and thank-offerings. They decorated the front of the temple with golden wreaths and ornamental shields. They renewed the gates and the priests' rooms, and fitted them with doors. There was great merry-making among the people, and the disgrace brought on them by the Gentiles was removed.

Then Judah, his brothers, and the whole congregation of Israel decreed that the rededication of the altar should be observed with joy and gladness at the same season each year, for eight days, beginning on the twenty-fifth of Kislev [I Maccabees 4:36–59].

Maccabaeus with his men, led by the Lord, recovered the temple and city of Jerusalem. He demolished the altars erected by the heathen in the public square, and their sacred precincts as well. When they had purified the sanctuary, they constructed another altar; then, striking fire from flints, they offered a sacrifice for the first time for two whole years, and restored the incense, the lights, and the Bread of the Presence. This done, they prostrated themselves and prayed the Lord not to let them fall any more into such disasters, but, should they ever happen to sin, to discipline them himself with clemency and not hand them over to blasphemous and barbarous Gentiles. The sanctuary was purified on the twenty-fifth of Kislev, the same day of the same month as that on which foreigners had profaned it. The joyful celebration lasted for eight days; it was like the Feast of Huts (Sukkot), for they recalled how, only a short time before, they had kept that feast while they were living like wild animals in the mountains and caves; and so they carried garlanded wands and branches with their fruits, as well as palm fronds, and they chanted hymns to the One who had so triumphantly achieved the purification of his own temple. A measure was passed by the public assembly to the effect that the entire Jewish race should keep these days every year [II Maccabees 10:1–8].

These passages seem clear: Hanukkah was a kind of rerun of Sukkot, the Festival of Huts, because the Maccabean guerrillas had been unable to celebrate Sukkot in its proper season. That is why Hanukkah lasted eight days, the term of Sukkot plus its conclusion, Sh'mini Atzeret. It celebrated the Maccabean victory and the rededication of the Temple. Since the First and Second Temples were both dedicated at the season of Sukkot, the reenactment of Sukkot may have seemed especially appropriate to rededicate the Temple. So from I and II Maccabees, the story seems fairly clear and simple.

But Jewish tradition about Hanukkah is not so simple. The books of the Maccabees themselves became an issue. They seem to have been treated as holy books by the Greek-speaking Jews of Alexandria. But the rabbis never regarded them as holy, never entered them among the books that made up the Jewish Bible. And it was the rabbis who determined what became Jewish Tradition. Ironically enough, these books that celebrated the Maccabees' victory over Hellenism survived not in Hebrew but only in the Greek language. Greek became one of the common tongues of the eastern Mediterranean as Hellenism grew stronger over the next few centuries. And it was the most Hellenized Jews who most honored these memorials of resistance to Hellenism.

Indeed, the Maccabean books survived into modern times only because some of these Hellenized Jews became recruits to Christianity, and brought with them the assumption that these Books of the Maccabees were holy writings. The Christian Church then included *Maccabees* among its version of what it called the "Old Testament." They were among the books, available in Greek rather than Hebrew, that the early Church father Jerome called "the Apocrypha." But they held no honored standing among those Jews who continued being Jewish.

For the classic Jewish view of the origins of Hanukkah, therefore, we must turn to the Talmud. Here we find Hanukkah in a most peculiar position. It is the only one of the traditional festivals that does not have a place in the *Mishnah*—the earlier level, or layer, of the Talmud. And in the later layer—the *Gemara*—it is treated in a very off-hand way, without the focused attention that is normal for deciding how to observe a holy day.

The rabbis are discussing what kinds of candles may be used for Shabbos when one of them asks, rather casually, whether the rules for Hanukkah candles are different. They explore this for a bit, talk about how the candles are to be lit, and then one of them says, as if he cannot quite remember, "What is Hanukkah?" They answer him:

> Our rabbis taught: On the twenty-fifth of Kislev [begin] the eight days of Hanukkah, on which lamentation for the dead and fasting are forbidden. For when the Greeks entered the Temple, they defiled all the oils in it, and when the Hasmonean dynasty prevailed over them and defeated them, they searched and found only one bottle of oil sealed by the High Priest. It contained only enough for one day's lighting. Yet a miracle was brought about with it, and they lit [with that oil] for eight days. The following year they were established as a festival, with *Hallel* and Thanksgiving [Shabbat 21b].

And at once the rabbis go back to discussing the candles. They have no more to say about the internal divisions of the Jews, the revolt against Antiochus, the victory of the Maccabees, the rededication of the Temple. Why this cautious attitude toward Hanukkah?

The reason is that the rabbis were not happy with the Maccabean approach to Jewish life. They were writing in the period when similar revolts against Rome, seeking to win the Jews political independence, to turn Judea into a rocky fortress, and to toughen the Jewish people had been systematically and brutally smashed by the iron fist of Rome. Only the rabbinical kind of power—the power not of rock but water, fluid and soft from moment to moment and yet irresistible over the long run—had survived. Only the rabbinical kind of power had protected and preserved Jewish peoplehood.

Moreover, the Maccabees had made themselves and their offspring kings, after expelling the Syrian–Greek empire. In itself, that was a violation of the ancient Israelite constitution, which requires the priests and the king to come from different tribes and thereby created a check-and-balance system between religious and political power. Even worse in the eyes of the rabbis, the Hasmonean kings—despite their anti-imperial, anti-assimilationist origins—had invited the Roman Empire to become protectors and overlords of the Jewish kingdom, paving the way for the ultimate Roman conquest. And worst of all, the Hasmonean kings sided with the Sadducees, the priestly upholders of the primacy of Temple sacrifice as a channel to God, against the Pharisees—forerunners of the rabbis who saw prayer and the study and interpretation of Torah as the path to God.

All these Maccabean ways of exercising power seemed to the rabbis a subtle surrendering to the habits of the Gentiles—ironically, a form of assimilation—as distinct from pursuing a life-path that the rabbis saw as authentically Jewish. So in retrospect the rabbis were critical of the meaning and ultimate outcome of the Maccabean revolt. And so, without utterly rejecting the national liberation movement, they refocused attention away from it toward God's miracle—toward the spiritual meaning of the light that burned and for eight days was not consumed.

As a later commentator suggested, the single bottle of oil symbolized the last irreducible minimum of spiritual light and creativity within the Jewish people—still there even in its worst moments of apathy and idolatry. The ability of that single jar of oil to stay lit for eight days symbolized how with God's help that tiny amount could unfold into an infinite supply of spiritual riches. Infinite, because the eighth day stood for infinity. Since the whole universe was created in seven days, eight is a symbol of eternity and infinity.

It was this way of understanding that became the Jewish norm—and remained so till very recently. Yet even this exploration of the internal debate over Hanukkah within the Jewish people does not exhaust the question of its origins. Is it merely accidental and historical that the date of the desecration of the Temple in 169 and of its rededication in 166 was the twenty-fifth of Kislev—at the waning of the moon nearest the winter solstice?

There is a great deal of evidence that in much of the eastern Mediterranean and the Middle East, the winter solstice was a time for imploring the sunlight to return and celebrating its readiness to do so. In Rome, the twenty-fifth of December was the birth-day of the Unconquerable Sun. In Persia, at the winter solstice the common people set great bonfires and their rulers sent birds aloft bearing torches of dried grass.

It is a short leap to surmising that the Syrian Greeks may have chosen the twenty-fifth of Kislev as a time to desecrate the Temple by making their own sacrifices there precisely because it was a time of solar and lunar darkness, the time of the winter solstice and the waning of the moon. And it is a short leap to surmise that the Maccabees, when they took the anniversary of that day as the day of rededication, were rededicating not only the Temple but the day itself to Jewish holiness; were capturing a pagan solstice festival that had won wide support among partially Hellenized Jews, in order to make it a day of God's victory over paganism. Even the lighting of candles for Hanukkah fits the context of the surrounding torchlight honors for the sun.

Some commentators have objected that Hanukkah cannot be a solstice festival because it is tied to the lunar, not the solar, cycle. But this objection ignores the fact that the festivals that are most clearly solar—Sukkot and Pesach, the festivals of fall and spring—are nevertheless tied to the full moon for their dates. The objection also ignores the fact that Judaism insists on keeping the sun and moon cycles in tension with each other in its entire calendar—never adopting either a purely lunar or a purely solar calendar, but insisting that each be corrected by the other. Moreover, if Hanukkah is not merely a solstice but a darkness festival, then the twenty-fifth of Kislev is the perfect time. In some years, the solstice day itself would be a night of bright full moon—especially powerful in an agrarian-pastoral culture with few artificial lights. So even the solstice itself would feel less like the darkest day of the year on such a moonlit night. By setting Hanukkah on the twenty-fifth of the month, the Jews made sure that the night would be dark. By setting it in Kislev, they made sure the day would be very short and the sun very dim.

It may even be that the Maccabees' desire to celebrate a late Sukkot, or to celebrate this newly Judaized solstice festival in ways reminiscent of Sukkot, was tied to Sukkot's earlier career as in part a festival of the sun. As we have seen in our examination of Sukkot, the Mishnah goes out of its way to preserve the memory that "Our forebears turned toward the East, to the Sun . . ." and the torches of Sukkot, juggled by the Levites as they danced through Jerusalem, may have been reminders of the sun.

If we see Hanukkah as intentionally, not accidentally, placed at the moment of the darkest sun and darkest moon, then one aspect of the candles seems to be an assertion of our hope for renewed light. Just as at Sukkot we poured the water in order to remind God to pour out rain, perhaps one reason for us to light the candles is to remind God to renew the sun and moon. Indeed, the miracle of eight days' light from one day's oil sounds like an echo of the Mishnah's comment that at the Sukkot water pouring, one log (measure) of water was enough for eight days' pouring.

Through almost two millennia, Hanukkah remained a real but secondary festival of the Jewish people. Beginning late in the nineteenth century in central and eastern Europe, Hanukkah had a second birth. There were two major factors in this second birth, both of them stemming from the emancipation of the Jewish people and their increasing day-to-day contact with the Christian and secular world. One of these factors was that as secular, non-religious, or rational religious ideas grew during the Haskalah or Jewish Enlightenment in the nineteenth century, there was a special disdain for the notion of such a miracle as the eight days' light from one day's oil in the Temple. Secular notions of Jewish peoplehood—including the Zionist notion of the Jews as a nation needing political rehabilitation through politico-military action—became more and more powerful. In that atmosphere, the Maccabees began to seem less dangerous and more heroic than they had throughout the centuries of rabbinic tradition. Indeed, many Zionists identified the rabbis' fear of militant action against oppressive governments as a major element of exile mentality to be transcended in rebuilding the Jewish people.

Thus the miracle of the lights declined and the Maccabees advanced in attention and popularity from about 1890 on. Hanukkah became more and more important as a celebration of Jewish political courage and military prowess. Meanwhile, the Christian Apocryphal books of the Maccabees were becoming more accessible to Jews, as the barriers between the Jewish and Christian worlds crumbled.

And meanwhile also, among Christians in Europe and North America the celebration of Christmas was becoming more and more a major society-wide event. Jews who were becoming semi-assimilated to the broader (Christian) society felt themselves both attracted and threatened by the joyful and pleasant Christmas celebrations and especially by their attractiveness to children. Looking for some answer to this assimilating tug, many Jews found

Hanukkah—both because of its date and because of its anti-assimilationist content—a useful tool for strengthening Jewish identity.

Out of these twin facts, Hanukkah was reborn with much more emphasis on the Maccabees, on resistance to assimilation and the defense of religious and ethnic pluralism, on the giving of gifts, and on the pleasure of children. The ancient ironies of assimilation and pluralism that had characterized Hanukkah from the beginning acted themselves out again, as, in an attempt to differentiate themselves from the peoples around them, the Jews made Hanukkah more like the holidays of those very peoples.

◆》》 PRESENT PRACTICE 《《◆

The most striking ceremony of Hanukkah is the lighting of the candles. In Talmudic times there was a debate between the school of Shammai and the school of Hillel. Shammai urged that eight lights be lit on the first night and the number be reduced by one each night. Hillel urged that one candle be lit the first night and the number be increased by one each night. The tradition, as it did on almost every issue, decided that Jewish practice during normal history should follow that of the school of Hillel—reserving the more austere approach of Shammai to be put in practice only when Messiah comes.

The reasons the Talmud gives for their disagreement are instructive. First it gives the obvious reason: Shammai thought the candles should represent the number of days of Hanukkah still to come, Hillel that it should represent the days already fulfilled. But then, unsatisfied, the Talmud suggests that Shammai had in mind the fact that on Sukkot, while the Temple stood there was a sacrifice of bulls in which the number of animals killed was reduced by one on each of the seven days of the festival. Perhaps Shammai had in mind that Hanukkah was originally a substitute Sukkot. In any case, the Talmud explains that Hillel argued we should increase holiness rather than diminish it. A modern sensibility, taking into account the sense of Hanukkah as the turning point from darkness to light, might speculate that during normal history—the realm of Hillel—the normal human fear of darkness would be best soothed by increasing light; but that after Messiah comes—when our practice will follow Shammai—human beings will be able to honor and celebrate the Divine Mystery that resides in darkness.

The candles are lit each night—at least one set to a household, and in many communities one set to a person. The candelabra are traditionally required to have the eight nightly lights in a row, with none higher than the others. Since the lights are not to be used to do any work like lighting each other or casting light on a book, the custom arose of having a *shammas* or *shamash*, a ninth light separated from the others that is used to light them.

Thus if anyone reads by the light of the candles, it is the *shammas* he or she is reading by.

The lamp is placed at an outside window or hung from the left-hand doorpost (as one enters), across from the *mezuzah*—in order to publicize the miracle of the Temple lights. The rabbis added, however, that at any time and place where there was danger of attack from non-Jews, the lamp could be placed on a table in the room. The candles should be large enough to burn for half an hour, and should be lit as soon as possible after the stars come out each evening.

On the first night of Hanukkah one candle is placed in the holder on one's far right, the *shammas* is lit, and three blessings are said before the *shammas* is used to light the candle:

Baruch atah adonai eloheynu melech ha-olam,
asher kid'shanu b'mitzvotav vitzivanu l'hadlik ner
shel Hanukkah.

Blessed be You, Lord our God, King of all space-time, Who makes us holy through his commandments and commands us to light candles for Hanukkah.

Baruch atah adonai eloheynu melech ha-olam
sheh-asah nissim l'avoteynu ba-yamim ha-heym
bazman hazeh.

Blessed be You . . . Who worked miracles for our forebears in those days at this very season.

Baruch atah adonai eloheynu melech
ha-olam sheh-hechianu v'ki'manu v'higianu lazman hazeh.

Blessed be You . . . Who has given us life, lifted us up, and brought us to this season.

Then the candle is lit and several songs sung afterwards. One of these is—

We kindle these lights on account of the miracles, the wonders, the liberations, and the battles that You carried out for our forebears in these days at this time of year, through the hands of Your holy priests. For all eight days of Hanukkah these lights are holy. We are not allowed to use them; they are only to look at, in order to thank and praise Your great Name on account of Your miracles, Your wonders, and Your liberations.

Among the Ashkenazic communities descended from central and eastern Europe, the household then sings "Ma-oz Tzur, Mighty Rock." Sephardic Jews descended from Spanish and Mediterranean communities chant Psalm 30: "You are my rock and fortress."

> Ma-oz tzoor y'shoo-aw-ti l'cha na-eh l'shah-
> bayach; tikon beit t'filati, v'sham todah n'zabayach;
> L'ayt taw-cheen matbayach mitzawr ha-m'nah-bay-ach,
> Oz eg-mor b'shir mizmor, chanukat hamizbayach.

And in English translation for the same tune:

> Rock of Ages, let our song
> Praise Your saving power;
> You, amid the raging foe,
> Were our shelt'ring tower.
> Furious they assailed us,
> But Your arm availed us,
> And Your word
> Broke their sword
> When our own strength failed us.
>
> Children of the martyr race,
> Whether free or fettered,
> Wake the echoes of the songs
> Where you may be scattered.
> Yours the message cheering
> That the time is nearing
> Which will see
> All peoples free,
> Tyrants disappearing.

On every night after the first, one more candle is added, beginning on the right-hand side of the lamp (facing it) and marching one candle at a time toward the left. The first candle lit each night, however, is the new one representing the new day—that is, the candle furthest to the left—and thus the candles are lit in sequence from left to right. The blessings are said after the shammas is lit and before the nightly candles are. After the first night, only the beginning two blessings are recited; Sheh-hechianu, "Who has kept us alive until this season," is not, because the season is no longer brand-new. We have already lived to see it.

The tradition goes out of its way to say that since women especially suffered from the sexual rapacity of Antiochus' viceroys, they too are obligated to light the Hanukkah candles. This was both an important and unusual ruling, because in much of Jewish tradition until the present century (and in Orthodox circles still) women have been exempted from the obligation to do certain acts at a certain time. The intention may have been to release women to deal with the never-ending, ever-present demands of growing children; the effect was often to isolate them into childrearing and to prevent them from having the honor of fulfilling the time-bound commandments on behalf of the community, as men could do.

The custom grew up that neither men nor women work during the time the candles take to burn each night, and in some Sephardic communities women do not work at all on the first and eighth days of Hanukkah—or even on all eight.

In the regular rhythm of daily prayer, there are two major changes for Hanukkah: the recitation of *Hallel*, the psalms of praise from Psalm 113 to 118, every morning of the eight days; and the insertion of a special paragraph called *Al Hanissim* into the standing prayer, the *amidah*:

> On account of the miracles and the deliverance, the triumphs and liberations and battles that you accomplished for our forebears in these days at this season—It was in the days of Mattathias, son of Yokhanan, the Hasmonean high priest, and his sons that there arose the evil Hellenistic empire to rule over Your people Israel, to force them to forget Your Torah and to violate the rulings that You willed. But You in Your great motherly compassion stood up to side with them and plead their case in their time of trouble. You delivered the mighty into the hand of the weak, the many into the hand of the few, those soaked in death into the hand of the pure, the wicked into the hand of the righteous, the arrogant into the hand of those who pore over Your Torah. For Yourself You made a great and holy Name in all the worlds, and for Your people Israel You made a great and liberating deliverance, till this very day. And after all that, Your children came to the shrine of Your house to cleanse Your Temple and purify Your holy place, to kindle lights in Your holy courtyards and to establish these eight days of Hanukkah so as to thank and praise Your great Name.

TORAH READINGS

The eight days of Hanukkah are the only long stretch of time during the year when the Torah is read every day. The reading is based on an analogy between the dedication of the original Shrine and the rededication of the

Temple. It is taken from the passage from Numbers 7–8 that describes the offerings brought by the chief of every tribe when the traveling shrine was dedicated in the wilderness. On the first day, Numbers 7:1 through the offering of the first day's tribe is read; on the second day, the second day's offering; and so on to the seventh day. On the eighth day, everything from the eighth day to the twelfth is read, plus the verses on lighting the Menorah (8:1–4) that end, "In accord with the appearance that the Lord had made apparent to Moses, in that way he made the Menorah."

On the first Shabbos of Hanukkah, the regular Torah reading in the yearly cycle is read, plus the appropriate passage from Numbers for that day of Hanukkah. The Prophetic *haftarah* is from Zechariah II:14–IV:7. It describes a mystical vision about the dedication of the Second Temple in Jerusalem, after the Babylonian Exile. Zechariah envisions an angel showing him the Menorah, but when he asks "What are these?" the angel answers, "Not by might and not by power, but by My spirit, says the Lord of hosts." So the Rabbis' choice for a Hanukkah *haftarah* not only calls to mind the miracle of light but warns those who might be tempted to identify the day with the might and power of the Maccabees: it is My spirit that has rededicated you and My holy places.

If Hanukkah begins on Shabbos and so has a second Shabbos on the eighth day, the *haftarah* is I Kings 7:40–50, describing the great brassworker Hiram's work on the holy bowls and ornaments of the First Temple, and King Solomon's provision of golden tools and menorahs for the golden altar.

HANUKKAH CUSTOMS

The Hebrew root of the word Hanukkah means education as well as dedication, and many Jewish communities have publicly addressed issues of Jewish education at Hanukkah time. Educational conferences have been held then, and some commentators trace the custom of giving children small amounts of money—Hanukkah *gelt*—to an effort to sweeten the process of Torah study.

On the other hand, the more frivolous custom of gambling with cards or *dreidls* also became identified with Hanukkah. (Gambling was forbidden throughout the year on the ground that transferring wealth without doing work for it must be robbery. But on Hanukkah, the rabbis relaxed—and the people usually gambled for nuts rather than money.) The *dreidl* or *s'vivon* (Yiddish and Hebrew, respectively, for spinning top) became the favorite game. On each face of the *dreidl* was imprinted a Hebrew letter: *nun*, *gimmel*, *hay*, and *sh'in*. In Hebrew they were said to stand for "Nes gadol ha-ya sham—A great miracle happened there." (In Israel the *s'vivon* is likely to have a *pay* for *po*—A great miracle happened *here*.) In Yiddish, however, the letters stood for *nits*, nothing; *ganz*, everything; *halb*, half; and *shtell-arein*, Put some in.

The rules of *dreidl* are flexible, but usually operate this way. All the players put some equal number of nuts in the pot. They take turns spinning the *dreidl*. If it comes up "nothing," nothing happens; if "half," the spinner gets half the pot; if "put some in," he puts in an agreed number of his own nuts; if "everything," the spinner gets everything in the pot and everyone puts in the starter amount again. Whoever is bankrupted drops out; the last survivor, of course, wins. The game is remarkably simple-minded—and if played with a spirit of childish earnestness, remarkably funny.

The ancient tradition of giving Hanukkah *gelt* to reward Torah study and the recent one of matching Christmas gifts have combined to encourage the giving of small gifts each night of Hanukkah. Some of these might be purely pleasurable in a secular way, others Jewish books or ceremonial art; some can be bought, others made by hand. In Israel, the custom has arisen of running a torchlight marathon during Hanukkah from Modin, the town where Mattathias first struck against Hellenistic idolatry, to Jerusalem.

The Hanukkah traditions have given rise to some customs concerning food. The Apocryphal story of Judith, who killed the invading general Holofernes, became a channel for the very Jewish approach of taking an idea and giving it physical reality in the form of food—so that eating the food would then recall the idea. The Book of Judith is written about the Assyrian invasion, but in Maccabean times and since, the story has been connected to the resistance against Antiochus. In the legend that emerged, a Jewish woman inveigled the tyrant general to eat a lot of thirst-provoking cheese. Then she gave him a great deal of wine to slake his thirst. When he fell into a drunken sleep, she cut his head off—and frightened his army into rout. Out of all this tale-telling arose the custom of making special cheese dishes for Hanukkah.

And as a way to honor the oil of the Temple miracle, the custom also arose to make some fried delicacies. In Eastern Europe, this came to mean *latkes* or pancakes; in Israel, *sufganiyot* or fried doughnuts.

And in celebration of both the heroism that lights up Hanukkah and the frolicking that keeps it warm, some modern songs have become deep favorites:

> Mi yimalel gvurot Yisrael
> Otan mi yimneh?
> Heyn b'chol dor yakum hagibor go-el ha-am. (2)
> Sh'ma! Ba-yamim haheym bazman hazeh!
> Makabi moshia oofodeh
> Oov'yamenu kol am Yisrael
> Yitacheyed yakum l'higa-el

> Who can retell
> The things that befell us?

Who can count them?
In every age,
A hero or sage,
Arose to our aid!

Hark! In days of yore, in Israel's ancient land,
Brave Maccabeeus led the faithful band.
But now all Israel must as one arise,
Redeem itself through deed and sacrifice.

◆》》》 NEW APPROACHES 《《《◆

As we have seen, the Rabbinic tradition was hostile to the Maccabees; and modern Zionism, identifying with the Maccabees, was often hostile to the Rabbis. Thus Hanukkah has been a kind of battlefield between "the Rabbi" and "the Maccabee" as models of Jewish life. Is there any way to integrate these conflicting orientations to Hanukkah?

From the standpoint of the Rabbi, Hanukkah celebrated God's saving Spirit: "not by might and not by power . . ." To the Rabbi, this spiritual enlightenment required a kind of inwardness and contemplation that was contradictory to insurgent politics.

From the standpoint of the Maccabee, Hanukkah celebrated human courage and doggedness, the human ability to make history bend and change. The need to organize, to act, to fight, to build might and use power, seemed in the aspect of the Maccabee to contradict study, prayer, and contemplation.

Can a new generation of Jews help to resolve this contradiction? If our forebears repressed and ignored the sense of Hanukkah as a festival of the darkened moon and darkened sun, what could we contribute by opening up to that aspect of the festival? What could we add by seeing Hanukkah as part of the nature cycles of the year and month?

Seen this way, Hanukkah is the moment when light is born from darkness, hope from despair. Both the Maccabeean and Rabbinic models fall into place. The Maccabean revolt came at the darkest moment of Jewish history—when not only was a foreign king imposing idolatry, but large members of Jews were choosing to obey. The miracle at the Temple came at a moment of spiritual darkness—when even military victory had proven useless because the Temple could not be rededicated in the absence of the sacred oil. At the moment of utter darkness in Modin, Mattathias struck the spark of rebellion—and fanned it into flame. At the moment of utter darkness at the Temple, when it would have been rational to wait for more oil to be pressed and consecrated, the Jews ignored all reasonable reasons, and lit the little oil they had.

The real conflict is not between the Rabbi and the Maccabee, between spiritual and political, but between apathy and hope, between a blind surrendering to darkness and an acting to light up new pathways. Sometimes the arena will be in outward action, sometimes in inward meditation. But always the question is whether to recognize the darkness—and transcend it.

The necessity of recognizing the moment of darkness is what we learn from seeing Hanukkah in its context of the sun and moon. There is no use pretending that the sun is always bright; there is no use pretending that the moon is always full. It is only by recognizing the season of darkness that we know it is time to light the candles, to sow a seed of light that can sprout and spring forth later in the year.

Seen this way, Hanukkah can become a time for accepting both the Maccabee and the Rabbi within us, seeing them as different expressions of the need to experience despair and turn toward hope. Seen this way, Hanukkah can become a resource to help us experience our moments of darkness whenever they occur throughout the year—and strike new sparks.

◆»» FOODS* «◆

POTATO LATKES
(POTATO PANCAKES)

6 medium-sized potatoes
1 small onion
1 teaspoon salt
1 egg

3 tablespoons flour, matzo
   meal, or bread crumbs
½ teaspoon baking powder

Wash, pare, and grate raw potatoes. Strain but not too dry and use juice for soup or sauce. If juice is retained, a little more flour will be needed for thickening. Grate and add the onion; add salt and the egg. Beat well. Mix remaining ingredients and beat into potatoes; mix well. Drop by spoonfuls into hot fat that is deep enough to almost cover the cake. Brown on both sides. Drain on absorbent paper. Serve with applesauce, if desired. Serves 4 or 5. Best if eaten immediately, but may be kept warm in the oven.

*Recipes by Hannah Waskow and Rose Gertz.

POTATO PUDDING

5 large potatoes	¼ teaspoon pepper
1 medium-sized onion	1 egg, beaten
1 teaspoon baking powder	2 tablespoons chicken fat
1 teaspoon salt	(or vegetable fat)

Wash, pare, and grate fine the potatoes and onion. Sift the dry ingredients together, and add with the egg and fat. Mix and pour into a greased 2 quart baking dish, dot with additional fat. Bake in a moderately hot oven (375° F.) for 1½ hours—until top is crusty brown. Serves 6.

SWEET AND SOUR STUFFED ROLLED CABBAGE
8 TO 10 ROLLS

CABBAGE

1 head of loosely rolled large leaf cabbage.
Sever each leaf at the core and remove carefully trying to keep from tearing. One large leaf for each portion or 2 small leaves to used as one. Small central leaves to be sliced as for slaw and used as bed for rolls. Boil water in large pot sufficient to cover number of leaves to be rolled. Put leaves into boiling water and allow to boil 4 to 5 minutes so they become pliable. Remove carefully and boil next batch. Depending on size of pot, handle 3 or 4 leaves at a time.

MEAT

Prepare ground meat as usual (1 lb.). Add ⅓ to ½ cup of cooked rice. Fill leaves handling the same as for blintzes.

COOKING

Slice 1 onion and add to sliced cabbage. Put into shallow pan such as covered frying pan, cover with water and bring to boil. Make up bag of spices (1 tbsp. mixed pickling spice tied securely in cheesecloth or white cloth) and put in pot. Lay stuffed cabbage rolls in single layer if possible. If not, double layer may be used with care taken on removal.
Cook for ½ hour. Add 1 can tomato paste, shake of ketchup, 2 tbsp. sugar, 3 pcs. sour salt, ½ tsp. salt, dash of pepper.
Cook for 10 minutes. Adjust to taste. More sugar if you like it sweeter, more sour salt if you like it tarter. You may need a little more salt. Break 4 ginger snaps into liquid. Make sure there is enough liquid as this mixture tends to thicken and may stick. If more liquid is needed during cooking use hot or boiling water. If gravy not thick enough add more ginger snaps. Pot should have tight lid.
Continue cooking ½ hour. Any left-overs may be frozen.

◆≫≫ GO AND STUDY ≪≪◆

See David Rosenberg, *A Blazing Fountain* (Schocken), an excellent collection of poetic translations and renderings of readings for Hanukkah; and Elias Bickerman, *The Maccabees* (Schocken) for an unsentimental, readable, brief, and pointed history of the Maccabean rebellion and civil war.

HINEI MATOV

"Behold how good and pleasant it is for brethren to dwell together in unity . . ."
(Psalm 133) The olive (i.e. children of Israel) stands at the foot of Mt. Sinai;
the wolf and lamb dwell together under the fig and the grape. Each of these
trees provides fruit for the Tu B'Shvat meal.

⬖⟫⟫⟫ CHAPTER SEVEN ⟨⟨⟨⬖

THE TREE THAT SUSTAINS ALL LIFE —TU B'SHVAT

Deep winter, still winter, but the days are visibly longer. The sun is visibly brighter. In the Land of Israel, it is still raining—but the rains are beginning to slacken. Already they have filled the deepest recesses of the earth.

Far underground, the roots of trees are beginning to suck at earth's replenished breasts. Their branches are beginning to grope toward the gathering light. There is barely any change to see; there is barely any change to hear. But the turn of the year has come. The still and quiet months are over; the seed is quickening, life is reasserting itself. In this hushed moment we celebrate the new year of the trees, and the reawakening of the Tree of Life.

⬖⟫⟫ ORIGINS ⟨⟨⬖

When the Temple still stood, one tenth of the income of Israelite farmers and shepherds was taxed—tithed—for the support of the priesthood, of the Levitical religio-legal functionaries, and of the poor. After the Temple was destroyed, the tithing system continued in the Land of Israel and for many Diaspora Jews. The income from the contributions went to those priests and Levites who were also Torah scholars—and finally to students of Torah whether they were priests and Levites or not.

The tithing system included a one-tenth tax on fruit. The tithe of fruit could only be given on behalf of the fruit crop of a given year out of the fruit

· 105 ·

that actually ripened in that year. So in order to organize the tithe correctly there had to be a tax year—an agreed date by which to define the end of the fruit crop of the previous year, and the beginning of the fruit crop of the next year.

By the time the *Mishnah* was codified (in the second century), there was a mild disagreement between the two great schools of rabbinic thought— those of Shammai and Hillel—on when the new year in regard to fruit comes. Should it be on the first or the fifteenth day of the month of Sh'vat? (Sh'vat is the eleventh month of the year, counting from the spring month of Nisan.) The view of the House of Hillel was adopted—as it almost always was.

Why was the late winter month considered the time to end and to begin the year of the fruit crop? Because, the *Gemara* explains, even though most of winter is still to come, most of the rain has already fallen—so the trees begin to drink from it, and their sap begins to rise.

Why did Hillel support and the rabbis choose the fifteenth, rather than the first, of Sh'vat; that is, the full moon, rather than the new moon? We know that the decisions of the House of Hillel tended to be more lenient and flexible, more in accord with the needs of the common folk, than the more austere decisions of Shammai. The full moon of Sh'vat, with its resplendent night of light, may have been a more practical and pleasant time for celebration than the barely glimmering new moon. And this particular full moon was exactly six months from the summery full moon of Av—celebrated with dances and betrothals. So the one may have been something of a midsummer day and the other a midwinter day. Hillel may have been choosing to identify the turning time of the fruit crop with a midwinter full-moon festival that was already popular—rather than add yet another festive day at a time nearby.

For hundreds of years, this midwinter fiscal new year for fruit trees was viewed as a minor holiday. Fasting and the saying of penitential prayers were prohibited. But the *Hallel* psalms of praise were not said as they were on the grand festivals, and the Talmud has even less to say about the day than it does about the midsummer fifteenth of Av.

Yet the minor festival hung on in gentle celebration. In the Ashkenazic communities of central and eastern Europe, the custom arose of singing Psalm 104 and the fifteen Psalms of Ascent (Psalms 120–134) which may have been sung by the Levites as they ascended fifteen steps into the inner court of the Israelites at the Temple. Along with these fifteen psalms went eating fifteen different kinds of fruit—especially some from the Land of Israel. A special association arose with carob or (in Yiddish) *bokser*—a tree mentioned as the chief food of the mystical rabbi Shimon bar Yochai during the years he hid from the Roman soldiery in a cave. In addition to carob, the fruits specially favored were olives, dates, grapes, figs, and pomegranates—all mentioned in the Torah specially as part of the goodness of the Land of Israel. The fifteen psalms and the fifteen fruits may be seen as simply celebrating the fifteenth of Sh'vat.

But they may have a deeper significance as well. Psalm 104 is a magnificent hymn to the Creator about the wonders of Creation. It celebrates the waters that God once allowed to flood the earth, but which now are constrained within the boundaries God sets—and come only as the rain that all life needs.

> The trees of the Lord have their fill;
> The cedars of Lebanon, which He planted,
> Wherein the birds make their nests;
> As for the stork, the fir trees are her house.

The feeling that Tu B'Shvat is in some more than legal sense a new year, the moment of ascent from the depths of winter into new life, may have kept its celebration alive when the tithing of fruits had long since been abandoned.

In the last 500 years, Tu B'Shvat has taken on more significance. From the community of mystics in the town of Safed above the Galilee in the sixteenth century, there emerged a new set of practices for Tu B'Shvat. The mystics of Safed got interested because one of the Kabbalists' images of the *S'phirot* or emanations of God is of a Tree.

The *S'phirot* represent the dynamic aspects of God through which the creation of the world continually takes place—aspects that begin in the unimaginable, undiscussable *Eyn Sof*—the Endless One—and become progressively more in touch with the created world and with human understanding. They are thus sometimes imagined as a Tree whose roots (above) are invisible and inexplicable to us and whose trunk and branches reach (down) toward us. Through this Tree there courses the ultimate flow of universal life, and its flow is what gives life to the whole palpable universe. The image is connected with the reference in the story of the Garden of Eden to a Tree of Life in the center of the Garden which is its ultimate treasure.

Since the Talmud refers to the fifteenth of Sh'vat as "the New Year of the tree," this can be taken as a New Year of The Tree. That is, the fifteenth of Sh'vat can be taken as the date on which the Tree of Life, the Tree of the *S'phirot*, renews the flow of life to the universe. The mystics of course viewed this as an awesome moment, to be guarded and mothered by those adepts who understood the process. It is as if this day were God's own Rosh Hashanah. Just as we need God's presence on our Rosh Hashanah to help us renew our days, so God, as it were, needs our presence on this one.

The mystics felt that this human intervention should take the form of eating fruit—the literal fruit that is the final product of the older generation of the earthly tree, which bears within it the seed of the next generation. The fruit is thus the symbol of the awesome moment in which the flow of life is renewed; and if human beings eat it in a holy way, with the proper blessing and directed intention, the flow is maintained and encouraged.

Out of this speculation among the Kabbalists of Safed came a practice, which was at first an oral tradition concerning a Seder for the night of the fifteenth of Av, in which the celebrants would eat a number of sets or courses of different kinds of fruit. In one version, there were three courses, made up of fruit with no shells, either outside or in, so that the entire fruit could be eaten (such as figs, grapes, carob, apples); fruit with an inedible internal pit (such as dates, olives, plums); and fruit with a tough outer shell (pomegran-ates, coconuts). These three kinds of fruit represented three of the four levels of the process of creation: *assiyah* or action, the physical world around us; *yetzirah* or formation, the level analogous to Plato's forms in which the ideal version of our world is set; *beriah* or creation, in which the inner dynamic processes that result in the forms are set in motion; and *atzilut* or emanation, in which God-energy infuses the processes with their initial life. *Atzilut* is so soft as to be utterly ethereal, beyond representation by the fruit; *beriah* is palpable but so soft that it needs no protection and is represented by fruit without shells; *yetzirah* needs protection, but only at its heart, and so is represented by fruit with an inedible pit; and *assiyah*, in the real world, needs full protection—and so is represented by fruit with tough shells on the outside. Within each set of fruit in this version of the Tu B'Shvat Seder, there are ten different species of fruit to be eaten—representative of the ten S'phirot.

Saying blessings over these fruits would help to release the holy sparks of life-flow in them. Moreover, actually chewing the fruit would have an even more profound effect—since we have 32 teeth, and the word *Elohim*, God, appears 32 times in the story of creation. Instead of hoarding the holy sparks on earth, the person who joined in the Seder would be returning them to the Creator, to the Tree of Life—to keep the life-flow going.

The Kabbalists' Seder for the fifteenth of Sh'vat also included the drinking of four cups of wine, beginning with a cup of white wine; then a cup of mild pink made by mixing some red wine into the white; a cup of deep rose; and a cup of red with just a drop of white in it. These four may have represented the shift in the yearly seasons from the paleness of winter through the awakening spring into blooming summer and the riotous color of fall. Or they may have represented the four letters of the most holy Name of God. The Seder also included readings from a range of Jewish literature on trees and fruit.

A slightly different version of the Tu B'Shvat Seder as it came from the Kabbalists of Safed ran this way:

At sunset people would gather at the *Bet Midrash* or at the home of one of the sages or honored members of the community. Candles were lit, the tables covered with white cloths and decorated with myrtle branches, flowers, and greenery, scented with rose water, and set with pitchers of two varieties of wine—white and red. The white symbolizes the dormancy and barren look of the plant world which began with the weakening of the sun's rays (near the summer solstice) on the fifteenth of Av. The red is a sign of the awakening of the plant to the flowering and growth which comes as the sun's strength begins to return—on Tu B'Shvat The forces of nature—cold and heat, winter and summer— struggle as one kingdom grapples with the other until the red triumphs and the kingdom of spring descends upon the world.

After reading thirteen biblical passages about the produce of the land, fruits, and plants, and studying excerpts from the Talmud (usually tractate Seeds, Zeraim) and the great 13th-century mystical text, the Zohar, the head of the assembly closes with this special prayer: "May it be Your will, O Lord our God and God of our forebears, that by virtue of the eating of the fruits of the trees, which we shall now eat and bless, they may be filled with the strength of the abundance of Your glory to grow and to flourish from the beginning to the end of the year, .for goodness and for blessing, for good life and for peace."

Then the first of the four cups is poured—entirely white wine. They serve wheat (in the form of tasty cakes), olives, dates, and grapes. One of the company makes the blessing over each fruit in the name of the entire group, making certain that the one who is blessing does not taste before he blesses from another fruit. Before they enjoy the fruit, each one reads over an appropriate selection from the Talmud or the Zohar. After eating the fruits they all bless the wine and they drink with great shouts of joy. Meanwhile the second of the four cups of wine is poured, mostly white with a trace of red. They bring the assembly figs, pomegranates, etrogs, and apples. After another reading from the Zohar, and the blessings as above, they drink the second cup with a great spirit of rejoicing. The third cup is poured, half white and half red.

Nuts (almonds or chestnuts), carobs, and pears are served. The company reads over a selection from the Talmud Berakhot and con- cludes with the study of Mishnah Kelaim. After discussing this selection, they raise their cups and drink to a year of goodness and blessing, fruitfulness and increase. Then they mix the fourth cup, red with a touch of white, and bring to the table a great variety of fruit: sorb apples, quince, cherries, crab apples, pistachios, sour cherries, and loquats. And just as they began with wheat, a grain, so did they finish the banquet with various seeds and peas, and drink the fourth cup with singing. Then the people get up from the tables and go out to dance (Sefer Hamoadim, Y.T. Levinsky, editor).

The new form of celebration made its way from Safed into the broader Jewish world first by oral tradition and then by its inclusion in a compendium of practices for holy days called Chemdat Yamim, published in the 17th

century. Early on this handbook got the reputation of having been written by
adherents of the false Messiah Shabbatai Tzvi, and so it was shunned by many
main-line Jewish thinkers. But several of the specific chapters about specific
festivals were so useful and attractive that they were published separately.
Among these was the passage on the Seder of the fifteenth of Sh'vat, called
Pri Eytz Hadar—Fruit of the Lovely Tree—published in 1753. *Pri Eytz Hadar*
brought about wider use of the Seder, especially among Sephardic Jews and
among the Chassidim in Europe.

The Festival of Trees took on another aspect late in the nineteenth
century. The growing Jewish settlements in Palestine were discovering that
planting trees was a crucial act of restoration of the land—bringing with it a
new ecological web of seeds and ground water, insects and small animals that
made possible the sowing of crops. Planting trees became both the practical
means and the symbolic representation of planting Jewish communities.
Perhaps in part influenced by the Arbor Day that was then current in
America and had been copied elsewhere in the world, the settlers began to
have their children plant trees on the fifteenth of Sh'vat. In the Diaspora,
under the auspices of the Jewish National Fund, the day become a day of
focusing on collecting money to plant trees in the Land of Israel.

◆»» PRACTICE «◆

The name used for the fifteenth of Sh'vat is almost as flexible as is
observance of the day. Since fifteen in Hebrew is *Chamishah Asar*, the
holiday is sometimes known as "Chamishah Asar B'Shvat." But more frequently it is called "Tu B'Shvat," from the Hebrew numerals that spell
fifteen. The Hebrew numeral system, like Roman numerals where the letter
"V" can mean the number "5," uses the letters of the alphabet for numbers.
The way to say "13" is to use the letters for "10" and "3"; the way to say "14"
is to use the letters for "10" and "4"; etc. But to say "15" raises a problem.
The letter for 10 is *yod* and the letter for 5 is *hay*. So 15 would be *yod-hay*. But
that is also one of the Names of God, and is half of the most sacred Name. So
it is not used. Instead the numerals for 9 plus 6—that is, *tet* and *vav*—are put
together. Pronounced like a word, they come out as "Tu" for 15. Other
names are *Chag Ha-Ilanot* and *Chag Ha-Perot*, Festival of Trees and Festival of
Fruits.

Observance of Tu B'Shvat is fairly fluid, since no legal authorities have
specified practice for the day. Recent observance has included a form of Tu
B'Shvat Seder based on the one developed by the Kabbalists of Safed, in
which the four cups of wine bracket the three sets of fruit. Each of the four
cups is preceded by the blessing "Baruch atah Adonai eloheynu melech
ha-olam borey p'ri hagafen. Blessed are You, Lord our God, ruler of space and

time, who creates the fruit of the vine." Each of the sets of fruit is preceded by the blessing. "Baruch atah Adonai eloheynu melech ha-olam borey p'ri ha-eytz. Blessed are You, Lord our God, Who creates the fruit of the tree." For any fruit that the celebrant has not eaten during the previous year, the blessing *Sheh-hechianu*—Who kept us alive—is added.

Songs, especially about trees, are often interspersed with the wine and fruit. So are readings about trees from the rabbinic commentaries, the *Midrash* (e.g., *Midrash Rabbah* on Leviticus, XXV, Soncino Engl. ed., pp. 313–324) and the great thirteenth century mystical work, the *Zohar* (e.g., 133a, 1158b–59a, III16a, 58a, 74a, 86a, 127a, 189b), from modern Yiddish and Hebrew poets like Saul Tchernichowsky, and from non-Jewish sources. Some time is often given for reflection and sharing of feelings about trees and about being soft, hard-centered, and hard-shelled.

Some congregations have, either at the beginning or end of the Seder, planted trees in their own communities in addition to collecting money for trees in Israel. The physical act of planting the tree has carried a powerful emotional charge, as well as asserting a sense of Jewish connection with and caring for the surrounding community.

◆》》 NEW APPROACHES 《《◆

In the early 1970s the many-layered Jewish imagery of trees—Biblical, Kabbalistic, and Zionist—became especially important to a number of Jews who were seeking to work in an explicitly Jewish way toward ending the Vietnam War. Most were young, but they included the venerable teacher Abraham Joshua Heschel. To them it became a special concern that United States government policy took as one of its tasks the destruction of Vietnamese forests—and to them it felt especially striking that Torah requires that even if one decides to make war against a city, its trees must be protected (Deut. 20:19).

Out of this focus on the tree they developed a Campaign for Trees and Life for Vietnam, which raised money for reforestation and reconstruction of devastated areas of Vietnam and which planted symbolic trees of peace in such places as the lawn of the U.S. Capitol. Often these plantings were done on Tu B'Shvat, and the day became (to a rather small number of people) a focus of caring and working for peace.

From the same command of the Torah not to destroy trees in wartime, the rabbis deduced the general command of *Bal Tash-chit* (Do Not Destroy), an entire ethic of protecting the natural world and the product of human labors. If even the trees of our enemies must be preserved, they said, all the more the earth and air and water when there is no war! So out of their own expansion of the verse of Torah that protects trees into a pattern of protecting the environment, we might draw a general expansion of Tu B'Shvat into a day of celebration and reaffirmation of the necessity of protecting God's world.

Indeed, Tu B'Shvat comes at precisely the most precarious moment in the cycle of nature. The darkness of Hanukkah may look more frightening to human eyes, but the actual danger to non-human life is greater when the cold has set in deeper. So deep winter, when trees and other vegetation must struggle to begin again, may be a specially appropriate moment to commit ourselves to protect the environment and to renew the flow of nature's life in our own generation, when it is most in danger.

The ancient Jewish sensitivity to the tree as a symbol and metaphor of Torah (the Tree of Life) and God (the Tree of the S'phirot) is what stirred the interest of the comparatively modern Kabbalists of Safed in Tu B'Shvat. We may extend their sensitivity by looking at the Most Holy Name of God as a calligraphic version of a tree in the cycle of its life: the Yod, a tiny seed; the Hay, a flowing, curving expanse of roots; the Vav, a tall trunk; the Hay, a flowing, curving expanse of branches. From the branches and their fruit comes the new seed, the new Yod. The tree, like the Yod-Hay-Vav-Hay, always begins anew; can always say, like the Yod-Hay-Vav-Hay, "EHYEH ASHER EHYEH. I AM WHAT I AM BECOMING."

These two approaches to the tree of Tu B'Shvat—seeing in it both the trees of the worldwide garden of endangered life and the Tree of the life-source in the Yod-Hay-Vav-Hay—can fructify each other. If we make Tu B'Shvat a day of politics and history, a day of recommitment to our nurturing, our gardening of the biosphere, we can help the Yod-Hay-Vav-Hay re-enter our lives. If we make Tu B'Shvat a day of meditation, contemplation of the Tree that sustains all life, we can renew ourselves . . . to sustain all life.

➔➔➔ SONGS ⬅⬅⬅

Atzey zeytim ohmdim la-la-la-la-la
Olive trees are standing.

Hashkediya po-rachat v'shemesh paz zorachat
Tzipporim marosh kol gan m'vashrot et bo ha-chag
Tu B'Shvat higia, chag ha-ilanot

The almond tree is growing,
A golden sun is glowing,
The birds sing out in joyous glee
From every roof and every tree.
Tu B'Shvat is here—
Hail the trees' new year!

◆»» GO AND STUDY «««◆

See Seymour Hefter, *Tu B'Shvat Haggadah* (Jewish Community Center of Wilkes-Barre, PA), which is useful even though it has little of the flavor of mysticism that should pervade the Tu B'Shvat Seder.

ESTHER II

"The king held out the golden sceptre towards Esther." (Esther 8:4) The commentators teach us that the bramble (Haman) was uprooted by the wolf (Mordecai), with the bear (Ahashverosh) sitting by as the myrtle (Esther) spreads influence over all.

CHAPTER EIGHT
SPRING FEVER— PURIM

It is early in the spring. The brown and sober trees of winter have put on gleaming costumes of bright green—not the darker, sedate green of later spring, but a sparkling elfin green. People act a little crazy—shedding heavy clothes while there is still a chill in the air, laughing a little wildly when there is no reason. The tyrant winter is not quite overthrown, but he is smelling musty.

Into this moment comes Purim, the Festival of Lotteries, the hilarious noisemaker among all the holy days, the day of merriment and buffoonery, parody and satire, the loony day of full moon in the pre-spring month of Adar. But the laughter of Purim is not a gentle laughter: it is a kind of angry, blood-red humor that celebrates the tyrant's overthrow.

For of course Purim recalls the tyrant Haman who would have murdered all the Jews—remembers that he cast lots with our lives, remembers that his own stupidity and greed would not have been enough to save us without the courage and tenacity of Mordechai and Esther. So even as a festival of merriment, Purim has its bloodier, darker underside of fear and fury.

ORIGINS

The origins of Purim are wrapped up in the Scroll of Esther—but it is not clear which way the wrapping goes: whether *Esther* led to Purim or Purim to *Esther*. For millennia, most Jews accepted the explanation of the text of

Esther: Purim was invented as a celebration of the victory of the Jewish community in Persia, led by Queen Esther and her cousin Mordechai, over a plot to exterminate them all that had been worked out by Prime Minister Haman and approved by King Ahasuerus.

In the past century, however, scholars have questioned whether the events described in the Book of *Esther* could have happened even approximately that way—given our historical and sociological knowledge about the Persian kingdom. They have suggested instead that the holiday came first; that the Book was written to explain and embellish it. They suggest that the Jews of Persia borrowed from their Persian hosts an early springtime feast of revelry and possibly of a mock battle between two sides. (Such springtime mock battles are found in many cultures—battles between winter and spring, between two political parties or great families, between two nations.) Such a celebration might then have gotten intertwined with the literary genre of a story about palace and harem intrigue, and with the memory of a struggle of the Jews against a hostile faction in the kingdom—intertwined in such a way as to produce the Scroll of Esther.

Some scholars have even suggested that the Scroll of Esther was written long after the Persian period, and was a kind of historical novel intended to comment on the situation of the Jews under Hellenistic rule. Indeed, there is a tale of Jewish danger and salvation under the Hellenistic Ptolemys of Egypt where the king's Jewish sweetheart is said to have saved the Jews that sounds like the Esther story.

In any case, the period of resistance to Hellenism was one in which Purim and another Jewish holiday struggled for mastery of Adar. The other holiday, Nicanor Day, was mentioned in Tractate Ta-anit, Fasts, of the Talmud. It celebrated the defeat of Antiochus' general Nicanor by the Maccabees. It was held on the 13th of Adar—the day before Purim. It may be that the anti-Maccabean rabbis who disliked Hanukkah also disliked Nicanor Day, and encouraged celebration of Purim as an alternative way of both enjoying early spring and commemorating a Jewish triumph over disaster. In such a view, Purim would have been most useful to the rabbis precisely because it predated the Maccabees and because the Scroll of Esther ignored them. It is clear that Purim won, and was described in the *Mishnah* and *Gemara* with great relish and detail. Nicanor Day was barely mentioned, and fell out of use entirely during the Talmudic period. Indeed, once the Fast of Esther was established on the day before Purim, Nicanor Day was obliterated in principle as well as in fact—for on the festive Nicanor Day, fasting had been prohibited.

The Scroll of Esther lends itself to the belief that it was written for an already hilarious Purim, because it seems so clearly a literary joke: a mobilization of hilarity and humor to cure the soul of fear and to shatter the pompous pretensions of all tyranny. The story is, indeed, the intertwining of two jokes. In one of them, Haman's efforts to impale Mordechai, destroy the Jews, and elevate himself are rewarded with precise irony: Haman himself is impaled, his own party is massacred, and Mordechai and all the Jews are elevated to great power and honor.

The other joke is very similar in structure, though sketched in ink less bloody: King Ahasuerus gets the whole story going by deposing Queen Vashti—so that he and all other husbands will never again have to take orders from their wives. He ends the tale by taking orders precisely from his wife—the new Queen Esther. As Haman's murderous anti-Semitism carries him to his own death, so Ahasuerus' contemptuous anti-feminism carries him to his own stultification. The joke is on the tyrant.

The joke is both bloody and bawdy. Blood? More than a few Jews have paled, along with others, as they have read in Chapter IX of the Scroll that not only a few hundred anti-Semitic mobsters in the capital city but also 75,000 in the provinces were killed by the aroused Jewish self-defense groups. But more than a few Jews have laughed at this fiction with a fierce and angry laughter: "Lift a hand against us, and you will be well repaid!"

As for the bawdy joke, think of the sexual overtones of the story: Vashti ordered to display herself, the months of perfuming to prepare Esther for the King's bed, the suspense as he reaches out his golden sceptre so that she can touch its end and save her life, the villain Haman collapsing in fear on the Queen's own couch while Ahasuerus raves that Haman is threatening to rape her.

God forbid that God should appear in such a story! And, of course, He doesn't. In this tale God is never mentioned. Even when it would seem most urgent that Esther, Mordechai, and the Jews pray to the Lord of liberation, they do not. They fast, they cry out, they wear sack cloth, they imagine salvation from another place if Esther cannot gather her courage—but they never pray, never look to God for help. The only other book of the Bible in which God's name appears not once is the Song of Songs. In the one case, the story is too bawdy. In the other, perhaps, it is too sublime—for God's Presence may be most sublime when the Presence is so totally suffused throughout Creation that God as a separate Other with a Name, out there, becomes invisible amid the consciousness of God in here, unnamed.

As H. L. Ginsberg, a modern scholar and translator of the Scroll, points out, *Esther* even ends with a joke on the *halacha*, that sacred life-path of Jewish law and lore. As an act of justice and equity, says the Scroll, the merry feast of Purim was instituted by the Sages to balance out the solemn fast-days they required in memory of destruction of the Temple. Fair is fair! If we must deviate from the original spiritual path of the year in order to fast and mourn, then we must also deviate to laugh too much and drink too much.

Indeed, in accordance with the atmosphere of hilarity that had characterized Purim from the beginning, the Talmud urges Jews to become so mellow on that night that they can no longer distinguish between "blessed be Mordechai" and "cursed be Haman." In Eastern Europe, this command to drunkenness was observed well enough that a proverb grew up to describe a foolish person: "He gets drunk all year and stays sober on Purim." Within the Talmud's call to levity there lurks yet another joke: using *gematria*, the mystical Jewish technique of counting the various Hebrew letters as the numbers they are used for in arithmetic, the letters in the words "Baruch Mordechai" and "Arur Haman" add up to the same number. So on a higher or a lower plane, the two profoundly different sentiments indeed become indistinguishable: a joke on feelings and reality.

It is hardly a surprise that in early spring there should be such a festival of laughter and excess. In many cultures there is such a bawdy celebration of the spring, of which the Christian carnival is only one (*carne vale*, "farewell to meat" before the Lenten fasting). In medieval Europe, indeed, an already lively Purim was quick to enhance its own hilarity by borrowing the carnival masquerades and mystery plays. Jews costumed as Vashti and Moses, Solomon and Mordechai, would stroll the streets to sing and shout. More formal plays about the various dangers and deliverances of the Jews, such as the story of Goliath and David, were concocted and publicly presented in European Jewish communities. The Purimshpiel or Ahashverosh-shpiel—a burlesque of the Purim story itself—became a staple of the celebration, sometimes sexually obscene enough that the rabbis tried to stop them. The custom grew of making Purim-Torah—parodying the prayers themselves on Purim night, parodying the rabbis' Talmudic debates and discussions over how to apply Torah to life-dilemmas. So Purim became a Jewish version of the widespread human custom of a season for relaxing the rules, even for making fun of the most serious parts of life. Nor was this alien to its beginnings. For if indeed the Book of Esther was a fictional tale explaining a spring revel, then the Scroll itself was in a sense the first Purimshpiel, the first act of Purim-Torah.

◆))) MAKING READY (((◆

The Scroll of Esther mentions that help must be given to the poor on Purim—as if to remind us that no merriment is full of heart unless everyone in the community is able to take part in it. In carrying out this command of the Scroll, the community made the whole Purim season a period of *tzedakah*—the righteous act of helping those in trouble.

The focus on *tzedakah* begins on the Shabbos just before Adar begins (or at latest on the first day of the new month, Rosh Chodesh, if that day itself falls on Shabbos). That Shabbos is set aside as Shabbos Shekalim, the day on which to the regular Torah portion is added the passage (Exodus 30:11–16) on the giving of shekels for support of the sacrificial offerings at the Holy Temple. (The Prophetic *haftarah* for the day is II Kings 11:17–12:17, in which King Jehoash collects funds for repairing the Temple.)

When the Temple stood, it was necessary to have the funds for sacrifices in hand and ready to be allocated by the beginning of Nisan, the month of spring proper when Pesach is celebrated. So the announcement of the due time was made a month early, and families used that month to make sure they had ready the required half-shekel per person. Even the poor, living on communal contributions, were required to contribute that much—and even the rich, owning large fields, were required to give no more; so for this purpose every Israelite was absolutely equal.

Nowadays, when the half-shekel commandment no longer applies because the Temple no longer stands, the tradition of reading the Torah portion continues for three reasons:

· As the Prophet Hosea said, with the passionate prayer and study of our lips we can fulfill the relationship to God that in ancient times was fulfilled by sacrifice.

· For some, the reading stands as a reminder of the fervent hope that when Messiah comes to bring the days of peace and justice, the Holy Temple can be rebuilt in Jerusalem.

· It underlines the universal obligation to share in communal upbuilding—to renew Jewish thought and culture, to rescue the oppressed, to feed the hungry, and to heal the sick. One of the Talmudic rabbis points out that it is with an offer of money that Haman persuades the King to issue the unholy order for the extermination of the Jews; it is therefore necessary for the Jewish people to give their money for a holy purpose before Purim, so that their lives and souls can be ransomed in advance. Today we might say that Shabbos Shekalim teaches us to hallow the money that could be used for deadly ends, by turning it toward life.

"When Adar arrives," says the Talmud, "multiply mirth." Yet the Shabbos immediately before Purim (one or two weeks after Shabbos Shekalim) emphasizes not mirth but the dangers of the Purim story. This is Shabbos Zachor—the Shabbos of "Remember!" The passage read from the Torah is Deuteronomy 25:17–19, and the *haftarah* is I Samuel 15:1–34. In the first, we read:

Remember what Amalek did to you on the road as you came out of Egypt—how he met you on the road and with no reverence for God, attacked all your stragglers in the rear, those who were famished and weary. Therefore, when the Lord your God gives you security from all your enemies around you, in the land that the Lord Your God is giving you for an inherited possession, you shall blot out the memory of Amalek from under heaven. Do not forget!

The *haftarah* describes how the Israelite King Saul, having destroyed all of Amalek except King Agag, spares Agag as if a brother King were due special consideration—to the wrath of God and the Prophet Samuel.

The two readings prepare us for Purim because the Scroll of Esther tells us that Haman is a descendant of Agag. In other words, he represents the radical evil that Amalek became when it made war not on warriors but on the weakest of the people. Not even the ancient slavemaster Egypt and the ancient conqueror Assyria are irredeemable in the eyes of Jewish tradition, but the ultimate wickedness of singling out the weak to be destroyed cannot be forgiven or forgotten. So beneath all the hilarity of Purim, the rabbis reminded us of the deadly danger of oppression and extermination—a danger to be remembered so powerfully and paradoxically that we must not forget to blot out the memory of such evil.

During the day before Purim begins—that is, from dawn to sundown on the 13th of Adar—we observe the Fast of Esther. Its timing accords not with that of Esther's own fast before she dares to explain to the King who she is, but with the dreadful day of fear and battle when groups of Jews and Haman's gangs were struggling for their lives in the towns and cities of Persia. So this day, too, underlines the anxiety and tension of the struggle to live under murderous oppression. Then, at nightfall, comes release.

◆≫≫ THE PRACTICE OF PURIM ≪≪◆

For all cities except those that have been surrounded by a wall since the days when Joshua led the Israelite conquest of the land of Canaan, the Scroll of Esther—usually called simply the *Megillah* (Scroll)—is read after sundown on the fourteenth of Adar. Because in the ancient Persian capital city of Shushan, the battles between Jews and anti-Semites lasted one day longer and the feasting and celebration thus came one day later, there is a Shushan Purim one day later. Shushan Purim occurs on the fifteenth of Adar, theoretically in all old walled cities, but nowadays in practice only in Jerusalem and Shushan itself, now the Iranian city of Susa.

Adar is the month that is repeated in the seven Jewish leap years that are designated in every cycle of nineteen years, in order to redress the imbalance of the solar and lunar calendars. So the question arose: in a year with two Adars, in which is Purim celebrated? The Talmud answers that in order to keep Purim close to Pesach, it should be celebrated in Adar II.

Wherever possible, Jews gather in their synagogues to read and hear the *Megillah*. Even in congregations that exempt women from most of the commandments that must be fulfilled at a specific time, the commandment to hear the *Megillah* applies to women. Children also come, except for the very youngest. If someone is too isolated on Purim night to join a *minyan*, s/he is obligated to read the *Megillah* anyway—even alone, if necessary.

As the congregation gathers, according to custom each participant gives to a *tzedakah* fund for the poor three halves of the unit coin of the country's currency—halves in honor of the half-shekel required when the Temple stood, and three because *terumah*—offering—is mentioned three times in the passage read on Shabbos Shekalim. In many households, the custom is to give three halves for each member of the household—including unborn children. This *tzedakah* is not considered a fulfillment of the obligation mentioned in the *Megillah* to give help to the poor during Purim.

As the congregation arrives, it is clear that this is to be no usual evening service. The children—and in many congregations the adults—are in costume. Many are carrying a range of noisemakers: pots and pans, *groggers* that rattle one piece of metal against another when swung in a circle, anything that will groan or screech or bang. In some congregations the grown-ups are carrying various kinds of mellowing drinks to share. (Recently in some *chavurah* congregations, some members may mellow themselves by smoking instead of drinking.) If the children are going to carry out the Purimshpiel tradition by presenting a Purim play, they may do it now—for after the service they will probably be too tired.

The evening service begins with levity. The words may get scrambled, someone may tie the cantor's shoelaces together. But in the standing, murmured *amidah* prayer, there is a more serious note of focusing on Purim. The passage that is inserted begins with the same formula as the prayer during Hanukkah:

> On account of the miracles and the deliverance, the triumphs and liberations and battles that you accomplished for our forebears in these days at this season—It was in the days of Mordechai and Esther in the capital city Shushan that there arose against them the wicked Haman. He sought to destroy, to murder, and to annihilate all the Jews, from child to hoary-headed sage, even babies and women, in one day—the thirteenth day of Adar, the twelfth month—and to plunder their property. But You in Your great motherly compassion frustrated his plot and undid his plan. You made his actions recoil upon his own head, so that [quoting *Megillah* 9:25] "they impaled him and his sons on the stake."

After the *amidah*, the congregation punctuates the service with a full *Kaddish* and turns to reading the *Megillah*.

Three blessings are said before the reading:

> Baruch atah Adonai eloheynu melech ha-olam asher kid'shanu b'mitzvotav vitzivanu al mikra megillah.

> Blessed are You, Lord our God, ruler of all space-time, who has made us holy with your commandments and has commanded us about reading the *Megillah*.

Baruch atah Adonai eloheynu melech ha-olam sheh-asah nissim l'avoteynu ba-yamim ha-heym bazman hazeh.

Blessed are You . . . Who performed miracles for our forebears in these days at this time of year.

Baruch atah Adonai eloheynu melech ha-olam sheh-hechianu v'ki'manu v'higianu lazman hazeh.

Blessed are You . . . Who has given us life, lifted us up, and brought us to this moment.

Then the reader spreads out the scroll and folds it, leaf upon leaf, because the *Megillah* refers to the letters that Mordechai and Esther sent to the people proclaiming Purim—and letters are customarily read spread out, not rolled like the Torah scroll. Since the commandment is that everyone should read or hear read every word of the *Megillah*, some congregants may bring their own copy to murmur aloud, so as not to miss anything in the hubbub.

For hubbub there is. When Haman's name is reached in Chapter III, the congregants try to drown it out. In joyful obedience to the Torah's command to "blot out the memory of Amalek" and in angry recognition of Haman's family resemblance to Amalek, they bang, rattle, swing, bash the noisemakers they are carrying. Some have written Haman's name on bits of paper—which they gleefully tear up and scatter to the winds—or on the soles of their shoes, which they joyfully rub upon the floor. Some have also written the names of later Hamans—monsters of anti-Semitism or of other tyrannies—who seem to be spiritual descendants of Amalek.

There are certain special customs for the reading. At the four verses of redemption, the congregation reads the verse aloud and then the reader repeats it: "There was a Jew in Shushan . . ." (2:4), "And Mordechai left the King's presence in royal robes . . ." (8:15), "For the Jews there was light and joy, gladness and honor . . ." (8:16), "For Mordechai the Jew ranked next to King Ahasuerus . . ." (10:3). The passage beginning "That night, sleep deserted the king" (6:1) is read with special emphasis and a different melody, for that is when the salvation of the Jews begins developing. And the recitation of the killing of Haman's ten sons and close lieutenants (9:6–10) is recited in a single breath. Presumably this is to emphasize their common fate for their common complicity in genocide; but the effect is to increase the breathlessness, the tumult, and the hilarity of the reading.

After the *Megillah* is completed, a blessing is recited:

Blessed are You, Lord our God, King of the universe, who has contended for us and defended our cause, avenging us by bringing retribution on all our mortal enemies and delivering us from our adversaries. Blessed are You, Lord, who delivers His people Israel from all their adversaries—God who saves.

And then two hymns are sung:

It was You who frustrated the wiles of the peoples and annulled all their scheming devices when there rose up against us the wicked Haman, arrogant offspring of the seed of Amalek. In his pride and vanity he dug himself a pit, and his overweening grandeur ensnared him. He planned to catch and he was caught, he sought to destroy and was fast destroyed. Haman revealed the hate borne by his fathers, and stirred in their progeny hate of their brothers. He did not remember the kindness of Saul, from whose sparing of Agag this cruel foe was born. The wicked intrigued to destroy the good, but the foul was caught by the hands of the pure. Mordechai's kindness overcame Saul's error, while the wicked Haman heaped sin upon sin, hiding in his heart his scheming intentions while addicting himself to carrying out evil. He stretched out his hand against God's holy ones, and gave of his wealth to cut off their name.

When Mordechai saw that this wrath was unleashed and heard edicts of Haman proclaimed in Shushan, he robed himself in sackcloth and was bound up in mourning, proclaiming a fast and sitting in ashes. Who then would arise to atone for past erring, winning pardon for ancestors' error and sin? A blossom sprang forth from the palm tree when Hadassah arose to stir those who slept. Her attendants hastened to Haman to cause him to drink snake's venomous wine. By his greed he had risen, he fell through his sin; he built a gallows and was himself hanged upon it. People the world over gaped in amazement when the *pur* (lot) cast by Haman became our Purim. The blameless were saved from the hand of the sinner, and the foe met his doom in their stead. The Jews then resolved to establish Purim for rejoicing and happiness every year. You, God, hearkened to the prayers of Mordechai and Esther, while Haman and his sons were given to the gallows.

The lily of Israel broke forth in rejoicing when they all saw Mordechai robed in royal purple. You have always been their Savior, their hope in every generation, making known that all who hope in You never shall be shamed, and all who trust in You never be dishonored.

Abhorred is the memory of Haman who sought to destroy us; but the memory of the Jew Mordechai is a blessing.

Abhorred is the memory of Zeresh, wife of him who appalled us; but the memory of the protective Esther is a blessing.

May Harbonah's memory be recalled for good.

Shosha-nat ya-akov tzoholoh v'somechoh birotom yachad techelet Mor-de-chai. T'shu-l-som ho-yita lanetzach v'tikvotom b'chol dor vodor.

Then the congregation completes the regular evening service. In some places, this may be the moment for the adults to put on their own more bawdy Purimshpiel and to get more mellow. Soon the congregants will wend their way home—perhaps a little staggered by their own hilarity, perhaps a little clearer than usual about the funnier confusions of the world.

On Purim morning, although work is not forbidden as it would be on the Torah festivals, it is viewed by many traditional Jews as better avoided. In any case, there will be a sense of relaxation, of loosening the juices and unbuttoning the formalities. At the morning service, the Torah passage of Exodus 17:8–16, is read. It describes the original attack of Amalek upon Israel, and ends, "The Lord will be at war with Amalek throughout the ages." Then the *Megillah* is read again—to the tune of somewhat less pandemonium—and a Purim-rabbi—a mock rabbi chosen for the occasion—might give a sermon that pokes fun at established traditions and institutions.

After the service, congregants will share *hamantaschen*. These three-cornered cookies filled with *mohn* or poppy seeds were originally called in Yiddish *mohntaschen*—poppy-seed pockets. The name was changed by folk custom and was said to refer to Haman's three-cornered hat shaped like Haman's pockets.

Since the *Megillah* mentions that Purim must be celebrated by sending gifts (specifically plural), the understanding grew up that at least two delicacies, *hamantaschen* or some other special cooked food, should be sent to at least one friend—*shalachmanos,* as they were called, or literally 'send gifts'.

Most households send many more *shalachmanos* to their friends in the community. Even more important, however, is the sending of help to the poor—food, clothes, or money. The tradition grew up that at least two different poor people must be recipients of a gift from each household. The command to give this *tzedakah* on Purim is separate both from the general obligation of *tzedakah* and from the contribution of those half-shekels before the Purim evening service. This command must be fulfilled during the day of Purim itself and must come from money specially set aside—not be deducted from one's general *tzedakah* fund. On Purim day, anyone who asks for charity must be given it—without investigating whether the beggar is worthy.

In traditional Jewish towns and neighborhoods, during the general scurrying to and fro to carry *shalachmanos* to friends and contributions to the poor, teams of Purimshpielers also tour the streets—juggling and singing, dancing and acting, wearing costumes and mugging, presenting playlets out of Jewish history. In Oriental Jewish communities (and until a few centuries ago among Western Jews as well) the children might hang and burn a rag-doll effigy of Haman that they had made before Purim.

After the afternoon service, households gather for the Purim-seudah, or celebratory meal. Among the traditional dishes are kreplach and peas—especially chickpeas (*nahit* or *bub*). For Queen Esther is said to have eaten chickpeas in the king's palace in order to avoid eating non-kosher foods. The table is dominated by a gigantic Purim challah or *koiletch*, so big it gives rise to a folk blessing. After someone had sneezed four or five times in a row and "Gesundheit" was clearly unavailing, the Jews of Eastern Europe might say: "Tzu voksen tzu kvellen vi lahng und vi breit vi a Purim koiletch—May you feel good and grow big—as long and as broad as a Purim challah."

After the New World fowl of turkeys became available to Jews, under the name *Tarnegol Hodu* or cock of India—the Americas here being mistaken for the Indies by Columbus—turkey meat became for some a special Purim food. For Ahasuerus reigned "from India to Ethiopia" and was a foolish king beside—the turkey!

In Tel Aviv, beginning in the 1920s the custom grew of having, on Purim afternoon, a parade and carnival called *Adloyada* from *ad lo yada*—until you don't know—from the Talmudic command to get mellow "until you don't know the difference between 'Blessed be Mordechai' and 'Cursed be Haman.'" Part of the festivities in Tel Aviv is a beauty contest to choose Queen Esther from among the women.

THE MEANING OF PURIM

There are two traditional sayings about Purim that raise profound questions about the festival. One takes a more formal traditional name for Yom Kippur—*Yom Hakippurim*—and reworks it as *Yom Haki-purim*, the day that is *like* Purim. How could there be any similarity between the most sublime and solemn day in all the calendar, when all bodily needs drop away, and the bawdiest day of the year, when the body's desires are fulfilled and overfulfilled?

One answer may lie in *ki-purim*, like a lottery. For on Yom Kippur lots are cast between the goats: one for sacrifice, one for sending into the wilderness. Purim gets its name from the lots cast by Haman to choose, as the day on which to destroy the Jews, the most propitious day for himself and the least propitious for the Jews. Another similarity between the days is that both remind us that chance has an important role in the world, but does not rule the world. There is absurdity in the world, but the world is not absurd. Do Purim and Yom Kippur both teach us that we must expect the unexpected, cope with the unpredictable—by tuning our responses to a sense of ultimate harmony and order?

The second comment of the rabbis is that "all the festivals will one day cease, but the days of Purim will never cease." That is, Purim will continue even in the Messianic Age.

Why, of all the festivals, will this one that reminds us of Amalek, of radical evil, survive even into the days when radical evil has dissolved? Precisely because *especially then*, when people will think that evil has disappeared, we must remember to keep blotting out the memory of Amalek?

And why, of all the festivals, will this one that celebrates the volcanic energies of laughter, sexuality, violence—the buried id—survive even into the days when the unconscious will have been integrated into a wholeness of personality? Precisely because *especially then*, when people will think the id has disappeared, we must open ourselves up to gusts of anger, bellows of laughter, waves of desire?

Or are these two comments—about Yom Kippur and the Days of Messiah—really one? Are both of them saying that the one holiday a serious-minded people might be tempted to disdain is really as important as Yom Kippur, as eternal as the Messianic Age? Are they reminding us that the excesses of Purim, its craziness, its bawdiness, are really its profound strengths—that we must remember how ultimately powerful are laughter and craziness?

◆》》 NEW APPROACHES 《《◆

That Purim is a gigantic joke on anti-Semitism (represented by the recoil of Haman's hatred on his own head) has been apparent for many centuries. That it is also a joke on anti-feminism (represented by the recoil of the King's contempt for Queen Vashti on his own head) has only become apparent in our own generation.

Or has it? What did it mean for the ancient *midrash* to say that Mehuman—the king's minister who advises him to get rid of troublesome Queen Vashti—is the same as Haman—the king's minister who advises him to massacre the troublesome Jews? What did Haman mean when he condemned "a certain people, dispersed in all your provinces, who keep themselves apart"? Did he mean the Jews alone—or also women? Did he mean Vashti, who kept herself apart?

Do we learn from the *Megillah* that those who will not treat Jews as human will also not treat women as human? That Haman and Mehuman are the same oppressor because they do the same oppression? That the hatred of the different ones—the ones who Haman says will not bow down, will not obey the King's laws—that hatred is one hatred? And that just as the oppression of women and of the Jewish people is intertwined, so their victories are intertwined? That the victory, the freedom of the Jewish people will only come with the victory, the freedom, of womankind?

We celebrate Purim one month before Passover. It is, in fact, a bawdy Passover. The destruction of Haman is a bawdy version of the destruction of the Pharaoh. And the victory of Esther is a bawdy version of the victory of the Song of Songs, which we read on Passover. It is a woman who leads the Song of Songs, and some modern readers think the Song celebrates a kind of flowing spirituality that arises from women's experience. Just as Passover according to tradition cannot be fulfilled unless we read the Song of Songs in addition to the Haggadah, so Purim could not be celebrated without Esther alongside Mordechai.

What does it mean that we celebrate a bawdy Purim just one month before the sublimity of Pesach? Why is it that—in exploring the same themes—at Purim we interrupt the Scroll with noisemaking, with laughter, and with getting drunk, while at Passover we interrupt the Haggadah with Four Questions and with four serious cups of wine?

When the original history happened, the sublime liberation of Exodus came long before the farce of Purim. But when we finish living that history and begin to learn it, absorb it into our lives, digest it so that we can make a holy future, then it may be important for us to laugh first, to let the farce come first. For power is funny, and those who hold power are ridiculous. The first stage of liberation is that we learn to laugh at them.

But power is also profound, and liberation is also at the root of all the universe. Having learned to laugh, we become ready to seek our freedom seriously. There is a time to laugh—and then there is a time to ask questions.

Out of this whole sense of Purim, what might we learn to do?

· Write Purimshpiels that mock male chauvinism as well as anti-Semitism; that make Vashti a heroine alongside Esther.

· Organize a center for battered women named the House of Vashti, and raise *tzedakah* money for it on Purim.

· Demonstrate in a Purimdik way against some center of oppression—political or sexual. The demonstration could take the form of ridicule rather than solemnity, could use costumes and street theater. Could the Purim style be used against a neo-Nazi demonstration, for example? Could Jews have dealt with the planned Nazi demonstration in Skokie by organizing an aggressively funny parody counter-demonstration—with large balloon-figures of Mussolini hanged and Hitler sprawling in the bunker, super-noisemakers, and burlesqued storm-trooper uniforms—that would have surrounded and drowned out the Nazis?

· Organize a festival of Jewish folk arts that emphasizes Jewish jokes—not only the story-telling kind of joke, but humor in dance, painting, cartooning, music, in the films of Lenny Bruce, and the songs of Tom Lehrer.

· As part of the cost of admission to the festival, require participants to make up, wear costumes, change roles, turn their identities inside out.

· Devote part of the proceeds of the festival to a *tzedakah* project. Perhaps give participants a ballot with a brief description of a few alternative *tzedakah* projects, and ask them to vote, or to give weights to the various choices.

· If there isn't time to organize a festival, gather some friends for an afternoon of singing, exchanging small gifts, and collecting *tzedakah* money for the poor. Pose a contest, bringing laughter to bear on some Highly Sacred Idol. For example—who can propose the funniest peace settlement for the Arab-Israeli conflict? (It might even work; it would be hard to find worse failures than all the serious ones that have been tried.)

◆》》 SONGS 《《◆

The boisterous and ironic songs of Purim have been important to its hilarity. A brief selection—one Yiddish, one traditional English, and a more recent song that follows up on the feminist view of Purim:

Heint iz Pur-im bri-der, S'iz der yom-tov grois.
Lo-mir zing-en lie-der, un geyn fun hoiz tzu hoiz. Lach
Mord-che-le lach, a yom-tov-'l mach, kinds
kind-er ge-denk-en dem nes. Zingt bri-der-lach, zingt, tantzt
frai-lach un shpringt, dem tei-er-en nes nisht far-gest.

Ho-mon iz a ro-sho, dos veist ye-der yid,
O-ber Got nish-ko-shoh, shveigt dem ro-sho nit,
Vart Ho-mon-ke, vart, du zei nit ge-nart
A nes hot ge-ton mit unz Got
Zingt kin-der-lach zingt, tantzt frei-lach un shpringt
Macht kin-der-lach gre-ser dem rod.

Oh, once there was a wick-ed, wick-ed man, And
Ha-man was his name, Sir, He would have mur-dered
all the Jews Tho' they were not to blame, Sir.
(Chorus)

Oh, to-day we'll mer-ry, mer-ry be, Oh, to-day we'll
mer-ry, mer-ry be, Oh, to-day we'll
mer-ry, mer-ry be, And "nash" some "Ho-men-tash-en."

And Esther was the lovely queen Of
King Ahasuerus, When Ha-man said he'd
kill us all, Oh, my how he did scare us.
(Chorus)

But Mordecai her cousin bold,
Said "What a dreadful chutzpah,
If guns were but invented now,
This Haman I would shoot, Sir."
(Chorus)

When Esther speaking to the King
Of Haman's plot made mention,
"Ha, Ha," said he, "Oh, no he won't!
I'll spoil his bad intention."

       (Chorus)

The guest of honor he shall be,
This clever Mr. Smarty,
And high above us he shall swing
At a little hanging party.

       (Chorus)

Of all his cruel and unkind ways
This little joke did cure him
And don't forget we owe him thanks
For this jolly feast of Purim.

       (Chorus)

Vashti's Song*

(Sing to the tune of "Artzah alinu")

Esther, mein shvester,
Esther, mein shvester,
The King will just pester you.
He will just use you,
He will abuse you,
He might just bruise you too.
Join me, sister—
Fight that mister!
Liberation—
Feel that sensation!
Emancipation, too.
Emancipation too . . .
Emancipation too!

*By Sue Roemer

◆>>> FOODS * <<<◆

HAMANTASCHEN

DOUGH cutter—3½ inch large size jar lid may be used

6 cups flour	dash of salt
3 teaspoons baking powder	grated rind of lemon
¼ cup water	1 scant cup sugar
3 eggs	½ cup oil
½ lb. vegetable fat (like Crisco)	

Mix flour, baking powder, salt, sugar. Add beaten eggs, fat, oil, lemon, and water. May add a little more flour and water if dough is too short to handle. Refrigerating increases workability, but not essential. Roll scant ¼ inch thick. I use spatula to help in lifting after filling. Will make about fifty hamantaschen.

POPPY SEED MIXTURE—MOHN (*enough for 50–60*)

1 tablespoon oil	½ cup honey
2 cups seeds (10 oz. box)	2 tablespoons bread crumbs
1 cup water	½ lb. walnuts
1 egg well beaten	¼ teaspoon cinnamon
½ lb. raisins	⅛ teaspoon each nutmeg, ginger,
2 or 3 tablespoons jam	cloves
½ cup sugar	dash of salt
1 lemon juice and rind	

Pour boiling water over seeds. Let stand until cool. Drain, put in pot, add 1 cup boiling water. Cook until dry. Watch and stir. May have a small amount of water to be drained off. Grind seeds, nuts, raisins. Add rest of ingredients. Mix well. Taste. May need a little more lemon and spices. Fill dough circles, bring two sides to center forming point and top down to meet with sides, forming a triangle. Pinch the seams closed and glaze with beaten egg mixed with 1 tablespoon water. Bake 350–375° until golden brown.

PRUNE MIXTURE (*enough for 50–60*)

1 lb. prunes	¼ cup bread crumbs
½ lb. raisins	¼ cup honey
½ lb. walnuts	¼ teaspoon cinnamon
1 grated apple	⅛ teaspoon each nutmeg, cloves,
4 tablespoons jam	ginger
1 tablespoon oil	1 lemon juice and rind

*Recipes by Hannah Waskow and Rose Gertz.

Cook prunes until soft, drain well, remove pits and grind with raisins and nuts. Add rest of ingredients. Mix well. Taste. May need a little more lemon and spices. Glaze with beaten egg and 1 tablespoon water. Sprinkle with cinnamon and sugar mixture. Bake 350–375° until golden brown. The sprinkle makes it possible to tell the difference between the prune and *mohn hamantaschen*.

NOTES ON HAMANTASCHEN RECIPE

Double the dough recipe if both kinds of *hamantaschen* are baked. If any mixture is left over it can be frozen for later use with cookie dough or yeast dough. Left over dough can be used for cookies.

All spices and lemon are approximate. Freshness of spices, and size and tartness of lemons make a difference. Adjust to taste. Fillings should be slightly tart, since baking removes some of the tartness. Orange rind and a little orange juice may be added to either filling. A little prune juice may be added to the prune mixture if it seems hard. The prune mixture tends to dry in baking. May need 2 or 3 tablespoons of juice.

1 lb. of seeds is 3 cups, 10 oz. container is 2 cups.

◆»» GO AND STUDY «««◆

See Philip Goodman, *The Purim Anthology* (Jewish Publication Society), and Irving Greenberg, *Guide to Purim* (National Jewish Resource Center, NYC).

MIRIAM

"*and Miriam . . . took a timbrel in her hand . . .*" (Exodus 15:20) Miriam led
the women in song and dance with her timbrel, or tambourine, at the sea
shore as the Jews crossed the divided Red Sea and left Egypt.

◀»» CHAPTER NINE ««▶
GIVING BIRTH
TO FREEDOM—
PESACH

The month of spring—the first month, says the Torah: time to begin.
As the flowers rise up against winter, so the Israelites rise up against Pharaoh.
The peoplehood of Israel is born—and we celebrate the freedom of new births
and new beginnings. The feverish hilarity of early spring, of Purim, becomes
a more directed, more devoted vigor.

◀»» ORIGINS ««▶

Many scholars believe that Pesach is a fusion of two early festivals—one
of shepherds, one of farmers—that welcomed spring in two quite different
ways. As the month of lambing begins in the flock, the shepherds may have
celebrated the flock's fertility by sacrificing a sheep, smearing its blood on the
doorposts of their tents, dancing a skipping Pesach dance around their
campfires.

As for the farmers—in preparation for the harvest of spring barley and
wheat, they may have cleared out from their homes and storehouses all the
chametz, the sour dough, the starter dough they used to make the bread rise.
It may have felt right to them to celebrate the new crop by starting over—not
only starting over for the year's new crop, but starting over in their history by
eating the most ancient bread of all, the flat unleavened bread that was the
beginning of the farmer's food.

So before the beginning of the people Israel there seems to have been a farmer's festival of unleavened bread and a shepherd's festival of the pesach (pass-over, skipping) sacrifice. When in Exodus 12 and 13 the Torah describes the birth of the people, it hints of these double origins even as it brings these two main elements of observance and ritual together.

When and how did the two forms get connected? Some scholars think that the shepherds' ceremony was transformed first: that the celebration of the lambing season was turned into the great festival of liberation. Some crisis stirred the people to a white-hot intensity that enabled them to melt down the old forms and recast them, proclaiming a new birth and a new purpose. The festival itself tells us what this was. Among some crucial nomadic shepherd clans that became the history-bearers of the People Israel, the eruption of a desire for freedom was so strong that it shattered their subjection to the power of the Pharaoh of all Egypt. Their desire for freedom was so intense that those clans experienced the direct intrusion into their own life-histories of the awesome Power that lay at the root of all history and all new birth.

As the story has come down to us, the small Israelite clans which came to Egypt under royal protection first prospered and multiplied there. But a change in royal politics or family brought to power Pharaohs who feared and despised them. So they were subjected to forced labor on the Pharaoh's city-building projects, and then to a concerted attack on their high birthrate: all their boy babies were to be killed at birth.

This decree triggered the first stages of resistance. Midwives—whether Hebrew or Egyptian or both is not quite clear—refused to murder babies. Even an Egyptian princess conspired with Israelite women to save one baby boy, Moses, who grew up to become a firebrand rebel.

Moses killed an Egyptian straw boss, fled Egypt in fear of his life, and then married and lived for years as a shepherd and political refugee in the nearby wilderness. He had a child, and only then was able to experience the intense and fiery God-energy toward freedom that transformed the rest of his life. (The story intertwines the birth of children and the birth of freedom, as if to teach that at the root of both is new potential, whether biological and personal or political and historical; as if to teach that the biology of spring and the sociology of freedom are in some deep sense the same.) At a mysteriously burning bush, Moses received God's charge to return to Egypt and to lead his people toward their liberation. With the help of Miriam his sister and Aaron his brother, Moses challenged Pharaoh, invoked ten disastrous plagues that finally shattered the Egyptian tyranny, and led his people into the wilderness of open space and choices.

From the intensity of thought and feeling that accompanied this moment of revolutionary change, there emerged a festival intended both to memorialize and to re-enact the moment—to keep it ever-fresh as a resource for renewal of the struggle to be free. In this new festival of Pesach—

Passover—the traditional sacrifice of the lamb in spring was re-explained as a ransom for the continued life of the Israelite first-born. For in the night of convulsion before the day of Exodus, the tenth plague or disaster struck, with the result that every first-born in the households of the Egyptian master-people died. Only where an Israelite had slaughtered a lamb and smeared its blood upon the doorpost did the plague of death pass-over and the first-born survive.

This connection between the Pesach lamb and the rescue of the first-born may have evoked deep feelings at the personal, family level as well as in the arena of political freedoms. For the passage in Exodus makes a close connection between the Pesach sacrifice and the command that every first-born calf or lamb shall be killed for sacrifice—and that every first-born son shall be specially redeemed, for his life and blood are also forfeit as a sacrifice.

It is not hard to feel that the Pesach lamb was partly a ransom against child sacrifice—partly a psychological substitute for killing one's own first-born son, as the ram on Mount Moriah was Abraham's substitute for killing his son Isaac. For the many years in which the sacrifice was carried on at local shrines and at the First and Second Temples, it may therefore (like circumcision) have helped discharge the tension between fathers and sons.

Jewish tradition understood this tension well when it said that the great task of Elijah the Prophet was to "turn the hearts of the fathers to the sons and the hearts of the sons to the fathers," and then welcomed Elijah to every circumcision and to every Passover Seder. In our own generation, modern psychologists have rediscovered the tension between the generations. If there were no way to discharge the tensions, some of them have said, they might explode into murder. So the Pesach ceremony may be a way of dealing with the most intimate struggles for life and freedom in the family, as well as the grand and glorious struggles of world history.

This speculation is strengthened by the emphasis in the first four chapters of Exodus on childbirth as the crucial element in the Israelite search for freedom and in the Pharaoh's denial of it. The effort to drown newborns, the midwives' frustration of that effort, the conspiracy of Miriam with Pharaoh's daughter to save the baby Moses, the birth of Moses' own son before he can experience God in the burning bush, and the uncanny circumcision of that son before Moses can become the liberator—all these suggest a strong connection between human birth, the protection of babies, and the liberation of a people. Each child comes through the narrow space to bring broad new possibilities of freedom to the world. Perhaps the oldest Pharaoh is the impulse many parents feel, at one or another moment, to strangle that unpredictability in the cradle.

In the long historical process of shaping the festival we know as Passover, there were many moments of change and growth. The crucial moment came when these separate sets of feelings about the new births in the flock of sheep, about newborns in the clan and family, and about the birth of political freedom were fused into a single extraordinary ceremony.

What was remembered as a great transformation of symbols in the intense emergency of the Exodus was preserved as a teaching of those transformed symbols even afterward. In the book of Exodus, indeed, the description of the emergency celebration and the command for future celebrations are tightly intertwined, moving back and forth from now to later. It is a way of saying that the later generations were to experience the first event as an urgent part of their own immediate lives. Once the connection had been made between the rebirthing powers of the flock and the human family, and the power of a people to politically rebirth itself, that connection was never forgotten.

But then where does the week-long Feast of Unleavened Bread join the story? Modern scholars feel that the nomad army of liberated Israelites may have brought their shepherds' festival of freedom to the settled farmers of Canaan. As many of the Canaanites responded to the fervent mixture of Israelite conquest and conversion, they connected their own history, legends perhaps of Abraham and Isaac, with the memories of the returning clans. The already settled farmers kept on celebrating their own spring festival of the unleavened bread and the new spring grain. They also accepted the shepherds' Pesach sacrifice into their celebration of the springtime. As the invading nomads settled down, they preserved their own ceremonial of birth and liberation, and joined with their neighbors in the week-long feast of matzah. Yet the scholars think the two festivals may have remained distinct for centuries. They may even perhaps have observed at two different times in the month of spring—the sacrifice at the full moon; the matzah feast whenever the barley harvest was ready to begin.

The scholars suggest that not until the Babylonian exile did the two festivals become one. Cut off from the nature-rhythm of their own barley harvest in regard to the one festival and cut off from the sacrificial altar at the Temple in Jerusalem in regard to the other festival, the Israelites in Babylon may have needed the two festivals connected and their dates fixed. In exile, their intense desire for exodus, for freedom and a return to the land of Israel, may well have burned hot enough to melt down the meaning of the ceremonial meal of matzah—to fuse it with the Pesach lamb as a memorial and a demand for exodus.

According to this theory, by the time the ancient oral traditions are woven into the text of the Book of Exodus, the matzah festival is connected with the liberation from Egypt by means of remembering that the haste of departure was so great that there was no time for the Israelites to let the dough rise in the emergency rations they had baked.

In any case, by the time of the Second Temple, the crucial personal and communal elements of Passover had been unified. It celebrated the spring equinox, the moment when the sun was born again—began anew to warm the northern hemisphere. It celebrated Spring in the lambing of the flocks and the harvesting of barley. It celebrated the life of every newborn child, and the joy of every family that the firstborn need not be offered up to God. It celebrated the birthtime of the people and their ability—not simply once, but now another time—to emerge from slavery to freedom and from exile to self-determination in their own land. And so Pesach had become the quintessential festival of newness, creation, creativity, freedom.

At this point, what Pesach meant was that on the tenth of the month of Nisan, each family acquired a lamb—or, if it were too small or too poor to deal with a whole lamb of its own, shared with a neighbor. In enormous multitudes—more than three million strong in the year 65 C.E.—the people Israel converged on Jerusalem to celebrate the festival. They would sacrifice the lambs as the day of the fourteenth of Nisan turned into dusk and moved toward the evening of the fifteenth. Until midnight they would roast and eat the paschal lamb, with bitter herbs to remember the bitterness of slavery and with matzah to recall the haste of liberation. For a week they would stay in Jerusalem, eating only unleavened bread, telling the tales of freedom, gathering again on the seventh day for another solemn day of dedication. Sometime during the week they would begin to wave before God's altar an *omer* of the earliest-ripened barley, starting the count of 49 days of awaiting the crop from different fields throughout the land of Israel as the barley ripened—a count that itself would ripen on the festival of Shavuot. And after the seventh day they would return to their homes.

Late in the period of the Second Temple, under the influence of Hellenistic and Roman culture, the Pesach feast became a carefully ordered meal that borrowed from the pattern of the Greek and Roman symposium, or discussion banquet. As this pattern developed, the *Mishnah*—a collection and codification of those traditions and practices of Jewish life approved by the early rabbis—laid out how to do the order, the Seder, of the Pesach meal. In its essentials, this Seder became the pattern that was put into the Haggadah—the telling of Passover—and thus became the pattern for the meal as we have it for our own generation.

One of the major elements introduced by the *Mishnah*, borrowing from the symposium, was the drinking of four cups of wine—two early in the meal, two after the meal was over. The custom of reclining during the meal as an expression of freedom also drew on Roman custom—for free citizens in Roman times would recline to eat a formal dinner.

There is also a tradition, passed on by word of mouth alone until our own day, that the Seder of Roman times which the Haggadah itself describes—the Seder in which Rabbi Akiba and four colleagues talk all night—was actually the occasion for discussing and planning an uprising against the Imperial power. Akiba's insistence on adding to the Passover Seder's blessing over God's redemptive power in Egypt, a passage looking forward toward restoration of the Temple that the Romans had destroyed, and Akiba's support for the Bar Kochba revolt against Rome as a Messianic event, were presumably connected with the discussion at this famous Seder in the town of B'nei Brak. This may have been the first occasion when Passover was consciously used not only as a celebration of God's gift of freedom in the past but as an incitement of collective human action for freedom toward the future.

Between the codification of the *Mishnah* (end of the second century C.E.) and the collection of the *Gemara's* commentaries on it (three centuries later), there were some changes in the text and arrangement of the Seder. The *Mishnah* lays out several questions to be asked by a child (in some texts three, in some four). One of these questions is about the roast lamb of the Pesach sacrifice. After the destruction of the Temple had not only occurred but lasted for several centuries, so that the restoration of the sacrifices no longer seemed imminent and the question about them was irrelevant to the actual Seder meal, the *Gemara* replaced this question with one about reclining. So at this point the child's questions became the Four Questions that we have today, all built upon the crucial question "Why is this night different from all other nights?" For on this night we eat only matzah; we eat bitter herbs; we twice dip food, into salt water and chopped fruit; we recline at the table. Why?

The *Gemara* also described a shift of the telling parts of the ritual from their earlier position during the meal to a place after only a symbolic green vegetable had been eaten and before the actual meal, probably to make sure the telling was done well and thoroughly before the effects of wine and food had dulled the abilities of the celebrants.

There were several debates among the Talmudic rabbis as to what the text of the telling on Pesach night should be. Some of these may seem at first glance picayune, but when we probe a little there is often revealed some basic moral issue. One of these disagreements was the one between Tarfon and Akiba over whether to refer to a future redemption and the restoration of the Temple. Another began out of a consensus that the story should start out by telling of the Israelites' original degraded status, and rise to their glorious redemption. But then the consensus turned into a dispute over what degradation to begin with: the slavery in Egypt, or the idolatrous beliefs of Abraham's family? This dispute was resolved by starting with both: "We were slaves to Pharaoh in Egypt . . . " and "Our forebears served as slaves to idols . . . "

Even the cup of Elijah results from a debate over whether there should be four or five cups of wine. The compromise was to have a fifth cup but not to drink from it or say the blessing, and in time this became known as the cup that awaited Elijah's visit to announce the Messianic redemption (may it come soon and in our own day).

Another, much more playful, debate arose over how many plagues really happened in Egypt—ten, fifty, two hundred? This debate is presented verbatim in the Haggadah—and takes on a more profound meaning when we notice that the various proposed numbers of plagues add up to 613, which is also the total number of God's commandments according to a traditional view. So the Haggadah hints that the ten plagues of Egypt stand opposite the Ten Commandments of Sinai; and that there are 613 plagues standing opposite the 613 commandments. For every commandment unfulfilled, there is a plague . . .

In the Gaonic period in Babylon, these discussions continued and gradually the results crystallized into a more-or-less agreed text and order of a service for Passover night. This text first appeared as part of the earliest Jewish prayerbook in the ninth century. By the eleventh century, the text was almost identical with the traditional Haggadah used today, with the exception of the verses beginning "Pour out Your wrath," which were added as a furious response to anti-Semitic outbursts during the Crusades. The earliest appearance of a separate Passover Haggadah seems to have been in the twelfth century. The songs sung after completion of the regular service first appeared in the fourteenth and sixteenth centuries.

During the past century, under the stimulus of profound changes in Jewish life, a number of modified Haggadahs have been used by parts of the Jewish community, beginning with Reform and Reconstructionist editions in the United States and with new versions published by hundreds of non-religious socialist kibbutzim before and after the establishment of Israeli independence. During the late 1960s and early 1970s in the United States, political and religious upheavals among young Jews led to the publication of a number of different Haggadahs. Some of these expressed more or less radical political feelings, others expressed the determination of Jewish women to enter Jewish life as full equals with men, and some presented a variety of alternate readings from inside or outside Jewish traditional thought that could be used to strike up open discussion and debate at the Seder in the spirit of the Z'man cheruteynu, season of our freedom.

◆➤➤➤ MAKING READY ◄◄◄◆

REMOVING THE LEAVEN

Preparations for Pesach are the most elaborate of all the Jewish year. They take place in both the physical realm of preparing the household by removing leaven, and the spiritual realm of clearing away deadliness and idolatry by means of prayer and Torah study. We act in the two realms simultaneously in parallel; here we will look at the physical first.

Renewal of the body can begin on Rosh Chodesh (the New Moon) of the month of Nisan, for that is when the reordering of the house and the cleaning out of last year's leavening can start. The Torah's command is that no *chametz*, leavening or souring agent, shall remain in one's house during Pesach. In our own generation, different Jews apply this rule with more or less stringency.

In removing the *chametz*, there are some traditional customs and regulations to keep in mind: regular bread is the most obvious candidate for removal. With it traditionally went all cereals and grains, especially wheat, barley, spelt, oats, and rye—all mentioned by the rabbis—but also corn (maize), not discovered until after 1492. Rice, millet, peas, and beans (including peanuts) were forbidden for Ashkenazic Jews, descended from Northern European communities. The Mediterranean-based Sephardic communities and the Oriental Jews did not feel—as did the Ashkenazic rabbis—that these foods might be ground into flour, get confused with the originally prohibited grains, and seduce Jews toward eating those grains.

Alcoholic liquors based on grain (which include beer and practically all other alcohol except wine and pure fruit brandies like slivovitz) also contain *chametz*. So does vinegar, if it is made at all from grain. Pure apple cider vinegar, however, even though it is sour is not considered *chametz* and may be used during Pesach. Many canned, bottled, and processed foods contain cornstarch, corn syrups, flour as a thickening agent, etc. All these are traditionally forbidden. So are non-foods that contain *chametz*—some cosmetics, inks, glues, toothpastes, etc.

There are several approaches to consider in dealing with this *chametz*:

· The very nooks and crannies of the household probably bear *chametz* in their dust; so the custom has arisen of doing an extraordinarily thorough spring cleaning before Pesach.

· As for visible, palpable *chametzdik* foods, some people find it psychologically satisfying to finish half-loaves of bread, half-boxes of crackers, etc., in the two weeks before Pesach.

· What is left can be physically removed from the house. In some communities, the custom has arisen of taking such foods, together with some money, to soup kitchens or other places that feed the (non-Jewish) desperately poor. In this way both the *mitzvah* of removing *chametz* and the *mitzvah* of *tzedakah* are fulfilled. If the soup kitchen or other group chosen is also working toward the goal of freeing the poor from poverty and powerlessness, then the historic message of Pesach—liberation from slavery—is also carried outward to the broader world.

· The *chametz* can be separated from everything else in the house, put in a room or a large box that is sealed closed, and the *chametz* can then be formally and legally sold to a non-Jew. It may be advisable to arrange this through a rabbi, or other person trained in Jewish traditions, who is knowledgeable in this particular practice. Untrained individuals may find it useful to consult as a model the legal formulas for this sale printed on pages 36–39 of Section 3 on Festivals of the *Code of Jewish Law* (Ganzfried-Goldin, ed., Hebrew Publishing Co.). This arrangement allows the *chametzdik* food to be sold before Pesach and bought back for the same price afterward. In some congregations, the custom has arisen of making the sale to a non-Jewish charitable organization—for example, Oxfam, which tries to deal with the world hunger problem—and then donating part or all of the cost of the food after its repurchase.

· Traditionally, all food utensils used during the regular year either need to be locked away after thorough washing and left unused during Pesach so that utensils would be used that were saved all year (under seal) for Pesach use alone; or else the utensils were purified of leaven by putting them in large pots of boiling water and putting boiling-hot stones or bricks in the pots so that the water (still boiling hot) would overflow the rim. Burners on the stove can be covered with foil, a special tablecloth used on the table, etc.

· Special food intended for Passover is indicated by the special "Kosher L'Pesach" notation on the container with a rabbinic seal of *kashrut*. Fresh fruits and vegetables do not need this symbol; foods like fresh milk or foods that list ingredients and do not list any form of *chametz* are probably kosher in fact, but there is no way to be certain that *chametz* has not infiltrated. Individual households must decide whether to insist on rabbinic certification. Whatever the decision, after utensils have been changed or purified and the regular food sold or given away, only food intended for Pesach should be bought.

· Traditionally, the matzah intended to fulfill the positive command to eat unleavened bread (which is separate from the negative command to *not* eat leavened bread) is made of only flour and water and must be completely baked in less than 18 minutes from when the flour is mixed with water, so that it has no time to rise. Special egg matzahs, fruit juice matzahs, etc., that use no water are not *chametz*; they are not fully matzah either. Traditionally, therefore, they may be eaten during Pesach but not as the ritual matzah of the Seder. Some households use only *sh'murah matzah* (guarded matzah). Its flour has been watched all the way back to the time of harvesting the grain to make sure no water has touched it. Some *sh'murah matzah* comes from fields that receive only the merest minimal amounts of rainfall.

· The baking of ritual matzah can itself become a spiritually uplifting experience. The process requires an oven capable of very high heat that can bake in great speed; absolutely dry flour; and fresh spring water with which the flour is combined just before baking. Rows of holes are put in the matzah in order to permit air bubbles to escape rather than leaven the bread even unintentionally. Directions for baking can be found on pages 143–145 of *The First Jewish Catalog*. (But it is very unlikely that such private baking can meet all the traditional tests for kosher matzah; so some who like to do their own baking eat this matzah before Pesach begins.)

On the night before Pesach (or if it begins at the end of Shabbos, on the Thursday night before), there is a final hunt through the house to get rid of any *chametz* that has not been eaten, given away, or sealed off and sold. Many households give this search a ritual as well as practical character by having each member of the household hide a few chunks of bread around the house ahead of time—adding up to a *minyan*, a total of ten. Then the whole household can hunt. A candle—not some other kind of light—is used for this search, because (so the Talmud says), the human soul is God's candle to search out the innards of the world. A feather (which you may want to look for in a public park in a pre-Pesach spring walk that afternoon) or a palm-branch from the *lulav* that has been put aside from last Sukkot may be used to brush the pieces of bread from their hiding place into a paper bag—so that no one actually is contaminated by a crumb of leaven.

The search begins with a blessing: "Baruch atuh Adonai eloheynu melech ha-olam asher kid'shanu b'mitzvotav vitzivanu al biyyur chameytz. Blessed are You, Lord our God, Ruler of space and time, who has made us holy through Your commandments, and commanded us about the removal of leavening." After the symbolic ten pieces have been found and any other *chametz* found along the way has also been swept up, the bag of *chametz* is laid aside. The household members use the ancient popular language, Aramaic, to declare:

> Kol shamira v'chamiya dika birshuti, d'la chamitey ood'la bah-aritey ood'la yadana ley, livtil v'lehevey hefker k'afra harah.

> All leaven in my possession that I have not seen or removed or that I don't know about is hereby made null and void, and ownerless as the dust of the earth.

In the morning, after breakfast, this declaration is recited again and the bag of *chametz* is burned outside the house—beginning perhaps with the dried-out *lulav*. If Pesach begins Saturday night, then on Friday morning, leavening like challah for eating Friday night may be left; the rest should be burnt (since a fire cannot be kindled on Shabbos); and the declaration of nullity is delayed until after eating two briefly separated meals which use up all the remaining bread on Shabbos morning, so as to fulfill the *mitzvah* of eating three meals with bread every Shabbos. If later during Pesach an accidentally overlooked piece of *chametz* is found, a cup or pot should be placed upside down over it and then during the middle five days of semi-festival, it should be burned with the blessing, "Who has commanded us about the removal of leavening."

In addition to the special problems created by a Pesach that begins on Saturday night, there are special problems with a Pesach that begins on Wednesday night. In such a year, all day Thursday and Friday are festivals. In traditional homes, food can be cooked on these days for eating on these days or on the semi-festival days later—but food should not be cooked on the festival days to eat on Shabbos (and even more strongly, food should not be newly cooked on Shabbos itself). How then to cook for Shabbos? The rabbis ruled that if a family began cooking for Shabbos before Pesach began and continued on into the festival days, this was not the same as beginning the process during Pesach.

So if Pesach begins Wednesday night, some cooking for Shabbos begins during the day before. That food and some matzah are singled out, and the household does the ceremony of *eruv tavshilin*, mixture for cooking, declaring over this food:

> Blessed are You, Lord our God, Ruler of space and time, Who has made us holy with Your commandments and commanded us about the "mixture." By means of this mixture we may bake, cook, warm, kindle lights, and do everything necessary from holy day toward Shabbos—we and all Israel who live in this town.

After 9:30 of the morning before Pesach, it is forbidden to eat *chametz* and it is the custom not to eat matzah, so as to be able to savor fully the taste of the first matzah at the Seder.

First-born children traditionally do not eat at all during the daylight hours before Pesach, in recognition of the awesome fact that all the first-born children of Egypt died during the night and that the Israelite first-born were saved only by virtue of God's forebearance and the Pesach sacrifice of the lamb and the blood on the doorposts. However, it is a *mitzvah* to celebrate with food and drink the completion of a *mitzvah* such as the study of a part of the Bible, Talmud, or other text from the tradition. So the custom has arisen that the first-borns of a community gather on the morning before Pesach to study together, and then can eat a breadless *siyyum*, a festive meal to celebrate the *mitzvah*. In some households, the afternoon before Pesach is a time to walk for an hour or two in a park or woods, enjoying the spring birthtime before turning to the political-historical birthtime. In some traditional communities, it is a time to immerse in the *mikveh*, the ritual bath—not to become physically clean but to experience the purifying rest, the sense of oceanic union with the universe, that can come from total immersion. Bodies of pure running water—streams, lakes, oceans—can be used as *mikvehs*.

To some modern sensibilities, following the rather elaborate rituals for ridding the household of leaven may seem obsessive. The task may become so onerous—especially if it is loaded onto just one member of the household—that it seems to re-establish the slavery that the original Passover freed us from! If the toil of pre-Pesach cleaning is shared and then the Seder is greeted as a great shared liberation, the toil might even come to be used in a spiritually helpful way.

There is also a mystical outlook on the meaning of the removal of chametz that can be kept in mind. According to this view, chametz is what lifts us up throughout the year—leads to our working harder, searching deeper, loving more. It is the yetzer, or swelling-impulse, of the soul. But allowed to swell and grow without restraint, it becomes yetzer ha-ra, the evil impulse. It impels us not only to productivity, but to possessiveness; not only to creativity, but to competitiveness; not only to love, but to jealousy and lust. So once a year we must clean out even the uplifting impulse; we must eat the flat bread of a pressed-down people. Half a year after the Tashlich ceremony of Rosh Hashanah, we must clean out the pockets of pride that have grown big again. Half a year after Yom Kippur, we must again swallow hard and look again at what is eating us.

MIND AND SPIRIT

While the Temple stood, the approach of Pesach was a time for every Israelite to clear away any aura of contact with a death. For no one who had touched a dead body could offer up a sacrifice to the living God without first going through an exercise to clear away the taboo. Pesach was the only time that every Israelite family brought a sacrifice. (On other festivals the priests made the offering, and when it was a matter of an individual guilt-offering or something similar, the special occasion would apply to just one person.) So to prepare for Pesach, the whole people heard the Torah reading about how to clear away the death taboo.

Now, with the Temple gone, we read that Torah passage to cleanse ourselves of deadliness through the reading itself. The passage is about the red heifer or parah adumah, and we read it on the second Shabbos before the month of Nisan begins (or if it actually begins on Shabbos, on the Shabbos just before). This passage (Numbers 19:1–22) describes how the red heifer was sacrificed—its red blood sprinkled on the altar and its body burned with red cedarwood and the red spice hyssop, with a scarlet dye to make in the fire a cloud of red smoke. The heifer's ashes were then used to clear away the uncanniness of death from the person of anyone who had touched a corpse. Along with this passage, on Shabbos Parah we read a haftarah (Ezekiel 36:13–38) in which God promises to cleanse all Israel from our idolatries.

On the Shabbos after Shabbos Parah, we read a special Torah passage to announce that Nisan, the month of Passover, is upon us. This passage from Exodus 12, "This month shall be for you the head of the months; it is for you first of the months of the year," is added to the regular Torah portion of the week. Every new month is announced on the Shabbos before, but only Nisan is announced with a special Torah reading. This gives the month an extra honor, and gives the congregation a special electricity about Pesach. The Shabbos is called Shabbos Ha-Chodesh, Shabbos of The Month. It completes the four special Shabbosim that began with Shabbos Shekalim and Shabbos Zakhor before Purim.

Once Nisan actually begins, the community begins to collect money to help the poor celebrate Pesach fully. This *ma-oz chittin* or wheat money is intended to let the poor buy matzah—and by extension all their other needs in food, clothing, and fuel—in order freely to celebrate Pesach, the festival of freedom.

> Even if a man has already fulfilled the *mitzvah* of *tzedakah*, in complete accordance with the law, he cannot appreciate the full implication of freedom if he knows that his neighbor is hungry and in need. If he knew that there were hungry people in his town and he had not bothered to come to their assistance, he would be guilty of telling lies—God forbid—on this "watch night" when he says at the beginning of the Haggadah, "Let all who are hungry come and eat." If, however, he has busied himself to supply the needy with food, and then he says, "Perhaps there are still some poor people of whom I know not, I am ready to receive them at my table," then his words are clearly sincere and he is rewarded for saying this just as if he had only now fed the hungry and gladdened the hearts of the poor (Eliyahu Kitov).

Money for this Pesach aid is distributed to the poor before the Shabbos before Pesach, so that they should have time to buy what they need.

Although the practice of *ma-oz chittin* focuses first on the poor of one's own town or community, some Jewish communities in some years have lived under restrictions of their governments as to how much matzah and other Pesach foods they may prepare. Soviet regulations, for example, have changed from year to year. Sometimes as much matzah as needed has been allowed; sometimes very little. Organizations for support of Soviet Jewry have sometimes sponsored the sending of large-scale supplies of matzah; or if even this has been prohibited, have urged American Jews to mail matzah to the Soviet Embassy as a protest. It would be wise, perhaps at the time of Shabbos Shekalim before Purim, to check with these organizations or with groups in touch with other oppressed Jewish communities to see what the situation is.

At the beginning of Nisan in the second year of freedom for the Israelites in the wilderness, the *Mishkan*, the traveling Shrine for the Presence of God, was dedicated. In memory of this event and in hope for the Messianic redemption when God's Presence will again become palpable (and this time to all humanity), some very traditional Jewish communities spend the seven days at the end of Adar and the first thirteen days of Nisan in a special commemoration. On the seven last days of Adar, when Moses completed the Shrine of the Presence and offered up the dedicatory sacrifices, these communities pray for the great redemption. On the first 12 days of Nisan they read (not officially from a Torah scroll, but from a printed book, without a blessing) the 12 passages, one by one, about the gifts brought by the 12 tribes to the Shrine (Numbers 7:12–83); and on the thirteenth of Nisan, in honor of the priestly tribe of Levi, the passage on lighting the Menorah from Exodus 8:1–5. The first day of Nisan is observed as a daylight fast in memory and mourning of the deaths of Nadav and Avihu, Aaron's sons, on the very day they brought strange fire to offer at the dedication of the Shrine. Similarly, the tenth of Nisan is kept by the most observant as a fast day in memory of the death of Miriam.

Beginning on the new moon of Nisan, it is also customary to start studying the Passover story—especially to review the Haggadah and various ancient and modern commentaries on it, with an eye to using it on Pesach night. In households and congregations where it is customary to use variations on the Haggadah, Rosh Chodesh Nisan is a good time to begin gathering different Haggadahs and looking through them for passages that stir the mind and soul in one's present stage in life.

The two weeks between Rosh Chodesh and Pesach can be a time for serious exploration of the meaning of freedom, creativity, the birth and rebirth of identity. What mitzrayim, what tight spot, do I need to leave this year? What buds and sprouts of change do I see in myself and in the world around me? What questions do I need to ask? What tales do I need to tell? What songs do I need to sing?

The Shabbos just before Pesach, Shabbos Hagadol (either The Great Shabbos or Shabbos of The Great) was traditionally a point at which these questions—seen, it is true, through the lens of the ancient texts—might be intensified.

The Shabbos took its special name from the climactic lines about "the great and terrible day of the Lord," Yom Adonai hagadol v'hanorah, from the haftarah assigned for that day replacing the regular haftarah connected with the ordinary Torah portion in the regular cycle of readings. The special haftarah is from the last chapter of Malachi, the last of the Prophets. It ends:

For here! The day is coming that will burn like a furnace. All the proud, and all who do evil, will be stubble; and the day that is coming will set them ablaze, says the Lord of Hosts, so that it will leave them neither root nor branch. But for you who fear My name the sun of righteousness will rise with healing in its wings, and you shall go forth leaping joyfully like calves released from the stall. And you shall trample upon the wicked, for they shall be ashes under the soles of your feet on the day that I make, says the Lord of Hosts. Remember the Teaching of Moses my servant, which I commanded him in Horeb for all Israel—rules and judgments. Here, I will send you Elijah the prophet before the coming of the great and terrible day of the Lord. And he will turn the hearts of parents to children and the hearts of children to parents—lest I come and smite the land with utter destruction.

This *haftarah* clearly connects the ultimate Redemption with the impending Passover—as if to remind us in advance that the point of Pesach is to look toward the coming of Elijah, in the Pesach that will redeem all the peoples from all the Pharaohs. And how, in that great and terrible day, will Elijah do the work of redemption? By turning the hearts of the generations toward each other. By infusing with love the questions of the children and the answers of the parents on Seder night. By making of the Pesach sacrificial lamb a true substitute for the death of the firstborn child, just as Elijah comes to the circumcision of a newborn son to make that ceremony, too, a substitute for death between the generations.

And thus Shabbos Hagadol comes to remind us once more and in a new way that Pesach is the festival of birth, of generation, of creation—and of all the strains that emerge when the old gives birth to the new.

In the afternoon service on Shabbos Hagadol, the part of the Pesach Haggadah that runs from "*Avadim hayinu*, slaves we were," to the end of *Dayenu*, "to atone for all our sins," is read in some synagogues to prepare for Pesach. It may replace the chanting of Psalm 104, or be added to it.

THE SEDER PREPARATIONS

The last burst of preparations focuses on the Seder itself. This is a symbolic, ritual meal that uses real foods to embody ideas—literally to make them part of the body. Seder means order. The order of the meal and of the story-telling that precedes it has been carefully worked and reworked over centuries and is laid out in the book called Haggadah or Telling. But this is an order that looks toward freedom, and there is a free play of discussion and action within the basic pattern.

Since the Seder is built around a real meal, it is done around a dinner table with a plate of the symbolic foods upon it. Almost all Haggadahs describe how this Seder plate should be set, though few explain all the items: Pesach or *zeroa* (arm-outstretched-to-sow-seed) stands for the sacrificial lamb—now usually represented by a roast lamb shankbone; or a roast chicken neck or wing, among Jews whose tradition suggests avoiding any hint that the Temple sacrifices might still be valid; or a boiled beet, among vegetarians, in accord with a Talmudic suggestion of what foods might fulfill the command of eating two dishes.

Why two dishes? One representing the Pesach sacrifice and the other representing the *chagigah* or festival sacrifice that was offered on all of the pilgrimage festivals, not only Pesach. The roast egg on the Seder plate came to represent the *chagigah*.

On most Seder plates there are two forms of *maror*, the bitter herb: both a raw root of horseradish (to eat a slice separately from the matzah, but piled with *charoset*), and a dish of grated horseradish (to eat together with the matzah in memory of the Temple and in honor of Hillel, who urged that way of doing it).

There is also the mildly bitter green vegetable: parsley, lettuce, or celery, used for dipping in salt water at the beginning of the ritual. It is intended to foreshadow the bitter herb, and to trigger the children's questions because the procedure is so odd. And it may carry a second level of symbolic meaning in that the greens in salt water may represent the spring element of Pesach—with the salt recalling the sea, mother of life.

And there is the *charoset*, a paste or mixture of chopped nuts, apples or raisins, and wine, representing the mortar that the Israelite slaves used in laying bricks. The fact that *charoset* is so sweetly delicious may represent a dialectical truth about slavery: slavery is bitter, but its orderliness and secure dependability can also become sweet to the slave.

Among the other arrangements of the Seder are the following:

· Participants (or at least the one who is acting as leader) wear the white robe or *kittel* that is otherwise worn only for Yom Kippur, one's wedding, and one's burial. Thus the sense of purity-in-renewal is asserted for this festival of new birth.

· Salt water for dipping the greens at the start of the ritual and a hard-boiled egg at the start of the meal.

· Three pieces of matzah, representing—depending on the commentator—Abraham, Isaac, and Jacob; the three castes of Cohanim (priests), Levites, and ordinary Israelites; the two joyful sacrifices of Pesach and *chagigah*, plus the bread of the oppressed; creation, revelation, and redemption; the three aspects of life expressed in assertion (which requires one), tension (which requires two), and resolution (which requires three); and many other threads of meaning.

· Enough wine to make up four cups for each participant—representing the four verbs of redemption in Exodus 6:6–7 (*v'hotzeyti, v'hitzalti, v'ga-alti v'lakachti*—I will bring you out, I will deliver you, I will redeem you, I will espouse you).

· A wine cup to fill for the expected visit of Elijah the Prophet.

· Pillows to lean the left side on, especially when saying blessings over the wine and ritual food—as a symbol of freedom and relaxation.

◆»» THE SEDER «««◆

The Seder itself can be done in a more or a less ordered way, depending on the desires of each group of participants. Since all Haggadahs—traditional and experimental—lay out an order for the Seder, the most important task is to absorb how one or another Haggadah works and to decide how much openness you want. What seems most useful for us to do here is to sketch the basic structure and to mention different approaches that some people have used. For more detail, choose a Haggadah.

The basic structure is (a) a series of preparatory steps; (b) an introduction to the telling made up of an interplay of questions and partial answers; (c) the heart of the telling, a brief historical passage from Deuteronomy intertwined with a number of midrashic commentaries; (d) singing part of the *Hallel* psalms, praising God for past and future redemptions; (e) formally eating the ritual foods; (f) the regular meal, with songs; and (g) the post-meal recitation of grace after meals and the rest of the *Hallel* psalms, with several closing songs and rituals.

In all of these sections it is possible to pause—to add some ceremonial acts; read some poems, stories, commentaries from Jewish tradition or from non-Jewish sources, or additional prayers; make new *midrash* by sharing reactions to what is going on; or add new songs. Time and hunger may turn out to be the chief problems involved in enriching the Seder in this way. The group might decide to take the edge off hunger by eating a light snack beforehand or even (unobtrusively) at some point in the service and discussion.

The preparatory steps are lighting the festival candles; making the separation and hallowing of *kiddush* to bless the festival; washing the hands; eating the mildly bitter greens dipped in salt water; and breaking one matzah. The company might explore the meanings of this pattern. Does it evoke the process of the Creation, from the separation of light and dark to the breaking in two of Adam? Does it bring forth special memories of old Passovers? As an introduction and warm-up, a beginning for the festival of beginnings, what feelings does it arouse?

The heart of the Seder is the telling, in accordance with the command, "You shall tell your child on that day, saying . . .". Precisely the command to "Tell your child" directs the Seder in an intergenerational direction. The Haggadah examines the different approaches of four different kinds of children (or are all these different aspects of every person's makeup?) and suggests four questions that the youngest put to all the grown-ups. The Talmud makes clear that these questions are only a suggestion; it tells the stories of several Seders in which other questions were asked, and because they opened up the story, replaced the Four Questions at those Seder tables. It is especially interesting to note that only two of the Four Questions receive explicit answers in the Haggadah—as if to say that the elders can never fully answer questions, or that the next generation must constantly work out new answers.

After the questions and some partial answers, the Haggadah enters the heart of the telling. This is made up of reciting the verses of Deuteronomy 26:5–8, a brief history of the Israelites' entrance into and exodus from Egypt, together with a long and intertwined midrash or exegetical commentary on these verses. The passage in its original context is an unusual credo in the form of a history, a public statement to be made when bringing the yearly first fruits offering to the Temple. The statement is not the usual kind of credo in the sense of "I believe in the following general propositions about the world, my religion, and my self," but instead is a statement of memory—a recapitulation of the history of the Israelite people in its relation with God.

The Haggadah's midrash on this passage pauses at many of the words of this mini-history, linking them with similar words elsewhere in the Bible and thus enriching the story. The *midrash* may also be making some philosophical points in arguments that were going on among the sages as the Haggadah was being shaped. For example, the *midrashim* could have been so chosen as to glorify Moses. Instead, he is referred to only once (and then in a casual way) in the whole Haggadah. Presumably the intention was to emphasize God's leadership and de-emphasize the individual hero who might come almost to be worshipped.

The next portion of the Seder is a powerful living-out of the fusion of physical and intellectual—through eating foods that have a strong content of ideas and emotions. Some Jewish communities have not waited till the eating to make this fusion, but have made the telling itself more physical, in the tradition of the vigor and haste of the departure from Egypt. Some Oriental Jews get up from the table, put matzahs on their left shoulders, and with sandals on their feet and staves in their hands march around the table and into other rooms or even into the street—re-enacting the Exodus. Others act out a mini-play in which a dusty, exhausted traveler hammers on the door and is finally let in to describe how things were going in Jerusalem and how close the coming of Messiah seems. Some American Seders have included playlets on the ten different plagues, improvised dances expressing the feelings of the Four Children and of the different verses of *dayenu*, and mime representing the inner essences of the matzah, the bitter herb, the wine, the *charoset*.

The section in which the ritual foods are shared begins with a formal hand-washing and goes on with matzah, *maror* (bitter herb), and *charoset*. It includes pointing out the shankbone or its substitute without eating or even lifting it—lest it be thought the sacrifices are still in force without the Temple. Between the ritual foods and the regular meal there is in many households a strange moment that has the quality of both: the eating of a hard-boiled egg sliced in old salt water. The character and wide usage of this soup marks it as a ritual; yet there is no special explanation or blessing, and it is treated as the first course of the meal, before the real soup with matzah balls. The egg in salt water would seem to be a symbol of birth and fertility—celebrated but not discussed.

PRAYER AND TORAH-READING

The first day of Pesach is a holiday on which, traditionally, no work is done. Before the morning *amidah* a hymn is sung: "B'rakh Dodi . . . , Flee," or "Hasten, my Beloved," a phrase from the last verse of the Song of Songs. Here it is addressed to God. There are three separate hymns by different poets under this title. One of them is sung on the first day, one on the second day of Pesach, and one on the Shabbos in the middle of Pesach. Each of them looks forward to the Messianic redemption, and each ends, "For the sake of the forebears, please save the children and bring redemption to their children's children. Blessed are You, Lord, Who redeems Israel."

In the *amidah* itself, the same festival paragraph used for Sukkot is inserted, except that the festival is given the special name "Chag Hamatzot, z'man Cherutenu, Festival of Unleavened Bread, the season of our liberation." After the *amidah*, all of *Hallel* is recited on the first day as it is on Sukkot.

The Torah readings of the first day of Pesach are made up of Exodus 12:21–51 and Numbers 28:16–25. These are, respectively, the passage that intertwines the story of the Passover night of Exodus with the command for future celebrations of Pesach; and the recitation of the sacrifices required for the seven days of Pesach while the Temple stood.

The *haftarah* for the first day is from Joshua 5:7–6:1, plus 6:27. In it, after having just led the Israelites across the Jordan River into the Promised Land, Joshua arranges the circumcision of all the Israelite males—for all who had been born in the wilderness during the forty years after the Exodus from Egypt had remained uncircumcised. He did this just in time to celebrate Pesach—evidently for the first time since the Exodus, since only circumcised men could take part in Pesach. When the people ate unleavened bread, the manna which had fed them since the Exodus stopped falling, and from then on they ate of the grain of the land of Canaan.

In the first blessing of the *amidah* in the *musaf* or additional service on the first day of Pesach, there is inserted a prayer for God to begin sending dew. This prayer marks the turning of the seasons in the Land of Israel. With Pesach begin the six months of the year in which there is almost never any rain; so the prayers for rain end. But some continuing moisture is essential to keep the land fertile, and so the rabbis decided to ask God for dew. The phrase "mashiv haruach u'morid hageshem, Who makes the wind blow and the rain fall," is simply dropped by Ashkenazic Jews from Pesach to Sh'mini

Atzeret, and among Sephardim is replaced with the phrase "u-morid hatal, Who makes the dew fall." One of the great liturgical poets, Eleazar Kalir, wrote a hymn that is used on the first day of Pesach in most congregations. Its last stanza:

Give dew, precious dew, that we our harvest reap,
And guard our fatted flocks and herds from leanness!
Behold our people follows Thee like sheep,
And looks to Thee to give the earth her greenness, *With dew.*

In the Land of Israel and among Reform Jews, as with all the other festivals (except Rosh Hashanah) there is celebrated only one first day of Pesach. Among non-Reform Jews of the Diaspora, two first days of festival are celebrated. On the second night of Pesach, therefore, there is a second Seder. Some households have developed ways of making the two experiences quite different: for instance, one in a family or small group of friends, the other in a larger communal setting; one indoors, the other outside—even as the culmination of a hike; one with a traditional Haggadah, one with a new one; one focused on political liberation, one on spring. It is on the second night of Pesach that the Counting of the *omer* begins, which we will deal with in the next chapter.

On the morning of the second day of Pesach, congregations that recognize it as a festival day* chant again a full *Hallel*, the psalms of praise from Psalm 113 to 118. From the Torah they read Leviticus from 22:26–23:44, and the same passage from Numbers as on the day before. The Leviticus passage contains the cycle of all the festivals of the year. The *haftarah* for the second day, II Kings 23:1–9 and 23:21–25, describes the efforts of King Josiah in the seventh century B.C.E. to cleanse the whole land and people of idolatrous practices and symbols—some of which had even been introduced into the Temple itself. Then Josiah called upon the people to make pilgrimage to Jerusalem to keep Pesach according to all the laws laid out in a book of Torah that had just been discovered (probably Deuteronomy). The people assembled in multitudes to keep such a Pesach as there had not been in all the days of the judges and the kings before.

With the end of the second day of Pesach, the intermediate days of *chol hamoed* (ordinary part of the festival) begin. In the morning service, only parts of *Hallel*, the psalms of praise, are chanted (omitting Psalms 115 and 116). We do this because on the seventh day of Pesach the Egyptian army was drowned in the Red Sea. According to the rabbis, when the angels began to sing for joy, God rebuked them: "Are not these also the work of My

---

*See Appendix I on the second day of festivals.

hands?" So in accord with God's desire we reduce our joy—so that we should express no pleasure over death, even the death of our enemies.

The obligation to eat no *chametz* continues through the rest of Pesach. Traditional Jews avoid strenuous or demeaning work during the whole week of Pesach; but cooking or other work for the holidays, and crucial business whose neglect would mean substantial losses, may be carried on. Most Jews now continue at their work during the week, but with a festive air.

On the Shabbos that comes in the middle of Pesach, the tradition teaches that the Song of Songs should be read before the Torah reading. The Song is a flowing set of interwoven love poems, some of them rich in erotic imagery and imagery of springtime. There was an argument among the rabbis over whether it should be preserved as part of the Bible at all—an argument resolved by Akiba's insistence that "All the writings are holy, but the Song of Songs is the holy of holies."

Why did the rabbis assign the reading of the Song to Pesach?

· The traditional understanding of the song is that it is about the love between God and Israel—a love poem especially appropriate at Pesach, which might be viewed as the onset of the love affair that culminates fifty days later at the Marriage between God and Israel at Sinai.

· Rabbinic and Kabbalistic midrash on the Song saw in it many specific metaphorical references to the night of watching, hope, and dread, just before the Exodus from Egypt; to the Exodus itself; and to the sojourn in the wilderness.

· The themes of spring and sexuality in the Song go well with Pesach as a festival of spring and birth.

· In the Song, God's name is never mentioned, and the spiritual life is one of flow, spontaneity, openness, and process—God as Inner. It thus complements the spirituality of the Haggadah, which is based on God as Other and on the rhythm set by clock and calendar. Perhaps both spiritual modes must be experienced and integrated if Messiah is to come—and if Pesach is to teach toward the Messianic redemption, then Pesach must hold and share both modes of being.

The Torah readings for Shabbos Chol Hamoed Pesach are from Exodus 33:12–34:26 and Numbers 28:19–25. The former describes Moses' seeking out and achieving a close and loving knowledge of God's loving-kindness, and hearing as a friend God's pattern of Pesach in the pilgrim festivals. The latter details the burnt-offerings for Pesach.

The *haftarah* is the extraordinary chapter of Ezekiel 37, in which Ezekiel experiences the valley of dry bones—the dead and hopeless house of Israel. God promises to breathe life and hope into the bones, to restore full vigor and spirit to the people, and to return them to their land. By placing this passage as a Pesach reading, the rabbis reasserted the connection between the redemption of the past and the redemption of the future.

According to tradition, the seventh day of Pesach is the day on which Pharaoh's chariots overtook the Israelites at the Reed Sea, and were plunged into the sea while Israel marched through it on dry land. In commemoration of the event, the seventh day (and eighth, for non-Reform Jews in the Diaspora) is a full holiday when work is forbidden and the people reassemble for a holy convocation. The morning service for the seventh day includes a hymn to be sung just before the amidah—Yom L'Yabasha. It is by Yehuda Halevi, perhaps the greatest of the Spanish-Jewish poets (twelfth century). It begins by celebrating the salvation of Israel at the Reed Sea, and then looks forward to the future great redemption with the refrain, "Shira chadash shibchu g'eulim, Then a new song sang Your redeemed throng." The Torah portion (from Exodus 13:17–15:26) also focuses on the encounter at the Sea. It includes the song of triumph Miriam, Moses, and the people sang. The haftarah underlines the theme of victorious song. It is made up of David's chant of triumph at his delivery from danger at the hand of King Saul: "The Lord is my rock and my fortress!"

On the eighth day, the Torah portion (Deuteronomy 14:22–16:17 if the eighth day is also Shabbos; if not, Deuteronomy 15:19–16:17) focuses on the command to celebrate Pesach in the context of the other festivals. The haftarah (Isaiah 10:32–12:6) again looks to the future:

And the wolf shall dwell with the lamb, and the leopard shall lie down with the kid, and the calf and young lion and fatling together, and a little child shall lead them. . . . None shall hurt or destroy in all My holy mountain, for the earth shall be full of intimacy with the Lord as the waters fill the sea.

It is on the eighth day that the community remembers its dead in the yizkor service.

COMPLETION

After nightfall ends the eighth day of Pesach, there is a havdalah (separation) ceremony—a truncated version of the havdalah that ends Shabbos. The paragraph before the wine and the blessings of spices and fire are omitted (unless the eighth day is also Shabbos):

Baruch atah Adonai elohenu melech ha-olam borey p'ri hagafen.

Blessed Are You, Lord our God, ruler of space and time, Who creates the fruit of the vine.
(Drink the wine.)
Baruch etah Adonai elohenu melech ha-olam hamavdil beyn kodesh

l'chol, beyn ohr l'choshech, beyn Yisrael l'amim, beyn yom hashvi'i
l'sheshet y'mey hama-aseh. Baruch atah Adonai hamavdil beyn kodesh
l'chol.

Blessed are You, Lord our God, ruler of space and time, who distinguishes between holy and ordinary, between light and darkness, between Israel and the other peoples, between the seventh day and the
six work days. Blessed are You, Lord Our God, Who distinguishes
between holy and ordinary.

In many households, people will then go out together to buy and eat
some *chametz*: ice cream perhaps, or a specially well-baked bread, or beer and
pizza.

The custom of a *chametz* party has been brought to its highest level by
the Jews of North Africa, who hold a great celebration called *Maimuna* on
the evening and day after Pesach. That day is believed to be the *yahrtzeit*
(death-anniversary) of Maimon ben Joseph, the father of Rambam or Maimo-
nides, one of the greatest of the rabbinic commentators and codifiers.
Maimon was himself a leading scholar of his generation, lived in the Moroc-
can city of Fez, and died about 1170. Much of his work focused on Islamic–
Jewish relations; it both took Islam seriously as a monotheistic religion, and
offered Jews who had been forcibly converted to Islam ways of continuing
their adherence to Torah. His work was therefore of great significance to Jews
living in Muslim countries—which may help explain the fact and the name
of the celebration on his *yahrtzeit*.

Maimuna itself begins with an evening meal of dairy foods symbolic of
birth and fertility—milk, figs, ears of wheat, and pancakes with butter and
honey. Often a live fish, swimming in a bowl, is on the table, along with a
bowl of flour in which golden rings are hidden. There is a great bustle of
visiting and sharing foods from one household to another. On the following
day there are large picnics at beaches, fields, and cemeteries. In Israel, Jews of
North African background carry on the *Maimuna* tradition, including a large
get-together in Jerusalem.

◆⟫⟫ NEW APPROACHES ⟨⟨◆

For centuries or millennia, three major themes have been interwoven in
Pesach: the birth of a people into political freedom; the rebirth of the earth
into springtime life; and spiritual rebirth of the individual (especially in the
symbolism based on removal of *chametz*). All these, of course, continue to be
profoundly important. In our own generation, the Pesach story might also
serve as a framework to deal with a new birth that embodies some elements of

all these three. That is the emergence of new forms in the relationships between women and men.

There are two main elements of Pesach tradition that might lead us in that direction: the story of the first stages of the birth of freedom, in the first four chapters of Exodus; and the Song of Songs. To this generation, the issues of the freedom of women and the place of women in the struggles for universal freedom are important. To such a generation, rereading the first four chapters of Exodus opens up some unexpected possibilities.

Those chapters keep asserting the importance of women and their experience of childbirth as the guide to freedom. First there are the mid-wives—who are the first to resist Pharaoh's decree that all the Israelite newborn boys be murdered. They obey God, not Pharaoh—even though they have never heard God's voice. They do not need to hear the Voice, because they hear it in the cry of each new baby. It is the voice of newness, unpredictability, creativity, the voice of "I will become who I will become," the Name that God's Own Self later adopts at the burning bush. Even more than mothers, they understood childbirth—because they had mothered so many births, so many mothers. And from giving birth to children, they learn to give birth to freedom. For the newborn carries at the biological level the same message that freedom carries at the historical-political level: it is possible to start over. It is possible for there to be possibility.

In Exodus, the women keep on teaching the lesson. Pharaoh's daughter and Miriam conspire to save the life of a baby boy by giving him a second birth from the waters of the Nile—and he grows up to be Moses. But even Moses must receive more education from women before he can become the liberator. His first clumsy efforts at liberation only send him bursting forth from Egypt like tumultuously sown seed. He settles among seven women at a well (a symbol of the womb), marries one of them, has a child—and *only then* can meet God at the burning bush and hear the Voice and Name of freedom. Even this is not enough: on the journey back to Egypt, Moses—in danger of death—has to learn from his wife Tzipporah how to fulfill the birth of his son by renewing the covenant of circumcision. Not till then can he take on the task he has been assigned.

So these chapters teach us that women—and the quintessentially female process, giving birth to children—were crucial to the Liberation from Egypt. Even the liberation itself—out of *mitzrayim*, the tight spot, across the broken waters of the Reed Sea—was a birth, or a conception in the first stages of what became a birth on crossing Jordan. Torah shows us that the process cannot be fulfilled until men are also part of it. But it is the women who first understand the path, because they bring to it something unique in their own life-experience.

◆>>> FOODS <<<◆

Perhaps the most thoroughly explored of all the aspects of Jewish food is that of how to cook for Pesach. In addition to some traditional recipes, we are making some available in one unexplored area. In the last decade the number of Jews who are vegetarians has grown considerably—and vegetarians who want to keep kosher for Pesach and who adhere to the special Ashkenazic prohibition on rice, peas, and beans find themselves in an unusually difficult position. Where do you find protein if meat, fish, and most of the grains and lentils can't be used?

Rose Sue Berstein, an Ashkenazic vegetarian who is a member of the *chavurah*-style group Fabrangen in Washington, DC, has collected a number of recipes for foods that are high in protein, low in cholesterol and calories, and fulfill both Jewish and vegetarian obligations.

STUFFED EGGPLANT

For each two servings, use 1 medium (approx. 1 lb.) eggplant, 1 small green pepper, 1 medium onion, 6–8 large mushrooms and 4 oz. Kosher-for-Passover Cheddar cheese, grated. Slice eggplant lengthwise. Carefully scoop out inside, leaving shells intact. Chop into small cubes. Saute—using as little oil as possible—eggplant with sliced green pepper, onion and mushrooms until soft. Season with basil and ground black pepper. Fill eggplant cavities with this mixture, place in oiled baking dish and bake at 350° for 15 minutes. Then top each eggplant half with grated cheese and return to oven until cheese melts, about 10 minutes.

ZUCCHINI SOUP

Use approx. 1½ lbs. zucchini, sliced in ¼ inch rounds. Saute the zucchini with 1 sliced onion, then pass through food mill or puree in blender, but reserve several slices for garnishing. Stir pureed zucchini into 4 cups milk over low heat. When thoroughly blended continue cooking over medium heat, for about 15 minutes, but do not bring to boil. Season to taste with salt, pepper and chives. Garnish with remaining zucchini slices. Can be served hot or cold; if served cold, add a spoonful of yoghurt or sour cream.

STUFFED PEPPERS

For four green peppers use 8 oz. farmer cheese, 2 eggs, 4 tablespoons chopped green onions, 1 teaspoon rosemary, salt and pepper as desired. Hollow out peppers, and fill with cheese mix. Then sprinkle grated cheddar cheese on top of each one, (use 2–3 oz. altogether) and top with sliced almonds. Place in oiled baking dish and bake at 350° approx. 30 minutes.

BRUSSELS SPROUTS CASSEROLE

1½ lbs. brussels sprouts
1 medium onion
butter

5 medium tomatoes
1 cup grated cheddar (can substitute) cheese

Saute sliced onion in butter until transparent. Scald, peel and slice tomatoes. Arrange brussels sprouts in casserole with onions and tomatoes. Add up to ½ cup water, then cover and bake at 325° for 45 minutes. When brussels sprouts are tender, sprinkle with grated cheese and place under broiler to brown. 4 servings.

RED CABBAGE WITH APPLES

1 red cabbage
1 medium onion
⅓ cup lemon juice
¼ cup honey
2 apples
handful raisins

½ teaspoon salt
1 tsp. cinnamon
(opt. 6 caraway seeds, 6 cloves, 4
  whole allspice, 2 bay leaves)
3 tablespoons oil or margarine
½ cup water

Gently saute sliced onion in oil, then add water, lemon juice, honey, and flavorings. Mix well, then add finely sliced or grated cabbage. Cover and cook over medium heat about 15 minutes, then add sliced apples and raisins. Continue to simmer about 10 minutes longer. Tart apples work best, and if you wish, you can tie the spices in cheesecloth for easy removal. 6 servings.

LEEK SOUP

2 large leeks
4 tablespoons butter
1 large potato

1½ cup milk
salt
pepper

Wash leeks well, slice, and saute in butter, but don't brown them. Peel and slice the potato very finely, add to the leeks and cook very slowly, stirring gently until soft. Add milk, salt and pepper. Force through a sieve, return to saucepan and serve warm. 4 servings.

POTATO CAULIFLOWER SOUP

1 cooked cauliflower
3 cooked and cubed potatoes
4 cups milk

2 tablespoons butter
1½ teaspoons salt
¾ cup minced onion

Heat milk in a large saucepan, add water in which you cooked the vegetables, stir in butter and salt. Sieve cauliflower and potatoes in small quantities and return to saucepan when smooth enough for your taste. (If you can use a blender this is much easier—be sure to put enough liquid in with each batch of vegetables). Simmer while you add the onion. Optional vegetables for additions include diced celery, carrots, fresh chives, and/or parsley. 2 quarts.

Some more traditional Pesach recipes, from Hannah Waskow and Rose Gertz:

MATZAH MEAL PANCAKES (LATKES)

½ cup matzah meal
¾ teaspoon salt
1 tablespoon sugar

¾ cup cold water
3 eggs

Combine matzah meal, salt, and sugar. Separate the eggs. Beat yolks slightly and combine with the water. Add the liquids to the dry ingredients. Allow to stand for ½ hour. (May be mixed this far the night before and kept in the refrigerator to save time the next morning.) Beat the egg whites until stiff. Fold into the matzah meal mixture. Drop by tablespoon onto a hot, well-greased frying pan or griddle and brown on both sides. Makes 10 to 12 latkes. Serve with cinnamon and sugar, sour cream, apple sauce, or syrup.

MATZAH BALLS

2 tablespoons fat
2 eggs slightly beaten
½ cup matzah meal

1 teaspoon salt
2 tablespoons soup stock or water

Mix fat and eggs together. Add matzah meal and salt which were first mixed together. When well blended, add soup stock or water. Cover mixing bowl and place in refrigerator for at least twenty minutes. (May be refrigerated until convenient to cook.) Using a two or three quart pot, bring salted water to a brisk boil. Reduce flame and into the slightly bubbling water drop balls formed from above mixture. (About the size of walnuts.) Cover pot and cook 40–60 minutes. Cut one matzah ball in half. If center is solid, return to pot and cook an additional 10 minutes. Have soup at room temperature, or warmer, and remove matzah balls from water to soup pot. When ready to serve allow soup to simmer for a few minutes. Will make eight to twelve balls. Packing these balls in 4's or 5's they may be frozen. To thaw, heat in small amount of boiling water and then transfer to soup. Very good in pea soup or noodle soup during the year. This recipe may be doubled with slight decrease in salt.

UNLEAVENED BAGEL

1 cup water
⅓ cup chicken or vegetable fat or margarine
1 cup matzah meal (full)

1 tablespoon sugar
4 eggs
¼ teaspoon salt

Bring to a boil fat, water, sugar, and salt. Then stir in matzah meal, boil a second more, and remove from fire. Mix thoroughly, and when cooled a little, beat in eggs one at a time. Grease or wet hands and roll dough into balls of about 2 inches diameter. Place on greased sheet, then dip forefinger in water and press a hole in center of each ball or omit and use as rolls. Bake at 425° for 20 minutes and at 375° for 25 minutes. They should sound hollow. Let cool in stove with door ajar.

SPONGE CAKE

7 eggs
1½ cups sugar—sifted
Grated rind of 1 lemon
dash of salt

juice of lemon
1 cup (light) potato
starch, sifted twice

Separate 6 eggs. Beat 6 yolks and one whole egg together with rotary egg beater until frothy. Gradually add 1 cup of sifted sugar, lemon juice, and grated lemon rind until thick and well mixed. Beat the 6 egg whites until stiff and add the rest of the sugar gradually. Mix potato starch and salt and add to egg yolk mixture. Fold in beaten egg whites. Finely cut nuts may be added to batter or sprinkled on top.

Pour mixture into ungreased 10 inch tube pan. Bake 350° 45–50 minutes. Turn over on funnel until cold. Remove from pan by sliding a knife gently up and down between cake and pan to loosen.

UNLEAVENED MEAT AND POTATO KNISHES

3 cups mashed potatoes (regular or instant)
1 beaten egg
½ teaspoon salt
5 tablespoons fat (chicken or margarine or combination)

Enough hot water (about ½ cup) to make a loose mixture. Add matzah meal to make a dough that can be shaped into biscuit-like form. (Wet hands before handling dough.)

FILLING
If *gribenes* (cracklings resulting from rendering chicken fat) are available, use.
If not, sautee:

large onion	½ lb. ground meat
garlic clove	¼ lb. liver (chicken or beef)

Grind *gribenes* and meat mixture (or sauteed onion and meat). Add:

beaten egg	½ cup mashed potatoes
salt	dash of oregano
pepper	pinch of sugar
parsley flakes	

Taste. May need a little more fat. Should have a smooth, velvety well-seasoned taste.
Wet hands, form patty of potato dough, hollow center, insert a walnut-size piece of meat mixture and form dough over meat. Put on greased pan 2 inches apart. Lightly grease top. Bake about ½ hr., 400° or until light brown and crusty. Any left over filling may be frozen. Will make 12–15 knishes, depending on size.

GRIBENES
2 cups fat and skin of chicken, duck or goose cut into small pieces. Melt in large heavy saucepan over medium low heat until almost completely rendered. Add 1 large diced onion and cook until onion is golden brown. (When adding onion be careful because the fat boils up and may catch on fire.) Cool and strain. Refrigerate fat. Freeze *gribenes* for later use.

◆⟫⟫ GO AND STUDY ⟪⟪◆

Haggadahs multiply. For me the most useful have been Nahum Glatzer and E. D. Goldschmidt, *The Passover Haggadah* (Schocken); Michael Strassfeld, *A Passover Haggadah* (Rabbinical Assembly); Central Conference of American Rabbis, with Leonard Baskin, *A Passover Haggadah* (CCAR); *Haggadah for a Secular Celebration of Pesach* (Sholom Aleichem Club of Philadelphia, 443 E. Wadsworth Ave., Philadelphia, PA); *Pesach Haggada* (Hashomer Hatzair, available through Americans for Progressive Israel, NYC); *Haggadah for a Crocus Festival* (Martin Buber Institute, Sebastopol, CA); Aviva Cantor, ed., *A Jewish Women's Haggada*, available from *Lilith Magazine*, NYC; and my own *The Freedom Seder* (Holt, Rinehart & Winston) and *The Shalom Seder*, available from *Menorah*, 1747 Connecticut Ave., N.W., Washington, DC.

See also Marcia Falk's translation of *The Song of Songs* (Harcourt Brace Jovanovich) as well as the one in *Five Megillot and Jonah* (Jewish Publ. Soc.). And see Ruth Gruber Fredman, *The Passover Seder: Afikoman in Exile* (Univ. of Pennsylvania), and Irving Greenberg's *Guide to Passover* (National Jewish Resource Center, NYC).

OMER CALENDAR

The first 49-day period is remembered by the representation of the seventy
palms and twelve springs of water which the Jews encountered at Elim.
(Exodus 15:27)

CHAPTER TEN

TREK THROUGH ANXIETY AND HOPE—COUNTING THE OMER

Seven weeks of seven days. Day by day, week by week, the community watches the spring grain grow, watches with hope and with anxiety. Day by day, week by week, the community moves forward from the moment of freedom's first explosion—moves forward with hope and with anxiety. Will the earth succeed in unfolding its fruitfulness? Will we succeed in finding rest and new truth in our freedom?

Day by day, week by week, the community counts the days of growing grain—and through them counts the unfolding of the earth and of our own potential. Day by day, week by week; for this is no holy day, not even a week-long festival—but truly a season of the year. A season full of hope, full of anxiety that hope may fail.

⬥⟫⟫ ORIGINS ⟪⟪⬥

The most ancient level of the counting of the *omer* is that the counting linked two moments of harvest, moments on which depended the prosperity of the year. In the Torah, the dating of these moments was imprecise—for it depended on the ripening of the grain. Barley is the quickest ripening grain and the most fertile—and so it was the quintessence of the fruitfulness of the land. The barley crop came to ripeness early in the spring—during or just after Pesach. Late in the spring—fifty days later—the wheat crop was ready.

So the Torah prescribed the waving of the *omer* (that is, a sheaf of barley) at the beginning of this period, "the time the sickle is first put to the standing grain" (Lev. 23:10–11; Deut. 16:9). Then seven full weeks were to be counted off, and on the fiftieth day, two loaves of wheat bread were to be waved as an offering. The fiftieth day was celebrated as the Festival of Weeks (Shavuot), celebrating the completion of the weeks of anxiety and hope.

The relationship between Pesach and Shavuot—and therefore the nature of these 49 days that connected them—became a matter of intense struggle between the priestly and rabbinic factions of Jewish leadership during the last two centuries before the destruction of the Temple. One passage of the Torah says that the counting of the 49 days should start when the sickle is put to the standing grain (Deut. 16:9); another, on the day after Shabbat (Lev. 23:11). The one date was indeterminate; the other, unclear. The priestly faction, the Sadducees, insisted the Shabbat in question was the Shabbos during Pesach. The Pharisees, forerunners of the rabbis, insisted that in this context Shabbat meant day of rest, not literally Shabbos, and that the day of rest intended was the festival day of the first day of Pesach. So they began the counting on the night beginning the second day of Pesach, and waved the omer of barley on the second day of Pesach.

According to the Mishnah, when the Temple still stood, the cutting of the omer of barley for the wave-offering would proceed this way:

> How was it made ready? The messengers of the court used to go out on the eve of the Festival day and tie the grain in bunches while it was yet unreaped to make it the easier to reap; and the towns near by all assembled there together that it might be reaped with much pomp. When it grew dark he called out, "Is the sun set?" and they answered, "Yea!" "Is the sun set?" and they answered, "Yea!" "Is this a sickle?" and they answered, "Yea!" "Is this a sickle?" and they answered, "Yea!" "Is this a basket?" and they answered, "Yea!" "Is this a basket?" and they answered, "Yea!" On the Sabbath he called out, "On this Sabbath?" and they answered, "Yea!" "On this Sabbath?" and they answered, "Yea!" "Shall I reap?" and they answered, "Reap!" "Shall I reap?" and they answered, "Reap!" He used to call out three times for every matter, and they answered, "Yea!" "Yea!" "Yea!" Wherefore was all this? Because of the Boethuseans who used to say: the omer may not be reaped at the close of a Festival day.

The Boethuseans were the priestly faction, the Sadducees under another name. The Mishnah is the record written by the rabbis. It is making a deliberate public statement that if the second day of Pesach happened to be a Shabbos, they reaped the omer even on Shabbos—when cutting grain would ordinarily be utterly forbidden—and did not reserve the reaping for the day after Shabbos as the Sadducees wished.

The Mishnah continues:

They reaped it, put it into the baskets, and brought it to the Temple Court. They used to parch it with fire to fulfill the ordinance that it should be parched with fire. So R. Meir. But the Sages say: They used to beat it with reeds and the stems of plants that the grains should not be crushed; then they put it into a hollow tube wherein were holes so that the fire might prevail over all of it. They put it in a grist mill and took therefrom a Tenth (of an *ephah* of flour) which was sifted through thirteen sieves. The priest then waved the *omer* in the six directions of the world: east, south, west, north, up, and down.

The struggle between the priests and the forerunners of the rabbis over when to start the countdown toward Shavuot may have been much more important than a battle over dates. For it was probably connected with the rabbinic assertion that Shavuot was not only the Festival of First Fruits, as the Torah calls it, but also the Festival of the Giving of the Torah. To assert this, the rabbis had to show that the date of Shavuot was the date of the revelation of the Torah at Mount Sinai. The written Torah never says this; it leaves unclear both the date of Shavuot and the date of Sinai. (In Chapter XI we will examine this struggle over the dates of the *omer*, Shavuot, and Sinai in more detail.)

Once the rabbis identified the two moments—the moment of celebrating the wheat harvest and the moment of receiving the Torah—they gave a new significance to the period of the 49 days. The period then became the time of ascent from political liberation to spiritual revelation—the period in which the newly free people move toward a new devotion, a new service and servitude to the God of freedom. Taken in this sense, the counting became relevant to the city-dwellers who were the Pharisees' constituency and for whom the spring harvesting may have become a distant, not highly significant process.

With the destruction of the Temple, the Pharisees and rabbis won. The importance of the priesthood shrank once the sacrifices became impossible. And with the waving of the *omer* and of the wheat bread gone as well, the sense of the period of the 49 days as a spiritual journey grew much stronger.

The rabbis decided that the counting of the 49 days should continue even after the wave-offerings had been prevented by the destruction of the Temple. Sometime during the next seven centuries, the 49 days took on the tone of a limited, moderate mourning. Except for the two new moons that come during the 49 days—Rosh Chodesh for the months of Iyar and Sivan— and for the day of Lag B'Omer—the 33d day of the *omer*—it was prohibited to have weddings or to play musical instruments or to get haircuts. When and why this tone of mourning was adopted is not clear. Some hypotheses:

· It may have been part of the observance from its early days, as a way of acting out the anxiety that pervaded the grain-growing season and the march

from Egypt to Mount Sinai. On this hypothesis, Lag B'Omer was the relaxation of this tension in midstream, a sigh of relief that the people heaved
before taking up the tension again. It is analogous to the ancient May Day
celebrations in many European cultures.

· It may have grown up only after the Destruction of the Temple, out of
mourning for the Temple and for the impossibility of waving the barley and
the wheat bread there.

· It may have grown up still later, out of a deadly epidemic that befell
the rabbinical students of Rabbi Akiba in the second century C.E.—a plague
that began with the *omer* and paused or ended on the 33d day. Alternatively,
the Talmud's reference to the death of Akiba's students may have been a
code-word reference to Akiba's soldiers. These were the soldiers of Bar
Kochba's revolt against Rome, which Akiba supported. Perhaps many of
them died in a terrible defeat during the *omer* period; but perhaps some of
them escaped or the battle ebbed on the 33d day.

· It may have been borrowed from a spring mourning period of the
Romans, during which the souls of the dead were thought to wander on earth
and marriages were avoided.

Some of these hypotheses, of course, may overlap. Thus a profound
sense of anxiety and hope during the spring growing season may have been at
the root of a Roman spring mourning period as well as at the root of the
Jewish counting of the *omer*. When the Jews discovered and felt the similarities, they may have borrowed some of the practices that others used to
express their feelings. And suppose that one or several stretched-out calami-
ties befell the Jews at approximately the same season, like a plague or a
bloody but indecisive battle. Their anxiety may have accentuated and become identified with that of the *omer* season.

As the connection of the *omer* with agriculture grew more remote, the
sense of the period as one of spiritual growth toward receiving Torah grew
stronger. As the saying goes, "It was relatively easy to get the Jews out of
slavery—but not so easy to get slavery out of the Jews." In this atmosphere,
the *omer* became a time of self-scrutiny and spiritual self-improvement.
Among the Kabbalists and the Chassidim who followed their approach, the
omer period became identified as a season for strengthening the virtues
intimated by the seven *S'phirot*, emanations or aspects of God, which had a
direct effect upon the world.

By the time these ideas get further refined in the Zohar [the great
Jewish mystical text, written in the thirteenth century] we are dealing
with a movement from the 49 Gates of Defilement [in *mitzrayim*]
through the Gates of Understanding [toward Sinai]. Since we have to
count 7 times 7 weeks, the number is not accidental. There is a pattern
in which 7 times 7 produces both cosmic and personal significance.
The Kabbalists taught us that the seven weeks represent the periods in

which one or another of the Seven Holy Attributes represented by the seven names not-to-be-erased appear in 49 different combinations. The attributes are listed in the following order: *Chesed* (Loving-kindness), *Gevurah* (Severity), *Tiferet* (Beauty), *Netzach* (Victory), *Hod* (Glory), *Yesod* (Intimacy), *Malchut* (Majesty). The seven attributes correspond to the seven archetypal persons: Abraham, Isaac, Israel, Moses, Aaron, Joseph, and David. The Seven *S'phirot* are manifested in us either on the side of holiness and order, or on the side of defilement and chaos. They are virtues on the holy side and vices on the side of evil.

DIVINE S'PHIROT	ARCHETYPAL PERSON	VIRTUE	VICE
Chesed (Loving-kindness)	Abraham	Love	Lust
Gevurah (Severity)	Isaac	Respect	Fear
Tiferet (Beauty)	Israel	Compassion	Indulgence
Netzach (Victory)	Moses	Efficiency	Pedantry
Hod (Glory)	Aaron	Esthetics	Vanity
Yesod (Intimacy)	Joseph	Loyalty	Promiscuity
Malchut (Majesty)	David	Leadership	Stubbornness

Accordingly, each of the 49 days of the *omer* period represents one of the possible combinations of the Divine *S'phirot*, in this fashion:

Omer Calendar

WEEKS	DAY 1	DAY 2	DAY 3	DAY 4	DAY 5	DAY 6	DAY 7
1	1 Chesed-Chesed	2 Gevurah-Chesed	3 Tiferet-Chesed	4 Netzach-Chesed	5 Hod-Chesed	6 Yesod-Chesed	7 Malchut-Chesed
2	8 Chesed-Gevurah	9 Gevurah-Gevurah	10 Tiferet-Gevurah	11 Netzach-Gevurah	12 Hod-Gevurah	13 Yesod-Gevurah	14 Malchut-Gevurah
3	15 Chesed-Tiferet	16 Gevurah-Tiferet	17 Tiferet-Tiferet	18 Netzach-Tiferet	19 Hod-Tiferet	20 Yesod-Tiferet	21 Malchut-Tiferet
4	22 Chesed-Netzach	23 Gevurah-Netzach	24 Tiferet-Netzach	25 Netzach-Netzach	26 Hod-Netzach	27 Yesod-Netzach	28 Malchut-Netzach
5	29 Chesed-Hod	30 Gevurah-Hod	31 Tiferet-Hod	32 Netzach-Hod	33 Hod-Hod	34 Yesod-Hod	35 Malchut-Hod
6	36 Chesed-Yesod	37 Gevurah-Yesod	38 Tiferet-Yesod	39 Netzach-Yesod	40 Hod-Yesod	41 Yesod-Yesod	42 Malchut-Yesod
7	43 Chesed-Malchut	44 Gevurah-Malchut	45 Tiferet-Malchut	46 Netzach-Malchut	47 Hod-Malchut	48 Yesod-Malchut	49 Malchut-Malchut

(Adapted from Zalman Schachter-Shalomi in the B'nai Or Newsletter)

◆»» PRESENT PRACTICE «««◆

In our own generation, the period of the *omer* has been somewhat altered by several factors. One is that among practically all Reform and many Conservative Jews, the actual counting of the days and many of the mourning practices have fallen into disuse. Lag B'Omer survives as a special day of celebration; we will examine it in more detail later in the chapter. Another aspect of change is that two special commemorative days have been introduced in the period: one memorializing the victims and the resistance in the Nazi Holocaust, and the other commemorating the declaration of Israeli independence in 1948. These will also be taken up in their specific places. The result of these changes is that the tone and approach of the period from Pesach to Shavuot is to some extent now in flux. More experiment and more re-evaluation seems likely before the old patterns are renewed or new ones worked out.

PRACTICE OF THE COUNTING

The Hebrew for counting is *s'phirah;* so the practice and the period are known as *S'phirat Ha-Omer* or often simply as *S'phirah.* The count begins on the second night of Pesach—traditionally, at the end of the evening prayer service, but in many families where there is a second Seder, in the part of the Seder after the meal. The heart of the counting is the recitation of the Biblical verse that commands the counting, followed by a blessing and the count itself.

Even on the first night, *Sheh-hechianu,* the blessing "Who has kept us alive until this season," which is usually said at the onset of a new season or festival, is not said because the *omer* is felt to be partly a preparation for Shavuot—so *Sheh-hechianu* is most legitimately said then.

Hin'ni muchan u'mzuman l'kayem mitzvat aseh shel s'phirat ha-omer, k'mo sheh-katuv batorah: U'sphartem lachem mimacharat hashabat miyom havi-achem et omer ha-tnufah sheva shabatot t'mimot tih'yena ad mimacharat hashabat hashvi-it tispr'u chamishim yom.

Baruch atah Adonai elohenu melech ha-olam asher kid'shanu b'mitz-votav vitzivanu al s'phirat ha-omer.

Ha-yom . . . yamim, sheh-heym . . . shavuah . . . u' . . . yamim la-omer.

Here I am, ready and prepared to do the command of counting the *omer,* as is written in the Torah: "You shall count for yourself from the day after the day of rest; from the day of bringing the sheaf of the wave-offering, there shall be seven full weeks; until the day after the seventh week you shall count—fifty days.

Blessed are you, Lord our God, ruler of time and space, who makes us holy with His commandments and commands us about counting the *omer*.

Today is the _____ day, comprising _____ weeks and _____ days, for the *omer*.

Among Chassidic Jews and others influenced by the mystical Kabbalah, the counting is preceded by a spoken or murmured *kavannah* or directed intention that the command is being fulfilled in order to bring closer the reunion of the masculine and feminine, the transcendent and ever-present aspects of God, the rebuilding of the spiritual Temple and the advent of the Messianic Age. In some households, the count is followed by another prayer: "May the Compassionate One restore the holy service to the Holy Temple in her place for us, speedily and in our own days."

Traditionally, anyone who forgets to do the counting in the evening may do it the following day, but without saying the blessing, and may then say it at night from then on, with the blessing. But anyone who misses counting the day altogether should pick up the count when s/he remembers, but without saying the blessing. This omission is because the blessing recognizes the fulfillment of the command, and the command is to do the *whole* counting—so missing one day is a failure to fulfill the command.

Conversely, one should not fulfill the command to count lightly and without attention—for example, by saying casually to someone, "Today is the fortieth day of the *omer*." Instead, if people forgot what day it was they traditionally told each other what yesterday's count was.

In order to remember from night to night what the correct number in the *omer* was, some households have made or bought *omer* counters. These can be simple notebooks where the pages can be turned and will lie flat to show a number—perhaps one that is calligraphed or illustrated—or small machines of more or less artistry where a knob can be turned or a dial twisted.

In some traditional communities, it is the custom not to do work from sunset till dawn—and among Sephardim, there is an especially strong custom that women not work at night during the *omer*. One commentary says that this custom is a memorial to Akiba's students—who were buried at night so that the daytime work of the whole Jewish community in Judea would not be disrupted by their funerals. (For the funerals of students and teachers of Torah, everyone stopped working; and so many died that every town would have been closed down.)

Except on the festive days during the *omer*—Rosh Chodesh (New Moon), Lag B'Omer, and for some Israeli Independence Day—haircuts, weddings, and musical concerts or other public celebrations are avoided.

Running parallel with the *omer* is the public reading in synagogue of *Pirkei Avot*, Ethics of the Fathers. This reading begins at the end of the afternoon service on the Shabbos after Pesach, when it replaces the reading of Psalm 104 and the Songs of Ascent (Psalms 120–134) that run through the winter season. *Pirkei Avot* is a section of the *Mishnah* with five chapters, and a sixth section was added for public reading so as to make it possible to read one chapter each Shabbos from the one after Pesach to the one before Shavuot. Sephardic congregations stop there; Ashkenazic ones start over again, reading a chapter a week in a spiral of four readings that are completed the Shabbos before Rosh Hashanah. (On the last two readings in this pattern, two chapters are read so as to finish *Pirkei Avot* before Rosh Hashanah.) *Pirkei Avot* contains a number of pithy aphorisms, which lend themselves to discussion by a public not deeply versed in Torah study:

If your deeds outreach your wisdom, your wisdom will endure; if your wisdom outreaches your deeds, your wisdom will not endure . . .

Who is wise? Whoever learns from everyone. Who is strong? Whoever subdues the impulse toward evil. Who is rich? Whoever is content. Who is honorable? Whoever honors all that is created.

HOLOCAUST MEMORIAL DAY

The twenty-seventh of Nisan, twelfth day of the *omer*, was set aside in 1951 by the Israeli Knesset (Parliament) as *Yom Hashoah v'Hagvurah*, Day of the Destruction and Heroism. (It is usually called simply Yom Hashoah, Holocaust Day.)

It is not totally clear why the Knesset chose that particular day. It falls somewhat after the date of the uprising of the Warsaw Ghetto against the Nazis (the first day of Pesach in 1943), and may be taken to symbolize the fall of the Ghetto. The mournful tone of the *omer* period may also have helped determine the date. In 1953 the Knesset created the Yad Vashem Authority to perpetuate the memory of the Holocaust, and specified that one of its tasks is to strengthen awareness of the memorial day. In 1959 and 1961 the Knesset provided for public observances and memorials on Yom Hashoah, and for closing entertainment places on the evening of the day.

The process of working out a ceremonial practice for Yom Hashoah is still under way. In the Diaspora, observance is growing but is still undertaken by a minority and in a wide variety of ways. Not all observances are on the twenty-seventh of Nisan. Among many who were themselves survivors of the

Holocaust and especially of the various Jewish uprisings, the custom grew up of holding public meetings on April 19, the anniversary in the Western calendar of the beginning of the Warsaw Ghetto Uprising. Among others, a weekend day or evening nearest to Yom Hashoah is, for convenience, frequently chosen as the time for observance. Some leaders have suggested that the Nazi Holocaust be incorporated among the disasters commemorated on Tisha B'Av, the Memorial Day for the Destruction of the Temple (see Chapter XII).

Forms of observance are even more diverse. There seems to be a growing custom for congregations and individuals to light six *yahrzeit* memorial candles, in memory of the six million Jews who were murdered in the Holocaust. Many observances include recitation of the Mourners' Kaddish and *Eyl Maleh Rachamim*, parts of the traditional service for mourning the dead. Some congregations, particularly *chavurot* (intimate participatory congregations or fellowships) and Hillel houses on university campuses, have used an extraordinarily powerful liturgical drama by David Roskies, *Nightwords: A Midrash on the Holocaust. Nightwords* intertwines modern poetry in Yiddish, Hebrew, and English with passages of bald recitation of the facts of the Holocaust, with traditional passages of prayer. Parts for recitation and acting out can be assigned to 36 people (in accord with the tradition that only the continuing existence of 36 fully decent people makes possible the survival of the world). The overall effect of *Nightwords* is a profound and harrowing collision between traditional pieties about God, the world, and the Jewish people—and radical questions put to all those traditional understandings. (The text is available from the national Hillel office.)

Various forms of secular public gatherings have been another approach to observance of Yom Hashoah. Some such gatherings have recited and heard Yiddish poetry, in the original and in translation, and the playing of Jewish music from Eastern Europe. The goal here has been to assert that the Nazis' effort to annihilate Yiddish culture failed; and that instead that culture continues, though wounded, to live and to enrich the emerging Jewish cultures of the next few centuries. Another kind of public gathering has focused upon speeches that reassert the lessons of the Holocaust.

One song of the Jewish Resistance movement has become a motif of Yom Hashoah observances. The tradition of Holocaust survivors is to sing it always standing:

Zog nit keyn mol az
du geyst dem letstn veg,
Chotsh himlen blayene
farshtein bloye teg.
Kuman vet noch undzer
oysegebenkte sho-

S'vet a poyk ton undzer
trot-mir zaynen do!

Fun grinem palmenland
biz vaysn land fun
shney,
Mir kumen on mit undzer
payn, mit undzer vey,
Un vu gefain s'iz a
shprits fun undzer blut,
Shprotsn vet dort undzer
gvure, undzer mut.

S'vet di morgnzun bagildn
undz dem haynt,
Un der nechtn vet farsh-
vindn mitn faynd,
Nor oyb farzamen vet
di tzun in dem kayor-
Vi a parol zol geyn
dos lid fun dor tsu dor.

Dos lid geshribn iz mit
blut un nit bit blay,
S'iz nit keyn lidl fun
a foygl af der fray,
Dos hot a folk tzvishn
falndike vent
Dos lid gezungen mit
naganes in di hent!

Never say that you are
going your last way,
though leaden skies
blot out the blue of day.
The hour for which we
long will certainly appear.
The earth shall thunder
beneath our tread—we
are here!

From lands of green
palm trees to lands all
white with snow,
We are coming with our

pain and with our woe,
And wherever a spurt
of our blood will light,
there will sprout our
courage, our might.

For us the morning sun
will gild the day and
the enemy and past will
fade away. But should
the dawn delay or sun-
rise wait too long, then
let all future genera-
tions sing this song.

This song was written
with our blood and
not with lead,
This is no song of free
birds flying overhead,
But a people amid
crumbling walls did
stand,
They stood and sang
this song with rifles
held in hand.

ISRAEL INDEPENDENCE DAY

The proclamation of the birth of the modern State of Israel was made on the 5th day of Iyar, 5708 (May 14, 1948) the twentieth day of the *omer*. The anniversary is a public holiday in Israel. A date nearby—usually the Sunday before or after—has become a day of rallies and celebrations for many Jewish communities in the Diaspora, especially in the United States.

In Hebrew the day is known as *Yom Ha-atzma-ut.* That is usually translated Independence Day, but *atzma-ut* comes from the Hebrew root for bone, and hints at the positive affirmation of an identity, at standing on one's own feet, rather than at the rejection of a hanging-on past as does the English word in-de-pendence. So a better translation might be Identity Day or Self-Affirmation Day. In this light, Yom Haatzma-ut celebrates not only a past event but the continued striving in the present and future to affirm one's own identity.

In Israel, Yom Ha-atzma-ut begins after a day of deep mourning: *Yom Hazikkaron* or Remembrance Day, in honor of those who died defending

Israeli independence. The transition from mourning to strong celebration is remarkable. As night falls, and Yom Ha-atzma-ut begins, people go out to dance in the street and shoot off fireworks. All the next day there are parades, public rallies, announcements of literary and artistic prizes, hikes to historic sites, and family picnics.

There are both secular-national and religious liturgies for the day. At Mount Herzl, near the grave of Theodore Herzl who in the 1890s initiated the modern political movement to create a Jewish state, the speaker of the Knesset lights a torch, which in turn lights twelve torches representing the twelve tribes of Israel. There is a gun salute; the number of rounds fired corresponds to the years of independence.

Rabbinical authorities of various orientations in Israel have worked out different—sometimes conflicting—liturgical patterns. For some, the day is treated as a festive break in the *omer* mourning. Some congregations blow the shofar at the end of evening services and pray that as the dawn of redemption has begun to shine forth, they hope to hear the shofar of Messiah, come speedily in our own day. Most Israeli Orthodox congregations in the morning service recite the *Hallel* psalms of praise, but some do only part of *Hallel* (as on the later days of Pesach or on Rosh Chodesh), and some omit the blessings before and after *Hallel*. These limitations are a way of compromising between the desire to praise God for Israel's independence and the desire not to deduce a divine command to do so or to make a major festival on a day not authorized by ancient tradition.

Some congregations read a Torah portion—some Deuteronomy 7:1–8:18; others, Deuteronomy 30:1–10. The former is a rather rigorous and harsh-minded passage from Moses' address to the people about their impending entry into Canaan, and the dangers of idolatry and of forebearance they may face there. The latter is a somewhat gentler forecast of a re-entry into the Land of Israel much further in the future, after an exile of punishment—a re-entry into delight and well-being rather than harsh danger.

In the Diaspora, few congregations have adopted these liturgical changes into their practice and prayerbooks. In cities where there are large Jewish communities, Yom Ha-atzma-ut, or the nearest Sunday to it, has become a day of public demonstrations of solidarity with and political support for Israel. (In New York City, there are both an Israel Independence Day parade and a Solidarity with Soviet Jewry parade, both on Sundays in May or June.) The basic pattern is that of the ethnic parade with political implications, initiated by Irish-American communities a century ago as the St. Patrick's Day Parade, and since adopted by Italians and other ethnic groups. There are often speeches by politicians, parades with floats and high-school bands, and contingents from a wide variety of organizations. In recent years, some efforts have been made to incorporate Jewish folk fairs in which Jewish arts, crafts, and music can be displayed and learned.

Celebrations of Yom Ha-atzma-ut usually include the singing of *Hatik-vah*, The Hope, which was originally the song of Zionist activists and became the national anthem of Israel:

> Kol od baleivav penima
> Nefesh Yehudi homiya
> Ulfa-atei mizrach kadima
> Ayin leTzion tzofiya
> Od lo avda tikvateinu
> Hatikva shnat alpayim
> Liyot am chofshi be-artzeinu
> Eretz Tzion vi' Yerushalayim.
>
> As long as a Jewish heart
> beats, the Jewish soul
> longs, and Jewish eyes
> look eastward to Zion,
> Our two thousand year old
> hope to be a free people
> in Zion and Jerusalem
> is not lost.

LAG B'OMER

In the pattern of Hebrew counting where the letters represent various numbers, *lamed* stands for 30 and *gimel* for 3. *Lamed-gimel* or *lag* therefore is 33, and the 33rd day of the *omer* is therefore *Lag B'Omer*. On this 33rd day of the *omer* (which comes on the 18th day of the month of Iyar) there is a special festival. Why it comes on that day is utterly unclear. There is one legend that the plague that decimated Akiba's followers ended on that day. There is another that on that day Akiba defied the Roman authorities by taking his students into the wilderness to study Torah, and disguised his intent by taking bows and arrows along as if they were, like Romans, hunting game. For that reason, goes this version, Jews have celebrated Lag B'Omer with archery contests in the woods.

Still others see Lag B'Omer as simply a relaxation and release from the mourning that dominates the *omer* season. And others connect it and its arrow-shooting and bonfire celebrations with the ancient Anglo-Germanic custom of shooting arrows at demons on May Day, when they are thought to be especially dangerous, and the Celtic and Swedish customs of lighting May Day bonfires to frighten demons and witches away.

Another cluster of legends has it that on Lag B'Omer one of the great Talmudic rabbis—Shimon bar Yochai—either was ordained by his teacher

Akiba, or emerged from the caves in which for years he had hidden from the Romans who were seeking his arrest, or he died. Since Shimon bar Yochai became identified as one of the great mystics, and since the greatest book of Jewish mysticism, the *Zohar*, names him as its author even though it was written twelve centuries after his death, he became one of the greatest models and heroes of the Kabbalists. They celebrate Lag B'Omer with pilgrimages to Shimon's grave at Meron, near Safed in Israel. The pilgrimage has become a gigantic outpouring of Chassidim and others who identify with the mystical tradition. Great bonfires are lit and a festival of wedding between heaven and earth is celebrated.

Since haircuts are not permitted during most of the *omer* but are on Lag B'Omer, many three-year-olds get their first haircuts at Meron on that day. Why three-year-olds? Abraham and Sarah's son Isaac (the first child to be Jewish from birth) was weaned when he was three years old, according to rabbinic midrash. So this was traditionally defined as the age for a child (traditionally, a boy) to move into the first level of responsibility to obey the commandments. One of these is to wear a four-cornered garment with *tzitzit*, ritual fringes—and this is undertaken when the child is three by wearing a *tallit katan*, a miniature version of the prayer shawl in the form of a pull-over undershirt with *tzitzit* at the four corners. Another is beginning to wear the hair with *payot*, corners—that is, earlocks—in recognition of the commandment not to cut the corners of the beard. And so . . . the haircut. In a broader sense, the haircuts at Meron stimulate the feeling of shared community and the excitement of seeing a whole age-group of children entering the next stage of growing up.

In most present practice among American Jews, Lag B'Omer is a day of hikes in the woods, picnics, and playful archery among schoolchildren especially. Among Conservative and Orthodox Jews especially, it has become a day for weddings and for public concerts of Jewish music—since these are forbidden at most other times during the *omer* season.

YOM YERUSHALAYIM

On June 7 in the year 1967, which was equivalent to twenty-eighth of Iyar in the Jewish calendar, Israeli armed forces established their control over the Old City of Jerusalem and reopened Jewish access to the Western Wall of the ancient Temple compound. The Western Wall was the last remaining wall of the great structures built by King Hadrian as retaining walls and defenses for the Temple Mount. (It was not the wall of the Temple itself.) After the Roman army captured and burned the Temple in the year 70 C.E., they destroyed the other Hadrianic walls but left the Western Wall standing—according to one tradition, in order to show how mighty was the defensive system they had smashed.

From then on, Jewish tradition understood the Western Wall as the place to which the *Shechinah*, God's Presence in the world, had fled in exile. She represented still the contact point, weak but surviving, between God and the Jewish people. So the Wall became a sacred place of Jewish prayers and lamentations. It became known as the Wailing Wall, and the custom arose of leaving little prayerful petitionary notes to God, *kvitlech*, tucked between its massive stones.

After the declaration of Israeli independence in 1948, the ensuing war between Israel and its neighboring Arab states, and the achievement of a cease-fire between the Arab states and Israel in 1949, the cease-fire line ran through the city of Jerusalem. The original United Nations plan had been for a Jewish state, a Palestinian state, and an internationalized city of Jerusalem. But most of the Palestinians and the other Arab states had rejected this arrangement, and the fortunes of war left the old city of Jerusalem, including the Western Wall, together with most of the area originally intended for a Palestinian state, entirely under the control of the Kingdom of Trans-Jordan. Trans-Jordan renamed itself Jordan and announced it had annexed Jerusalem and the Palestinian areas called the West Bank of the Jordan River. But most governments did not recognize the annexations, viewing the region's future as unsettled, to be determined by negotiations. The cease-fire was not converted into a peace treaty, and hostility between Jordan and Israel remained so intense that Jordan refused to allow Jews any access to the Western Wall.

During the renewed outbreak of war between Israel and the Arab states in June 1967, the Israeli Army established its control over the West Bank areas formerly controlled by Jordan, including Jerusalem. When it was again possible for Jews to come to the Western Wall, there was an intense outburst of joy and thanksgiving among most Jews throughout the world. Shortly afterward, Israel announced it had annexed Jerusalem as part of Israel proper, but would allow free access for people of all religious groups to the holy places in the city. Most governments of other countries refused to recognize this annexation, again looking forward to negotiations that might decide the city's future. Some of them began to urge the creation of a Palestinian state that would include part of Jerusalem.

For both religious and national-secular reasons, the result of this history was the emergence during the 1970s of an effort by some Jews to celebrate the twenty-eighth day of Iyar, as Jerusalem Day—Yom Yerushalayim. The Israeli government and some secular Jews wanted to do this as a way of proclaiming permanent, non-negotiable Jewish sovereignty over all of Jerusalem. Some religious Jews viewed the reassertion of Jewish access to the Western Wall and Jewish control over the site of the Holy Temple as a fulfillment of ancient prophecy and perhaps a sign of the onset of the Messianic Era. So they, too, wished to celebrate the day. Other Jews who did not necessarily agree with the most far-reaching assertions about the meaning of the day nevertheless felt strongly about preserving the renewed Jewish presence in Jerusalem, especially at the site of the Temple and the Wall. They, too, wanted to celebrate the day. The result has been the emergence of a mixture of secular and religious celebrations of the twenty-eighth of Iyar. Their form is very fluid, both in Israel and outside it.

Films about Jerusalem, a day-long hike around the walls of the entire Old City, concerts of songs devoted to Jerusalem, prayers for its continued unity, have all been aspects of various celebrations. The numbers of people who take part in such observances is growing, but is still considerably smaller than those involved in some form of observing Yom Ha-atzma-ut. Whether Yom Yerushalayim will solidify into permanence, continue as it is, or fall into disuse, remains unclear.

◆≫≫ NEW APPROACHES ≪≪◆

Many modern American Jews do not see anxiety as an acceptable emotion for themselves; and the combination of mild mourning and ritual counting that characterize the traditional practice of the *omer* season are the quintessence of anxiety. Yet the process of coming to fruition, moving from birth to adulthood, is an appropriate time for anxiety. Will we find our way to Sinai, to some new path of life? Will the wheat crop flourish and the trees bear fruit? If not, what then?

The modern temperament seeks to *act*—so as to discharge the anxiety. When Fabrangen, a free-standing *chavurah* in Washington, DC, tried to develop its own approaches to the *omer*, it tried to infuse the anxiety-laden clock-and-calendar-rhythm of the *omer* with the more relaxing, fluid, and spontaneous rhythms of the Song of Songs—especially because the Song celebrates the springtime vividly. People tried to:

· Get to know a new flower each of the seven weeks of the *omer*: smell it, look deeply at it, watch it change, absorb its color, its shape, its patterns—with the sense that flowers could in some ways replace the growing grain as an aspect of springtime.

· Get to know a new person each of the seven weeks—either a nearby person with whom it was possible to meet, have lunch, play tennis, do a trust walk (in which first one person, then the other is blindfolded and is led into a variety of places and situations); or a new person in fiction or essays, a writer who has written autobiography, etc.

· Read one chapter a week of the Song of Songs—experiencing the chapter differently each night: its sounds and language patterns, its imagery, its story line.

· Give an amount of money for *tzedakah* that increased each week. (Giving 25 cents a night the first week, 50 cents a night the second week, 75 cents the third, and so on up to $1.75 a night the seventh week adds up to $49.)

These particular practices are only an example of what could be done. The goal should be to establish a regimen that recognizes the tension, hope, and anxiety of the March toward Sinai, and tries to act out the tension in such a way as to give relief—but only temporary relief. The full sense of full release can come only with the reaching of Sinai on Shavuot.

The *omer* season can also be seen as a microcosm of the Jubilee cycle. In this cycle of renewing the land and the society of ancient Israel, described in Leviticus 25, there were seven weeks of seven years each, culminating in the Jubilee of the fiftieth year. In the smaller, seven-year cycle, the seventh year was one in which the land lay fallow and all debts were annulled. Then in the year after the forty-ninth year, the Jubilee was proclaimed; the land lay fallow for the second year in a row, and every family returned to the equal share of land it had been allotted in the beginning. The rich were released from their surplus and the poor from their deficit; and all rested from their work together. Thus the primacy of God's ownership of the land was joined to the need for communal repose and for restoration of economic equality.

In the *omer* cycle, the seven weeks of counting are capped by Shavuot. To view the *omer* as a miniature version of the Jubilee cycle would suggest that a miniature community—a family, a household, a group of friends— agree to celebrate the *omer* together. On the seventh day of each *omer* week, the group could meet to share whatever the members most need: meditative time, food, help in dealing with a problem, study.

Finally, it would be possible to develop for such *chevras* or friendship groups the Chassidic notion of the *omer* weeks and days as evocations of the seven *S'phirot* in their various permutations with each other. Friends could work together in seeking spiritual development or unfolding.

◆»» GO AND STUDY «««◆

For Yom Hashoah, see David Roskies, *Nightwords: A Midrash on the Holocaust* (B'nai B'rith Hillel Foundations, Washington, DC). André Neher's *The Exile of the Word* (Jewish Publication Society) is an extraordinary modern midrash on the silence of God in the Bible and in Auschwitz.

SHAVUOT

"The time of the giving of our Torah." (*amidah* for festivals) The fifty kernels of wheat represent the forty-nine days from Pesach to Shavuot plus one for the festival. The pomegranates are symbolic of the Torah.

CHAPTER ELEVEN
PEAK EXPERIENCE— SHAVUOT

The spring comes to its climax, hovers on the edge of summer. The world is perfect: warm but not hot, ripe but not rotting. Those who had just given birth to a new self at Pesach have now matured their new identities, are ready to meet and encounter one another. The weddings that have been delayed all spring can now be celebrated. Both anxiety and hope are swallowed up in the moment of meeting.

So now comes the moment of the great Meeting, the great Marriage, with the Infinite Other. The people of Israel, on the trek from slavery, meet at the mountain—meet the Voice that becomes visible, meet the universe that sheds its silence and begins to Speak. The weeks of tension end in the Festival of Weeks—Shavuot.

ORIGINS

Shavuot is the only one of the great festivals for which the Torah gives no historical-political connection, but only mentions the natural and agricultural cycle. Yet later tradition identifies it as the anniversary of God's giving of the Torah at Mount Sinai.

The Torah prescribes that the "Israelites shall hold a festival for the Feast of the Harvest, of the first fruits of your work, of what you sow in the field" (Exodus 23:16). "You shall bring from your settlements two loaves of bread as a wave-offering . . . baked after leavening, as first fruits to the Lord

. . . On that same day you shall hold a celebration; it shall be a sacred occasion for you; you shall not work at your occupations" (Leviticus 23:17–23). "You shall observe the Feast of Weeks for the Lord your God, offering your freewill contribution according as the Lord your God has blessed you. You shall rejoice before the Lord your God with your son and daughter, your male and female slave, the Levite in your communities, and the stranger, the fatherless, and the widow in your midst, at the place where the Lord your God will choose to establish His name" (Deut. 16:10–12).

When the Temple stood, there were two special aspects of the sacrifices for Shavuot: the two loaves of bread offered up by the priests for the nation as a whole, and the freewill offering brought by every family according to its own means, according to how God had blessed them. These offerings were brought from bikkurim, the first fruits, of the seven kinds of food plants for which the Land of Israel is specifically praised in the Torah: wheat, barley, grapes, figs, pomegranates, olives, and dates.

Family by family, in pilgrim parties made up by clans, districts, and provinces, huge numbers of Israelites would travel to the Temple in Jerusalem. Each family carried baskets of the bikkurim: the rich, baskets made of gold and silver; the poor, willow baskets. By night on their journey they slept in the public squares of the towns they passed through.

The Mishnah describes the scene:

And at the rise of morning an official says: "Rise and let us go up to Zion, to the House of the Lord our God!" An ox walked before them, its horns covered with gold, and with an olive-crown on its head. The chalil (flute) was played before them till they reached the vicinity of Jerusalem. Upon coming close to Jerusalem, they sent word ahead and decorated their bikkurim. The important officials went out to meet them . . . and all the tradesmen in Jerusalem stood before them and greeted them: "Our brothers, the men of such and such a place, you have come in peace!"

The chalil was played before them till they reached the Temple Mount. Even King Agripas took the basket on his shoulders and carried it till he reached the courtyard. When the pilgrims reached the courtyard, the Levites sang: "I will exalt You, O Lord, for You have saved me and You have not rejoiced my enemies over me!"

With the basket still on his shoulder, the Israelite read: "I have told the Lord your God this day, that I have come to this land which the Lord swore to our fathers to give to us . . . My father was a wandering Aramean and he went down to Egypt and he sojourned there and he became there a great, mighty, and numerous people. And the Egyptians harmed us, and they afflicted us and they put hard labor upon us, and we cried out to the Lord, the God of our fathers and the Lord heard our voice . . . and the Lord took us out from Egypt with a strong hand . . . and He brought us to this place, and He gave to us this land, a land flowing with milk and honey. And now I bring the first fruit of the land which you have given me, O Lord." After completing the entire *parshah* the Jew places the *bikkurim* basket by the side of the altar, he bows down, and goes out.

And so every family publicly avows its share in the history of the people. Then the high priest acts on behalf of the people as a whole. He presented before the altar the special Shavuot wave-offering—two loaves of bread made of wheat, the first products of the spring wheat harvest that begins just as the barley harvest comes to an end. So Shavuot celebrates the success of the spring growing season—the growth of the new sprouts of spring into full-grown plants at summertime. But there is a special twist in this celebration of growth. The two loaves of bread are unusual—for they are explicitly the products of human labor. Not grain, not sheep or lambs or goats, straight from God's hand—but bread, mixed and kneaded and leavened and baked, is the distinctive offering of Shavuot. So Shavuot celebrates the partnership of human beings with God in giving food to the world. Having received from God the rain, the seed, the sunshine, we give back to God not just a dividend on the natural growth, but the value we ourselves have added to it.

So, into the period of the Second Temple, Shavuot was viewed simply as the festival of first-fruits. But toward the end of that period different understandings of Shavuot became part of an important debate within the Jewish people. At that point, deep disagreements were emerging between the Sadducees of the priestly caste who focused on the sacrificial system, and the Pharisees who were more interested in prayer and study of the Torah, and who were developing the theory of the two-fold Torah: written and oral. For the Pharisees, forerunners of the Talmudic rabbis, what was crucial was their sense of a continuing unfolding tradition that was truly Torah, stemming from Mount Sinai, but not written down. It could be worked out by doing *midrash*—searching for inner meanings in the Torah-text. It is necessary for us to understand how the Pharisees and later the rabbis felt about the Torah, if we are to understand what they came to believe about Shavuot.

For the Pharisees and later for the rabbis, the process of their own wrestling with Torah was the way for them to meet with God. They were not priests, whose sacrifices brought a kind of rhythmic physical illumination. Their sense of the Presence came only from engaging with God's Word. So powerful was their sense of the Torah as the contact point with God that they saw Sinai as the moment of a marriage between God and Israel, in which the Torah was the *ketubah*, the contract of the covenant.

And so, for them it was as important for everyone in every generation to stand at Sinai as it was for everyone in every generation to escape from slavery in Egypt. For only if everyone can stand at Sinai can the Torah be heard anew in every generation. Only if the rabbis themselves can see the

Voice can they feel they are discovering Torah—not inventing it—when they discern some new approach in the old letters.

How to inculcate this sense of presence at Sinai? There existed already, in Pesach, the holy day that brought everyone into tasting, literally tasting, the bitterness of slavery, the headiness of freedom, and the experience of sacrificing the Pesach lamb as their forebears had done on the awesome night of deliverance. Could there be such a holy day to teach the Jews to stand at Sinai?

Perhaps there could. But as things stood, the Torah nowhere named with clarity the date on which the Torah was received. If there were to be a Torah festival, the rabbis would have to search and find it, hidden in the text.

In what follows it is necessary for us moderns to try to imagine how the rabbis thought, in order to understand how they took the steps they did in transforming the meaning of Shavuot. Since we are moderns and they were not, we cannot be sure we understand correctly. The explanation may seem boring and obsessive. Yet because it involves an effort to understand Torah in new ways in order to meet new needs of a new society and era, it is an excellent example of one of the most characteristic modes of Jewish thinking.

Suppose that the rabbis hoped there was, concealed in texts of Torah, an explanation that one of the festivals was the moment of Sinai. Which festival was possible? There were two ways to discern this: through the mood and feeling of the festivals; and through the timing and succession of the festivals. Yet even though a logical deduction or a philosophic meditation might be enough to give a hint, to show the way, for the rabbis that would not be enough to prove the point. For that, a proof text from the Torah would be needed.

Very well. What could their logic and their feelings tell them? Most importantly, that the main point of God's liberating the Israelites from Egypt was to make possible God's giving them the Torah at Mount Sinai, and that since Pesach clearly celebrated that liberation, it would make sense that the next great festival, Shavuot, should celebrate the gift. Similarly, if Pesach celebrated the birth of the Jewish people, then it would make sense for the next great festival—Shavuot—to be the celebration of the wedding between the Jewish people and God. And finally, Shavuot already had special elements of celebrating the God–Human partnership, because of the partnership required to make the bread-offering; and therefore Shavuot already had hints of Covenant.

But there still needed to be a way of finding in the Torah itself that the date of Shavuot was, in the year of the Exodus from Egypt, the date of the Revelation at Sinai. So the ascertaining of these two dates became the crucial problem. There were two texts—one on Sinai, one on Shavuot—that had to be brought into contact with each other.

The passage on the date of Sinai is, on its face, indefinite. It is Chapter

19 of Exodus, which begins with a verse that can be translated either "On the third new moon," or "In the third month," "after the children of Israel had gone forth from the land of Egypt, on that very day they came into the wilderness of Sinai." The chapter goes on to explain that the people trekked to the foot of the mountain and Moses conferred with God about the impending encounter at the mountain, taking some period of time that is not specified. After that came three days of purifying and preparing the people. Then came the Revelation at the mountain.

To give a firm date for the Revelation would require knowing what the first verse of the chapter meant about the day the Israelites arrived in the wilderness of Sinai, and knowing how much time it took for the people then to reach the mountain and for Moses to confer with God.

Now, to look at the other side of the problem, there is the question of the date of Shavuot; for this too, as we have seen in Chapter X on the *omer*, is not clear. Shavuot is to come fifty days after "the sickle is put to the standing grain" (Deut. 19:9) or after "the day after Shabbat," where Shabbat has some unclear connection with Pesach (Lev. 23:11). When should counting begin?

First possibility: does the counting begin whenever the grain is first ripe? If so, the date and weekday of Shavuot would change from year to year and there would be no hope of connecting it with Sinai—since Sinai did actually happen on a specific day in a specific year.

Second possibility: is the "day after Shabbat" the day after the Shabbos that occurs during Pesach? This is what the priestly faction, the Sadducees, thought; so for them, Shavuot came always on a Sunday, but its date of the month changed from year to year because the Shabbos of Pesach came on a different date from year to year. This interpretation, therefore, would also make it impossible to pin down Shavuot to a date that could be matched up with the anniversary of the Revelation at Sinai—so it did not meet the needs of the Pharisees who were the prototypes of the Talmudic rabbis.

From the standpoint of the Pharisees and rabbis, the only way to fix the date of Shavuot was to understand Shabbat as a fixed date. What could it be? If Shabbat were understood not as a weekly Shabbos with its shifting date but as a day of rest, then the particular day of rest involved might be either the first day or the seventh day of Pesach. In the one case, Shavuot would come on the sixth of Sivan; in the second, on the twelfth of Sivan*. The community at Qumran on the Dead Sea which left the famous Dead Sea Scrolls used still other calculations that resulted in fixing Shavuot on the fifteenth of

---

*The Falashas or Beta Yisrael, a community of Jews in Ethiopia that became isolated from the rest of the Jewish people before rabbinic Judaism had developed and thus worked out and acted on their own interpretation, accepted the twelfth of Sivan as the date for Shavuot, and continue to celebrate it as the Festival of First-Fruits into our own generation.

Sivan. Of these three possibilities, which would fit best with the possibilities for the date of Sinai?

Let us now return to the passage about Sinai. The rabbis might have read the crucial verse about when the Israelites entered the wilderness of Sinai to mean three months *after* leaving Egypt, but that would have put the entrance into Sinai in the middle of the month of Tammuz, much later than even the fifteenth of Sivan, which seemed the latest possible date of Shavuot. Or they could have read it as on the third new moon that the people saw *after* leaving Egypt, but that would have put the entrance into Sinai still too late, on the first day of Tammuz. If they read the verse to mean in the third month *of the process* of leaving Egypt, that would give them the month of reaching Sinai as the month of Sivan.

If the rabbis read the phrase later in the verse, "on that very day," to refer to the full moon because that was the very day in Nisan that the Israelites left Egypt, then the Israelites would not enter Sinai until the fifteenth of Sivan—still too late to leave any time for the three days of preparation at the mountain and still have the Revelation coincide with Shavuot on the 6th, 12th, or 15th of Sivan. But if the phrase "on that very day" meant on the day of the *new* moon, that would mean the first day of Sivan was the day when the Israelites entered Sinai.

If the people entered Sinai on the first of Sivan and the preparations at the foot of the mountain took three days, then if the Revelation had come on the sixth of Sivan there would have been three days for the people to march to the mountain and for Moses to converse with God; if the Revelation had come on the twelfth of Sivan, nine days; if on the fifteenth of Sivan, twelve days. The shortest period seems best to accord with the tasks that had to be accomplished. So the Pharisees and rabbis concluded that the Shabbat which set the start of counting fifty days was the first day of Pesach; that Shavuot fell on the sixth day of Sivan; and that Shavuot was not only the Festival of First-Fruits, but the season of the Giving of the Torah.

And so it was, and so it came to be. The Jewish people accepted that Shavuot was the anniversary of Sinai. It became inconceivable that the Torah should specify no festival for its own anniversary, and inconceivable that the people could go forward in their wrestling with Torah unless they had some way of re-experiencing their original contact with it. And this the new aspect of Shavuot gave.

Indeed, once the Temple had been destroyed the continuation of Shavuot would have been most difficult if this new aspect had not been accepted. For the celebration of Shavuot described in the Torah is entirely limited to the sacrifices of the wheat bread loaves and several animals. Where Pesach has its matzah and its bitter herb and the command to tell the story; where Sukkot has the leafy hut and the four kinds of vegetation to be waved;

Shavuot has nothing. It was unimaginable that one of the great pilgrim festivals commanded by the Torah be allowed to fall into disuse.

It was not only intellectually unimaginable, but spiritually unworkable. For the cycle of celebration and the spiritual path that demands a season for birth demands as well a season for maturity and outreach. One cannot leap from birth to fulfillment, and from life-beginning to the ingathering of life-work—from Pesach to Sukkot—without achieving adulthood and partnership in the meantime. It would be like leaping from being born to giving birth without having espoused another in between: impossible.

In recognition of the importance of Shavuot in the motion of the yearly cycle, the rabbis gave it the name *Atzeret*. The root of this word means set a boundary, enclose, and thus, come to completion. Thus the rabbis pointed to its relationship to the Pesach festival—that what began in liberation could only be completed in revelation. They also hinted at a parallel between Shavuot—the *Atzeret*, completion, of Pesach, and *Sh'mini Atzeret*, the festival that completes Sukkot.

So it was crucial to the wholeness of the yearly cycle and to the health of the Jewish people that Shavuot be saved after the Temple was destroyed. The way in which it was saved shows forth an utter rightness, a deep congruence, between the method and the content. For the rabbis needed to find a festival of hearing Torah because their whole path of Jewish life was built on hearing Torah in new ways. How did they find this festival? Precisely by hearing Torah in new ways. If the date of Shavuot had been specified in the text of Torah, or if Shavuot had been specifically called the Festival of the Giving of the Torah in the Torah text itself, the task of the rabbis would have been much simpler, but—to a modern's mind at least—far less satisfying. They did *midrash* so as to discover, hidden in the text, the festival that makes it possible to keep on doing *midrash*.

Just as the ancient Shavuot meant that human beings took God's grain and shaped it into bread to offer up to God, so Shavuot since the Temple fell has meant that human beings took God's Torah, shaped it into *midrash*, and, as it were, offered the Torah back to God. Our own identity, grown tall, is able to join in partnership with God. The shift can be seen in a graphic physical image of the Exodus. First the Jews are in headlong flight. For seven weeks they can see only the back of the head in front of them. Then at Sinai they meet a boundary, an *Atzeret*: The Face of God's Own Self, face to face with them. They stop and for the first time face each other. They become a community, they receive the Torah which embodies their new freedom in the rules of a community.

◆⟩⟩⟩ ⟨⟨⟨◆

◆⇒⇒ SHAVUOT TODAY ⇐⇐◆

On the afternoon of the last day of the *omer*, traditional Jews prepare for Shavuot with a visit to the *mikveh*, the ritual bath, or to any free-flowing river, lake, or sea. There the ceremony of total immersion helps achieve the oceanic feeling of oneness with the universe, often sought before any of the festivals, but especially before receiving the Torah.

Meanwhile, the synagogue is being decorated with branches of green leaves—and in some places, roses on the Torah scrolls—as a symbol of the shift from spring to summer and as a memorial of the bringing of first-fruits to the Temple.

The celebration of Shavuot itself begins at home with the lighting of the candles after the blessing "Baruch atah Adonai eloheynu melech ha-olam, asher kid'shanu b'mitzvotav vitzivanu l'hadlik ner shel yomtov. Blessed are You, Lord our God, ruler of time and space, who makes us holy through Your commandments and commands us to light the candles for this holy day." The festival *kiddush* (similar to that for Sukkot) is said over wine, and with it *Sheh-hechianu*, the blessing "Who has kept us alive."

Households then congregate at the synagogue for the evening service. For most of the festivals, this service may be held a little early in order to add extra holy time to the time actually required; but not on Shavuot. Then the evening service is delayed until it is clearly dark and three stars are visible, since the counting of the *omer* before Shavuot must be seven full weeks, and the seven weeks would not be complete if Shavuot were begun early.

The evening service follows the regular festival pattern. In the *amidah*, Shavuot is referred to as the Season of the Giving of our Torah. In many congregations, there is a custom of staying awake all night to read and discuss different elements of Torah in the broad sense—the written Torah from the five books of Moses; portions of the Prophets and of the Holy Writings; parts of the Talmud; sections of the great (13th century) mystical text, the *Zohar*; and for some, more recent Jewish thought like that of Martin Buber, Abraham Joshua Heschel, and Rav Avraham Yitzchak Kook of Jerusalem. This custom, called *Tikkun Leyl Shavuot*, the Repair of the Night of Shavuot, arose among the Kabbalists of Safed in the sixteenth century. They saw the *tikkun* as a ceremony of bedecking the bride on the night before the great Wedding of Sinai.

One of the results of the *tikkun* is that it intensifies the experience that each person is directly and personally encountering the Torah, is actually present at Sinai. By drawing on the later Biblical, Talmudic, mystical, and modern interpretations of Torah, it also enriches the sense of Torah as not a one-time Revelation in the simplistic sense but a constantly unfolding process of Revelation in which everyone in every generation is able to be present.

The all-night study of the *tikkun* serves also to give Shavuot a distinctive and memorable ceremony of its own. No one who has done the *tikkun* can forget the sense of triumph with which the congregation, bleary-eyed but excited, greets the sunrise and begins the morning service.

In the morning service, all proceeds in the usual festival fashion through the *amidah* and the chanting of the full *Hallel*, the psalms of praise from Psalm 113 to 118. The Torah service begins as usual, but in Ashkenazic communities, after the first person is called up to the Torah, when the Scroll has been opened but before the reader recites the blessing, the poem *Akdamut* is chanted. The poem was written in Aramaic (a close relative of Hebrew, which was spoken by the common people of Talmudic times and which was the language in which most of the Talmud was written) by Rabbi Meir ben Isaac Nehorai of the German city of Worms in the twelfth century.

According to tradition, Rabbi Meir was forced to take part in a public debate with priests over the correctness of Judaism versus Christianity—a technique frequently used by some elements of the Church in the Middle Ages to attempt to humiliate the Jewish communities and bring about conversions—and wrote *Akdamut* as a song of spiritual joy to celebrate the Jewish people's commitment to Torah in the face of pressure from other peoples and faiths. Presumably, too, he wrote it in Aramaic to keep its contents available only to Jews—since only Jews understood Aramaic, while some Christian scholars knew Hebrew.

The poem begins with 44 lines whose first letters count off in order the 22 letters of the Hebrew alphabet—twice. These follow 46 more lines whose first letters spell out "Meir, son of Rabbi Isaac, may he grow in Torah and in good deeds, Amen. And be strong and of good courage!"

Three portions of the poem deserve special note:

· The ecstatic opening which says of God, "Were all the skies parchment and all the reeds pens, all the seas inks and everyone a scribe, God's grandeur still could not be near spelled out."

· A passage that carries forward the Shavuot theme of partnership between God and human beings by echoing an ancient legend: Just as traditional Jews on weekday mornings pray wearing the prayer-straps-and-boxes called *t'fillin*, bearing within them a parchment with the verses "Hear, O Israel, the Lord our God—the Lord is One," so God, as it were, wears *t'fillin* that say "Great is Israel, a unique people."

· A passage that looks forward to the Messianic moment when the beasts that symbolize ungovernable rage and evil, the sea monster Leviathan and the land monster Behemoth, will be slain at last by God's ultimate justice, to become the food of the upright in the Messianic banquet of harmony.

> You upright, having heard this hymn of praise,
> May you be in that blessed fellowship!
> You will deserve to sit among that circle

If you obey God's words of majesty.
For God, in the heights at Beginning and End,
Bent forward in love to give us the Torah.

After *Akdamut* is responsively chanted by the reader or cantor and the congregation, the reading of the Torah goes forward.

Sephardic and Yemenite congregations do not read *Akdamut*. Instead, just before the Torah reading there is read aloud a poetic *ketubah*, a marriage contract, between God and the People Israel. This reading echoes the rabbis' sense of Sinai as the moment of an indissoluble wedding. One of the most widely used of these *ketubot* is by one of the sixteenth century mystics of Safed, Israel Najara:

> Friday, the sixth of Sivan, the day appointed by the Lord for the revelation of the Torah to His beloved people . . . The Invisible One came forth from Sinai, shone from Seir and appeared from Mount Paran unto all the kings of the earth, in the year 2448 since the creation of the world, the era by which we are accustomed to reckon in this land whose foundations were upheld by God, as it is written: "For He hath founded it upon the seas and established it upon the floods" (Psalms 24.2).
>
> The Bridegroom [God], Ruler of rulers, Prince of princes, Distinguished among the select, Whose mouth is pleasing and all of Whom is delightful, said unto the pious, lovely and virtuous maiden [the people of Israel] who won His favor above all women, who is beautiful as the moon, radiant as the sun, awesome as bannered hosts: Many days wilt thou be Mine and I will be thy Redeemer. Behold, I have sent thee golden precepts through the lawgiver Jekuthiel [Moses]. Be thou My mate according to the law of Moses and Israel, and I will honor, support, and maintain thee and be thy shelter and refuge in everlasting mercy. And I will set aside for thee, in lieu of thy virginal faithfulness, the life-giving Torah by which thou and thy children will live in health and tranquility.
>
> This bride [Israel] consented and became His spouse. Thus an eternal covenant, binding them forever, was established between them. The Bridegroom then agreed to add to the above all future expositions of Scripture, including Sifra, Sifre, Aggadah, and Tosefta. He established the primacy of the 248 positive commandments which are incumbent upon all . . . and added to them the 365 negative commandments.
>
> The dowry that this bride brought from the house of her father consists of an understanding heart that understands, ears that hearken, and eyes that see. Thus the sum total of the contract and the dowry, with the addition of the positive and negative commandments,

amounts to the following: "Revere God and observe His commandments; this applies to all mankind" (Ecclesiastes 12.13).

The Bridegroom, desiring to confer privileges upon His people
Israel and to transmit these valuable assets to them, took upon Himself
the responsibility of this marriage contract, to be paid from the best
portions of His property.

All these conditions are valid and established forever and ever.
The Bridegroom has given His oath to carry them out in favor of His
people and to enable those that love Him to inherit substance. Thus
the Lord has given His oath. The Bridegroom has followed the legal
formality of symbolic delivery of this document, which is bigger than
the earth and broader than the seas. Everything, then, is firm, clear,
and established.

I invoke heaven and earth as reliable witnesses.

May the Bridegroom rejoice with the bride whom He has taken as
His lot and may the bride rejoice with the Husband of her youth while
uttering words of praise.

BIBLICAL READINGS

On the first day of Shavuot, and among Reform Jews and Israelis who
celebrate only one day, the Torah reading is the passage of Exodus 19 and 20
in which the Israelites enter the wilderness of Sinai, camp before the mountain, purify themselves, hear (or as the text says, see) God's Voice deliver the
Ten Commandments, and—overwhelmed by awe—send Moses forward to
hear the detailed requirements of Torah. There is also a brief reading of
Numbers 28:26–31, listing the sacrifices for Shavuot. It is customary for the
congregation to stand for the reading of the Ten Commandments.

The Prophetic passage assigned for the first day of Shavuot is from the
first chapter of the Prophet Ezekiel, plus the single verse of Ezekiel 3:12. The
chapter is one of the most astonishing passages in the entire Bible, a
description of a mystical vision that gripped Ezekiel:

In the thirtieth year, on the fifth day of the fourth month, when I was
in the community of exiles by the Chebar Canal, the heavens opened
and I saw visions of God. On the fifth day of the month—it was the
fifth year of the exile of King Jehoiachin—the word of the Lord came to
the priest Ezekiel son of Buzi, by the Chebar Canal, in the land of the
Chaldeans. And the hand of the Lord came upon him there.

I looked, and lo, a stormy wind came sweeping out of the north—a
huge cloud and flashing fire, surrounded by a radiance; and in the
center of it, in the center of the fire, a gleam as of amber. In the center
of it were also the figures of four creatures. And this was their appearance:

They had the figures of human beings. However, each had four faces, and each of them had four wings; the legs of each were [fused into] a single rigid leg, and the feet of each were like a single calf's hoof; and their sparkle was like the luster of burnished bronze. They had human hands below their wings. The four of them had their faces and their wings on their four sides. Each one's wings touched those of the other. They did not turn when they moved; each could move in the direction of any of its faces.

Each of them had a human face [at the front]; each of the four had the face of a lion on the right; each of the four had the face of an ox on the left; and each of the four had the face of an eagle (at the back). Such were their faces. As for their wings, they were separated: above, each had two touching those of the others, while the other two covered its body. And each could move in the direction of any of its faces; they went wherever the spirit impelled them to go, without turning when they moved.

Such then was the appearance of the creatures. With them was something that looked like burning coals of fire. This fire, suggestive of torches, kept moving about among the creatures; the fire had a radiance, and lightning issued from the fire. Dashing to and fro [among] the creatures was something that looked like flares.

As I gazed on the creatures, I saw one wheel on the ground next to each of the four-faced creatures. As for the appearance and structure of the wheels, they gleamed like beryl. All four had the same form; the appearance and structure of each was as of two wheels cutting through each other. And when they moved, each could move in the direction of any of its four quarters; they did not veer when they moved. Their rims were tall and frightening, for the rims of all four were covered all over with eyes. And when the creatures moved forward, the wheels moved at their sides; and when the creatures were borne above the earth, the wheels were borne too. Wherever the spirit impelled them to go, they went—wherever the spirit impelled them—and the wheels were borne alongside them; for the spirit of the creatures was in the wheels. When those moved, these moved; and when those stood still, these stood still; and when those were borne above the earth, the wheels were borne alongside them—for the spirit of the creatures was in the wheels.

Above the heads of the creatures was a form: an expanse, with an awe-inspiring gleam as of crystal, was spread out above their heads. Under the expanse, each had one pair of wings extended toward those of those others; and each had another pair covering its body. When they moved, I could hear the sound of their wings like the sound of mighty waters, like the sound of Shaddai, a tumult like the din of an army. When they stood still, they would let their wings droop. From above the expanse over their heads came a sound. When they stood still, they would let their wings droop.

Above the expanse over their heads was the semblance of a throne, in appearance like sapphire; and on top, upon this semblance of a throne, there was the semblance of a human form. From what appeared as his loins up, I saw a gleam as of amber—what looked like a fire encased in a frame; and from what appeared as his loins down, I saw what looked like fire. There was a radiance all about him. Like the appearance of the bow which shines in the clouds on a day of rain, such was the appearance of the surrounding radiance. That was the appearance of the semblance of the Presence of the Lord. When I beheld it, I flung myself down on my face. And I heard the voice of someone speaking.

Then a spirit uplifted me and I heard behind me a mighty, roaring voice: "*Baruch k'vod Adonai mimkomo.* Blessed be the radiance of God forth from His place."

Why is this vision assigned for reading on Shavuot? It is obviously intended as a comment on, a parallel to, almost an interpretation of, the communal experience of receiving the Torah. It reminds us that the throng who stood at Sinai—600,000 men, perhaps 2 million people—was made up of individuals like Ezekiel—each of whom had his or her own vision. Exodus describes that experience as awesome—thunder, lightning, earthquake, volcano, an impenetrable darkness where God was—so awesome indeed that the people could not bear to keep on hearing God directly. But Exodus gives no account of a personal experience so freaky, weird—there is no other word—as that of Ezekiel. Yet Ezekiel is able to stay with the vision; he does not back away.

So perhaps the connection between the two passages is teaching us, for one thing, that for every individual who stood and stands at Sinai, the lonely hearing of God's Voice was, is, so strange as to shatter all the categories of description. Perhaps it is only a communal sharing of the burden, and afterward a communal sharing and merging of the memory, that makes the experience more manageable.

There are several other remarkable aspects of Ezekiel's vision. One is that the vision *moves*. At Sinai, the people and the mountain both stood firm and fast. For all the other Prophets, and for the Patriarchs and Matriarchs, the experience of God was rooted in a single place. But motion fills Ezekiel's description of his vision. And the last line of the *haftarah* emphasizes not God's settled presence *in* The Place, but God's radiance coming *from* The Place.

Another is that Ezekiel emphasizes that he is seeing and recording not only far from the Land of Israel, but in captivity. At Sinai the people were newly free and on their way to the Land. The passage from Ezekiel may therefore be teaching us that God is available far from home—whether a physical home or the spiritual home of freedom. God moves, to be with us wherever we need the Radiance.

Ezekiel's vision continues beyond what is included in the *haftarah* for Shavuot; and this continuation was also in the minds of the rabbis who assigned the reading. In Chapters II:8–III:9, Ezekiel explains that the Radiance of God gave him a scroll, written with lamentations, dirges, and woes, and told him to eat the scroll: "Child of Adam, feed your stomach, fill your belly with this scroll that I give you." And Ezekiel ate, "and it tasted as sweet as honey to me."

Here the experience—especially felt in the context of Shavuot—seems to be teaching us that it is not enough to see and hear Torah. Torah must be taken into us, into our very bodies—must become part of our blood and breath and bone—for all its sorrows to be turned to sweetness. It is living Torah, not simply hearing it, that is to be the meaning of Shavuot.

At Sephardic and Oriental congregations, during the *musaf* (additional) or *mincha* (afternoon) service a poem of *Az-harot*, by the poet of the Jewish Golden Age in Spain, Shlomoisn Gabirol, is recited. *Az-harot* is a form of liturgical poem that recites those 613 commandments that, according to tradition, make up the full number of commandments in the written and oral Torah. The number of 613 was originally arrived at by adding 365, the days of the year, to 248, the number of bones that the rabbis believed were in the human body. The number thus metaphorically meant, "With every bone of my body, every day of my life, I will obey the commands of God in the Torah!" But once the number was set, generations of Jewish scholars made lists of what the 613 commandments were—often disagreeing with each other. And generations of Oriental and Sephardic poets wrote chants that listed them. For Shavuot, in congregations that use the Gabirol poem, the first day of Shavuot is devoted to the positive commandments—You shall do—and the second day to the negative commandments—You shall not do.

SECOND DAY

Jews outside the Land of Israel, except for congregations of the Reform movement, celebrate a second day of Shavuot for reasons arising from the ancient difficulty of being sure when the New Moon was. According to tradition, the second day of Shavuot was both the birthday and deathday of King David, the forebear and model of Messiah. So on the evening of the second day traditional congregations light a *yahrtzeit* candle to remember David. The congregants do not stay up all night, but stay together for a while after the evening service to sing some or all of David's psalms.

The Torah readings for the second day of Shavuot are Deuteronomy 15:19–16:17 (beginning earlier, at 14:22, if the day is also Shabbos), and Numbers 28:26–31. The *haftarah* is from the Prophet Habakkuk (2:20–3:19).

It begins, "The Lord is in His holy Temple; be silent before Him, all the earth." Then—astonishingly, since such a reading is never otherwise interrupted—among traditional Ashkenazic congregations the reading stops briefly for the recitation of an ecstatic poem about the gift of Torah, *Yatziv Pitgam*, that was written by the great twelfth century rabbi Jacob Ben Meir of Troyes, France—known as Rabbenu Tam.

The memorial prayers for the dead, *yizkor*, are recited on the second day of Shavuot by mourning families for specific individuals and by the whole community in memory of those who died as martyrs for *Kiddush ha-Shem*, to hallow the Name of God.

Depending on the congregation, at one or another time during Shavuot, traditional congregations read the Book of Ruth—assigned for this festival just as the Song of Songs is for Pesach. *Ruth* is about the Moabite woman who after her husband dies, follows her Israelite mother-in-law into the Jewish people: "Whither thou goest, I will go . . . and thy God will be my God." She asserts the right of the poor to glean the leavings of the barley harvest, breaks the normal rules of behavior to confront her kinsman Boaz, is redeemed by him for marriage, and becomes the ancestor of King David.

There are many intertwinings between *Ruth* and Shavuot. One is her kinship with David, whose *yahrtzeit* day this is. Probably more important, the barley-harvest setting of the story echoes the harvest that is just being completed as Shavuot arrives. Most important of all, Ruth accepts Torah in her own individual way—a way utterly different from that of Ezekiel in that it is simple, gentle, and based on her love of her mother-in-law Naomi.

CUSTOMS OF SHAVUOT

In an attempt to strengthen the sense of ever-presence at Sinai, Jewish communities have connected Shavuot with crucial steps in the education of children in Torah. In many European Jewish towns and villages, it was the custom to introduce young children to Hebrew and the Torah on Shavuot morning:

> At dawn, the children are taken to the Synagogue, as it is written: "It was on the third day, at the coming of morning." A tablet is brought on which the letters of the alphabet are written, as well as several individual verses: "Moshe commanded us the Torah," "My faith shall be in Torah," and the first verse in Vayikra. The teacher reads every letter, and the child repeats after him. The teacher puts a little bit of honey on the tablet and the child licks the honey from the letters. On a special honey cake verses from the Torah are written, and a Torah verse is written on a boiled egg.
>
> The teacher reads with the child everything on the tablet, on the cake and on the egg. After the children have finished their lesson, they

are given the cake and the egg to eat. When the children are taken from their homes to the teacher's home or to the synagogue, they are wrapped in a *tallit* or some special covering, in allusion to the verse: "And they stood at the bottom of the mountain." The child is set on the arm of the teacher who then puts the child on a seat, as it is written: "As the nurse carries a suckling child," and "I bore Ephra'im on my arms." After the lesson, the child is brought to a river's edge, since the Torah is compared to water, in allusion to the verse: "May your wellsprings overflow outward." The cake is made with much honey and milk, as it is written: "Honey and milk are under your tongue."

Rabbi Ya'akov Emden writes in his commentary to the Siddur:

"In truth, I do not know why they did away with this custom completely. Even though the custom of eating a cake on which verses of Torah was written, is questionable, nevertheless all the other customs which were observed (when children began the study of Torah) seems exceedingly proper. How then did it come about that so beautiful a custom as this, should be uprooted without reason? This could only be a result of a lack of reflection on a proper approach to the study of Torah" (Eliyahu Kitov).

More recently, Reform Jews introduced the custom of the confirmation of 16-year-olds in Judaism at Shavuot. They had concluded that in the conditions of modern society, when children did not become independent adults or even take on a more independent emotional and intellectual life at age 13, it was important to add to the *bar mitzvah* some way to recognize a later stage of development. In the early German Reform synagogues, confirmation of boys began in 1810 and of girls in 1817. At first a variety of days were used, but gradually the practice focused on Shavuot. On Shavuot in 1846, at a German (that is, Reform) synagogue on Henry Street in New York City, the youngsters sang psalms, heard the rabbi exhort them to adhere to Judaism and Torah, promised publicly that they would do so, and received a blessing from their parents and the rabbi.

Since then the Reform movement generally, many Conservative, and some Orthodox congregations have adopted the custom—usually in such a way as to reinforce the collective sense of a whole age-group receiving Torah together, rather than individually as in the *bar* and *bat mitzvah.* In some synagogues the entire class of 16-year-olds plans and leads the Shavuot service, introduces a creative element—such as a cantata on the themes of Ruth or Sinai, written and sung by the youngsters themselves—and then receives the priestly blessing from the rabbi.

For reasons that are not altogether clear, the custom has arisen that *milchig* or dairy foods are especially prepared for Shavuot. Some commentators connect the custom with a verse from the Song of Songs, "Honey and milk are under your tongue"—which they suggest refers to the sweetness of Torah, and is acted out by cooking foods of milk and honey. Others suggest that when Israel first received as part of Torah the laws of kosher food, they had to abandon eating the newly forbidden meats and had to make their utensils kosher—so chose to eat only dairy foods in the meantime. But to a skeptical ear both explanations sound like pleasant associations with a teaching message, but not real origination points for the folk custom.

Theodore Gaster points out that spring festivals in many areas of the world focus on cheese and other milk foods. To a pastoral society, the renewal of milk in cattle, goats, and ewes along with the spring birthings may have been the reason for this. Gaster points out that the Torah's prohibition on boiling a kid in its mother's milk is twice connected with the commandment of the first-fruits offering of Shavuot. Perhaps such a ritual was part of a Canaanite spring celebration, and in reaction to it the Israelites ate only milk foods at the first-fruits festival.

In Israel, the *kibbutzim* (collective farms) and other agriculture settlements have revived the first-fruits aspect of Shavuot. A procession of tractors, wagons, and trucks, filled with gardeners, poultry keepers, shepherds, orchardists, dairy workers, arrive from the fields—carrying grain, milk, eggs, honey. Carpenters, laundry-workers, child-care people, cooks, teachers join in parading to an open-air make-shift theater, where the fruits of the settlement's labor are presented to the community. The children read poems, show drawings, dance a circle dance. Some of the community's income may be dedicated to *tzedakah*, help for those in trouble.

One of the favorite Shavuot songs celebrates the giving of Torah as part of the whole process of relationship with God:

1.

Baw-rooch eh-lo-hay-noo
sheh-b'raw-noo li-ch'vo-do (3).
Od ha-pah-ahm, li-ch'vo-do (3).

Blessed be our God who created us
for His glory, who distinguished us
from those who err, who gave us the
Torah, and everlasting life.

2.

V'hiv-dee-law-noo min hah-to-eem (3).
Od ha-pah-ahm, min hah-to-eem (3).

3.

V'naw-tahn law-noo To-raht emet (3).
Od ha-pah-ahm, To-raht emet. (3).

4.

V'chah-yay o-lam naw-tah b'to-chay-noo
(3)
Od ha-pah-ahm, b'to-chay-noo (3).

In Eastern Europe, a special art form emerged in connection with Shavuot that has since become much broader: papercuts called *shavuoslech* (literally, little Shavuots) or *raizelech* (little roses). It may have developed when some rabbis tried to stop the custom of bringing greenery into the synagogue, fearing it was too like a pagan habit or looked too much like Palm Sunday in a Christian church. Seeking a form of decoration that would be acceptable, Lithuanian Jews may have hit upon the papercut as a way of showing greenery and flowers, letting the light shine through the cut-outs in the windows of homes and synagogues. The new art form spread beyond Shavuot-time; indeed, the illustrations in this book are based on papercuts and might be called grandchildren of the *shavuoslech*.

◆»» NEW APPROACHES «««◆

In the long history of Jewish celebration, Shavuot meant first the festival of first-fruits and then the festival of receiving the Torah. One—or the other. Is it possible in our generation to integrate these two? The sense that underlines both the first-fruits and Torah-giving aspects of the festival is the basic sense of Shavuot as the season of the maturing of a new identity to the point where it can enter a partnership with another. Can this basic sense be expressed in new ways that integrate Torah and the first-fruits?

The *kibbutzim*, together with Ezekiel's experience, may point toward some ways of integrating the intellectual and physical experiences of Shavuot. In a modern industrial society, not all the first-fruits of our labor are agricultural; yet the early summer is often a moment of completion, a moment when the project begun at Rosh Hashanah time in early fall has come to some harvesting. Imagine ceremonies where people brought and shared some product of their effort—their success in teaching a child; the new way they found of designing a building; their exploration of some new knowledge, art, or craft; their search for a new place to live; their frustration over a failed experiment. Show and tell could illuminate the growth of a new aspect of self, and reach out to other newly growing selves.

Ezekiel's sense of the bodily manifestation of God in a moving chariot and of Torah in an edible scroll may say to us something about using our bodies more vigorously in receiving Torah: motion, dance, mime, gesture, the re-examination of our eating habits to advance our sense of living by the Torah—all these might be ways of celebrating Shavuot.

Finally, there is a special legend from a marginal eddy in the stream of Jewish tradition that might offer us some new directions for Shavuot. The *Book of Jubilees* is a *midrashic* commentary on the Torah that was not part of either the rabbinic or priestly tradition. Indeed, one of the ways we know this is that it dated Shavuot on the 15th day of Sivan—neither the Pharisaic nor the Sadducean belief. The *Book of Jubilees* seems to have been connected with the independent communities at Qumran on the Dead Sea.

It treats Shavuot as the day of many covenants—not just the covenant at Sinai. It bases this *midrash* partly on a pun: Shavuot means weeks, *shevuot* means oaths—including oaths of covenant. Beer-sheva, for example, is the Well of the Oath where Abraham and the King Avimelech promised to make peace. This oath, says *Jubilees*, was made on Shavuot. And on Shavuot, too, says *Jubilees*, God made the covenant with Noah and the human race not to destroy the world again.

And it was on Shavuot, says *Jubilees*, that Abraham's two sons—Isaac, the forebear of the Jewish people, and Ishmael, the forebear of the Arab peoples—came together after their estrangement to be with Abraham while he was dying, to mourn his death together, and to make an oath of peace between them.

So it may be that on Shavuot we might seek the meeting between the peoples that would carry out the ultimate meaning of the Meeting between God and our people at Mount Sinai: the Meeting of the covenant of peace. If Shavuot is the season at which one newly mature adult can reach out to another, the season that celebrates King David, forebear of Messiah, then to seek on that day a dialogue between Arabs and Jews, Israelis and Palestinians, Americans and Soviets, would be a way to embody that adulthood and to act on Torah.

◆➤➤➤ FOODS * ◀◀◀◆

CHEESE BLINTZES

FILLING

2 cups dry cottage cheese
½ cup sour cream
1 egg
3 to 4 tablespoons sugar
½ teaspoon cinnamon
¾ teaspoon salt
½ teaspoon lemon rind
raisins if desired

PANCAKES

2 eggs
1 cup flour
½ teaspoon salt
1 cup milk or water
1 tablespoon oil or butter (about)

butter, sour cream, cinnamon and sugar, powdered sugar

*Recipes by Hannah Waskow and Rose Gertz.

Filling: Mix all ingredients together, cover and refrigerate.

Pancakes: Beat eggs until fluffy. Add water or milk, flour, and salt, to eggs. Heat oil in a 6-inch skillet. Spoon small amount of batter into skillet, covering the entire bottom, tilting quickly to help spreading. Fry gently only until batter is set. Turn out on dampened tea towel, stacking cooked side up.

Place about two tablespoons filling in center of each pancake (cooked side down). Fold over three sides, tucking in fourth to make an envelope. To cook, fry in hot butter until golden brown, carefully turning once. To serve offer sour cream, cinnamon and sugar, powdered sugar. Makes 8 servings of 2 each.

May be made ahead of time and stored in refrigerator for use later in the day or frozen for several weeks. If frozen they will take longer to fry. They may be baked instead of fried. Use a greased sheet and paint with melted butter.

DAIRY-NOODLE PUDDING
(Milchige Lukshen Kugel)

½ lb. medium noodles
½ to 1 cup large curd pot or cottage cheese
2 eggs, separated
3 tablespoons melted butter or margarine
½ teaspoon salt
2 tablespoons sugar
½ cup sour cream
½ cup raisins
1 teaspoon vanilla extract
½ teaspoon lemon extract
1 teaspoon lemon rind
¼ cup chopped nuts
¼ teaspoon cinnamon
¼ teaspoon allspice
1 tart apple, peeled and diced.

Break noodles in 2-inch pieces, in boiling salted water until tender. Drain, but not too dry, and do not wash. Stir the cheese into the noodles. Beat the egg yolks with the butter, salt, sugar, extracts, rind, and spices. Fold into the noodles the egg yolk mixture, sour cream, raisins, and nuts. Fold in egg whites beaten stiff but not dry. Butter and lightly crumb with dry crumbs a 2-qt. casserole or 9-inch square pan. Turn mixture into pan, sprinkle with crumbs and dot with butter. Bake in moderate oven (350°) for about 45 minutes or until top is light brown. May be finished under broiler but watch carefully so it won't burn. Will serve 6 to 9 people. Leftovers may be frozen and reheated wrapped in foil.

TUNA, MACARONI, AND CHEESE

1 6½ oz. can tuna
2 eggs, lightly beaten
1 cup small curd cottage cheese
1 cup shredded Monterey Jack cheese
6 oz. macaroni, cooked
¼ cup grated Parmesan cheese

Optional, ripe olives, mushrooms

½ cup dairy sour cream
¼ cup sliced green onion, including tops
⅛ tsp. salt
⅛ tsp, pepper
½ cup milk

Garnish: paprika, parsley flakes, oregano

Drain tuna. Combine eggs, cottage, Jack cheese, sour cream, onion, salt, pepper, nutmeg (olives and mushrooms). Stir in macaroni and tuna; pour into buttered casserole or 9 x 9-inch pan. Sprinkle with Parmesan, parsley flakes, oregano, paprika. Cover with foil and bake in 350° oven 45 minutes. Remove from oven and let set covered for 10 minutes before serving. Will serve four.

CHOCOLATE ROLL CAKE
(Yeast Dough)

1 cup scalded milk
1 oz or 1 dry package yeast
¼ lb. butter
½ cup lukewarm water
Grated lemon and orange peel

1 teaspoon salt
½ cup sugar
2 beaten eggs
5 cups flour

Dissolve yeast in lukewarm water. Add butter, salt, and sugar to scalded milk and allow to cool. Add yeast mixture and beaten eggs. Add flour until able to handle. Let rest 10 minutes then knead until smooth and elastic. Put in greased bowl turning to be sure entire surface is covered. Cover with cloth, put in *warm* (not hot) place and let rise until double in bulk. About 1½–2 hours. Punch down, knead several times and roll into sheets. Spread with melted butter, sprinkle *generously* with cocoa, cinnamon and sugar mixture, nuts, raisins, jelly, peel, minced apple, coconut and a few bread crumbs (about 1 teaspoon per sheet). Roll up. Cover and let rise until almost double. Paint with melted butter and sprinkle with cinnamon and sugar. Bake 375° until done. The mohn or prune mixtures may be used as fillings for this dough.

◆»» GO AND STUDY «‹◆

See Philip Goodman, *The Shavuot Anthology* (Jewish Publication Society) and Irving Greenberg, *Guide to Shavuot* (National Jewish Resource Center, NYC).

ZACHRAH YIRUSHALAYIM

"Jerusalem remembers in the days of her affliction and of her miseries all her pleasant things that she had in the days of old." (Lamentations 1:7) The fallen *keruv*'s wing, broken palms and blossoms are a metaphor for the destruction of the Temple. (see Kings I 6:29)

⬛«»» CHAPTER TWELVE »«»⬛
BURNT OFFERING—
TISHA B'AV

It is the heart of summer: hot as a furnace, dry as the tomb. A shower, a breeze are forgotten memories. The earth is panting in exhaustion—almost as if the birthing of her harvest has gone awry, as if the birth-pangs will go on forever but there will be no fruit. And people are exhausted too; their freshness and fertility, warmed and renewed by the sun of spring, has wilted as the sun grew still hotter. We feel burnt out. The whole world is being put to the torch.

On such a scorching summer day God's holy house on earth was burnt. The Temple in Jerusalem—microcosm of the holy Earth—was put to the torch by Babylon, by Rome. The Great Powers of their day, the empires ruled by Sun Kings, had from a distance, pulsed new energy into the simmering Jewish culture. But now that energy came far too close, turned into a raging fire. The Temple collapsed in flames, the people shattered into slavery and exile.

But we know that this moment of exhaustion and destruction is but a moment. We know that the earth passes safely through its too-hot exposure to the sun, that the crops coming to fruition in the fields do not burn up, that we will have a harvest and store the heat to keep us warm in winter. We know that our own eyes, blinded by the glare of the year's noonday, will once again be able to see clearly. We know that the Jewish people will harvest something new in exile, will harvest its shattered, scattered selves into a reunited holiness.

But to do this we need to experience fully the moment of burn-out, the moment of fire and thirst. And this the tradition does with Tisha B'Av—the ninth of the month of Av, the day that mourns for the destructions of the Temple (and the day set aside for the birth of Messiah, the beginning of redemption).

◆➤➤ ORIGINS ◄◄◆

Twice the Temple was destroyed—once by order of Nebuchadnezzar, king of Babylon, in 586 B.C.E.—and again by Vespasian, a general of the Roman Empire, in 70 C.E. On neither occasion did the actual destruction come on the ninth of Av. The Talmud (Taanith 29a) shows that the rabbis (writing after the Second Destruction) were puzzled by the fact that II Kings and Jeremiah give different dates for the First Destruction. One gave the seventh, one the tenth of Av. The rabbis insisted that the anomaly be cleared up and concluded that the Temple was captured by the Babylonians on the seventh, put to the torch on the ninth, and consumed by the fire on the tenth.

The very anxiety of the rabbis to justify the date of Tisha B'Av might be taken to support a theory of some modern scholars that the date was partly affected by the religious patterns of Babylon. Among the Babylonians, the ninth of Av was a day of dread and sorrow, a climactic moment in a month-long celebration focused on torches and firewood. (Perhaps this Babylonian holy season also had to do with midsummer and a sense of the raging sun.) Once the Jews had gone into the Babylonian exile, in seeking to commemorate the day of their disaster they may have chosen the fiery day already set aside by the Babylonians around them—the day whose date was so close and whose fiery significance echoed so well with the burning of the Temple.

When the Babylonian captivity ended and Jews returned to the land of Israel, they preserved the memorial day of Tisha B'Av—even though the prophet Zechariah said that God wanted them to live so justly that it could be made a festival of peace and joy.

After the Second Destruction—itself on the tenth of Av—the rabbis went further to legitimate the date and meaning of Tisha B'Av. They looked far back in Jewish consciousness—back to the second year of the Israelites' wandering in the wilderness after the Exodus from Egypt. They worked out a calendar of that year to show that on Tisha B'Av the people refused to enter the Land which God had promised to them. They refused in fear of the powerful nations that controlled the Land, a fear communicated to them by the spies whom they had sent to scout the territory. And as they waited in fear, the Holy One not only commanded that they wander in the wilderness for forty years till all that generation died, but said to them: "You have wept without cause; therefore I will set [this day] aside for a weeping throughout the generations to come."

The rabbis added that on the ninth of Av in 135 C.E. the Romans captured the city of Bethar, the last stronghold of the Bar Kochba revolt against Rome. And on the ninth of Av one year later, Romans ploughed the site of the Temple so as to build there a pagan temple and a Roman city, and forbade Jews to enter the town that had been Jerusalem.

All these events—even the one in the wilderness of Sinai—are connected with exile from the land—with the burning desire of the people to feel once more at home. But the rabbis did not view the Destruction of the Temple as merely a military defeat, nor even as only a political and cultural disaster for the Jewish people. The *Shechinah*—God's very Presence—went into exile, they insisted. God's own Self was shattered, and the world itself was riven. The Biblical book they assigned to be read on Tisha B'Av—*Eichah* or *Lamentations*—carries this theme into the spiritual life of the people by asserting that for *our* sins was Jerusalem destroyed. Tisha B'Av becomes a day not only to mourn the triumph of alienation, the loss of love and wholeness in the world, but to recognize our own complicity in that disaster.

And the rabbis point up the lesson for all human beings. They take the word that begins the Book of Lamentations, "*Eichah!*—How lonely sits the city!" and the word that God howls out to Adam in grief and anger after the shattering of Eden: "*Ayeka*, where are you?" These are the same word, they say—and indeed, in Hebrew they have the same root, only the vowels change. They are the same word, the rabbis say, because these two events are the same event. For Adam's was the first exile, the first alienation, the archetype of all loss ever since: the separation of the human psyche from God, the loss of utterly harmonious love. It is a loss burned into our consciousness by the flaming swords that burn and turn to bar our way to Eden.

How then do we experience this burning thirst—so fiercely as to learn the way to wellsprings? We learn it through a set of practices set forth by the tradition, beginning three weeks before Tisha B'Av and ending some seven weeks afterward, with Rosh Hashanah.

❖❯❯❯ PREPARATION ❰❰❰❖

Three weeks before Tisha B'Av is the seventeenth day of the month Tammuz. According to the Talmud, it was the day on which the Romans breached the walls of Jerusalem—and about a week distant from the day on which the Babylonians had done the same thing six centuries earlier. So it was the beginning of the end. It is a partial fast day—in which the fast is in effect only during the daylight hours. *

---

* A similar daylight fast, instituted for a similar reason but now observed in only the most traditional circles, is on the tenth of Tevet. On that day in 586 B.C.E. the Babylonians began their siege of Jerusalem.

Just as the rabbis reached forward and backward in Jewish history to explain and reinforce Tisha B'Av, so they did with the seventeenth of Tammuz. They found that it was the date of the celebration of the golden calf and of Moses' breaking the tablets of the Ten Commandments—a day in which Israel's own sinfulness dominates the mood and colors history. By tying that tradition to the fall of Jerusalem, the rabbis reinforced the connection in the Jewish mind between internal failing and external defeat.

Beginning on the seventeenth of Tammuz, weddings are avoided until after Tisha B'Av. So are haircuts, buying or wearing new clothes, musical celebrations. A general atmosphere of somberness and self-examination is encouraged. The atmosphere colors even the three Shabbosim of these three weeks, for on each of them a Prophetic passage is read that warns of the destruction of Jerusalem and rebukes the people for choosing a destructive path of life. The first two passages are Jeremiah I:1–II:3 and Jeremiah II:4–28 and III:4. The third—read on the Shabbat just before Tisha B'Av —is Isaiah I. After the initial words of the *haftarah*, *Chazon Yeshayahu*—A vision of Isaiah, the entire Shabbos is named Shabbos Chazon.

The atmosphere of mourning deepens on the first day of Av. Meat and wine disappear from the table. Washing and bathing are forbiddden, except when it is directly a matter of health. Shade trees are not planted. (These prohibitions on trees and water seem almost calculated to intensify our experience of the sun's heat.) Finally, just before Tisha B'Av itself, we eat a meal of mourning—lentils or hard-boiled eggs, traditionally eaten in a house of mourning, and some uncooked fruit or vegetables, perhaps a slice of bread dipped in ashes. And then begins the fast.

◆»»» TISHA B'AV «««◆

If the ninth falls on Shabbos, we postpone its observation until the next evening. This is clearly not just because it is a fast, for Yom Kippur is celebrated on Shabbos whenever the tenth of Tishri falls there. It is instead because this day is utterly different from Yom Kippur, the Joyful Fast. This is a day of deep mourning.

Beginning at sundown, we do not eat or drink at all; we do not wear leather, wash ourselves, anoint our skin or hair with oils or perfumes; we do not make love. And we go far beyond these prohibitions, which are the same as those for the Joyful Fast of Yom Kippur. We adhere to the traditional mourning customs because we feel almost like mourners, those whose dead have just been buried and who are just beginning to pray again, but sadly; who can share their grief with others, but not greet them; who cannot bear to look in a flattering mirror or sit on a comfortable chair. We study only sad and painful passages of the Bible and Talmud: the Book of Lamentations, Job, the sad parts of Jeremiah's prophecies; and commentaries on them.

We gather in the evening to a congregation of mourners. We do not greet each other as we enter. The Ark of the Torah is draped in black—or left open, empty, stripped of its holy scrolls. There are no bright lights—only candles casting a dim and flickering glow. In some Sephardic and Eastern congregations, even these candles are put out close to the end of the service, so that it ends in utter darkness. We find ourselves places to sit on the floor, or on low benches and cushions of the kind that mourners sit on.

We begin to chant the service in a mournful undertone. When we complete the murmured standing prayer, the *amidah*, the reading of *Eichah*, *Lamentations*, begins—to a limping, broken melody. In Chapter III the melody shifts to a more agonized howl—in keeping with the shift in content from public mourning to personal grief. When *Eichah* is finished, *kinot*— dirges—are chanted that were written in many of the later periods of anti- Jewish persecutions—from the Crusades, the Expulsion from Spain, pogroms in Eastern Europe, the Holocaust. Finally the service ends with *Alenu*, the homage to the King of Kings Who will someday be acknowledged through all the earth; Mourner's *Kaddish*, which on this *yahrtzeit* day of the defenders of the Temple may include us all; and perhaps with the singing of *Ani Ma'amin*, the song that looks forward—wistfully—to the coming of Messiah. Finally we leave, perhaps with a hug or a handclasp but without a word of farewell, without *Shalom Aleichem*—again as if we were all mourners, there is a death in every family.

The next morning we gather again. We do not wear *tallis* and *t'fillin*, the prayer shawls and leather straps-and-boxes—not out of the joy that makes them unnecessary on Shabbos and festivals but out of a sadness and anger that make them unbearable. We read from the Torah the portion of Deuter- onomy 4:24–40 that prophesies the Destruction, and the Prophetic portion is from Jeremiah 8:13–9:23. In some congregations the person called up to read the Torah says the broken blessing "Baruch dayan emet—Blessed be the Truthful Judge"—the blessing said upon hearing of a death. In some, the congregants sprinkle ashes on their heads. Again we read *Eichah* and again we chant *kinot*. Although there is no outright prohibition on work, some Jews follow the advice of Rabbi Akiba: "Anyone who works on Tisha B'Av will never see from that work any sign of blessing."

When we gather again in the late afternoon for the *mincha* service, the atmosphere has changed. For now the tradition comes to the fore that on this day of our deepest sadness, Messiah will be born and our greatest joy be celebrated. Now, having plunged ourselves into—and through—the deepest gloom, we are able to experience the first sense of joyful renewal. So—for the only time in all the year—we put on the *tallis* and *t'fillin* in the afternoon. In some Sephardic and Eastern communities, women put on perfume to welcome King Messiah. We begin to sense God's answer to the outcry at the end of *Eichah*—"Hashivenu adonai eylecha, v'nashuvah; chadesh yamenu k'kedem—Turn us around, Lord—turn us to You and we will be returned. Make new our days, as they were long ago."

After sundown, we break the fast together, wash our faces, and then go outside to do the joyful service of *kiddush levana*—hallowing the moon. There are Messianic overtones to this service, which echo the tradition that in the days of Messiah the moon will be restored to equality with the sun—perhaps a hint that women, long identified with the moon, will take on an equal rank with men in the religious sphere. *Kiddush levana* may be done at any time the crescent moon is visible during the first half of any month, but in Av most communities have a strong tradition to connect it with the end of Tisha B'Av.

In Israel, especially since 1967 when it again became possible for Jews to visit the ancient site of the Temple, new customs have emerged for Tisha B'Av. One is that hundreds of congregations come to the Wailing Wall itself—the only remaining portion of the fortified retaining walls built by King Herod around the Temple Mount—to pray and chant the Tisha B'Av services. Another is that groups of Israelis take Tisha B'Av hikes around the walls of the Old City of Jerusalem, and others visit the archeological sites where the ancient approaches to the Temple are being uncovered.

SONGS

The mood of most of Tisha B'Av is too mournful to admit of music. But in the atmosphere of Messianic hope and determined self-renewal with which the day ends, three songs (the first of them from *Eichah*, the Book of Lamentations) do seem appropriate. The first two are somewhat plaintive in tone, the third joyous and rousing.

Hashivenu, hashivenu, Adonai eylecha—
V'nashuva, v'nashuva
Chadesh, chadesh, yamenu k'kedem.

Help us turn to You, Lord, and we *will* return,
Renew our days as of old.

Ani ma-amin, ani ma-amin ani ma-amin b'emuna sh'lema—
B'viyat ha-mashiach, b'viat ha-mashiach ani ma-amin.
V'af al pi sheh-yitma-meyah
Im kol zeh ani ma-amin.

I affirm, I affirm, I affirm with a full and firm belief
The coming of Messiah;

And though he tarry, despite all that—
I affirm.

Achakeh lo, achakeh lo, achakeh lo
B'chol yom sheh-yavo
V'af al pi sheh-yitma-meyah,
Im kol zeh achakeh lo!
Achakeh lo b'chol yom sheh-yavo.

I will wait for him;
Every day while he is coming,
Despite all that I will await his coming.

THE SEVEN WEEKS OF COMFORT

The redemptive response to Tisha B'Av continues after the day itself. While the Second Temple still stood, there was a celebration that was observed just six days later. This was the celebration of Tu B'Av—the fifteenth of Av, at the full moon, exactly six months after Tu B'Shvat, the New Year of Trees. On this day, all the people brought firewood as an offering for the altar—and they celebrated by burning bonfires and torches. It was considered the last day on which wood for the Temple could be chopped, because thereafter the sun would no longer be hot enough to dry the wood. It therefore also represented the turning point of the sun's heat from scorching to bearable—a first hint of the revivifying autumn as Tu B'Shvat was the first hint of spring. On that day the maidens of Jerusalem lent each other white dresses—so that even if some of them had none to wear, no one would have to be ashamed of her poverty—and went out to dance and sing in the vineyards, calling out to the young men, "Lift up your eyes and see whom you choose for yourself."

The second way in which the redemptive process that begins on Tisha B'Av afternoon is continued and enriched is in the series of following Shabbosim. The Shabbos immediately following Tisha B'Av is called Shabbos Nachamu—the Shabbos of Comforting—after the beginning of the Prophetic passage (Isaiah 11:1–26) that is read, "Nachamu, nachamu, ami—Comfort you, comfort you, my people." It is the first of seven Shabbosim of comforting haftarahs that climb from the depths of Tisha B'Av to the renewal of Rosh Hashanah. All of them prophesy the redemption of Israel, its restoration to the Land, and the coming of the days of peace and justice.

These seven Shabbosim echo, in a very different key, the seven weeks of the omer that must be counted for the Jewish people to move from the liberation of Pesach to the revelation of Shavuot. They echo also, at a different tempo, the moment on Simchat Torah when we shift from reading the end of the Torah—the death of Moses—to reading the beginning—the creation of the world. Here it takes us seven weeks to move from the deathday of the whole people to the birthday of the human race. In these seven weeks we complete the circle of the year, moving from the burning sun of summer to the first cool breeze of autumn. From the hot and thirsty fast of Tisha B'Av to the wellsprings of Hagar and Abraham, and our own visit to the river for *Tashlich*. We complete the circle, from exhaustion to new life.

◆»» SOME NEW APPROACHES «‹‹◆

Several major events of the past generation have raised fresh questions and new possibilities in regard to Tisha B'Av. Two of these are the Holocaust and the emergence of the State of Israel, including its assertion of sovereignty over Jerusalem. On the one hand, some have argued that the mourning for the six million murdered Jews of Europe should be intertwined with mourning for the Temple. On the other hand, some have urged that Tisha B'Av mourning be relaxed in light of the emergence of a Jewish state in the Land of Israel—even in the absence of the rebuilt Temple and the Messianic Age.

The Holocaust has had a considerable impact on forms of commemoration of Tisha B'Av. In Israel, large numbers of people wearing tennis shoes can be seen at *Yad Vashem*, the Holocaust Memorial Museum and Study Center, on Tisha B'Av. The tennis shoes are the badge of those who are eschewing leather, part of the traditional observance of the fast because leather was a luxury. In some American congregations, poetry about the Holocaust—new *kinot*—has been incorporated in the service. In others, the liturgical drama by David Roskies called *Nightwords: A Midrash on the Holocaust* has been added to the service for Tisha B'Av night. (*Nightwords* is used in some congregations on Yom Hashoah, Holocaust Memorial Day, and is described at greater length in the Yom Hashoah section of Chapter XI.)

For many congregations, however, there is a major problem in connecting the Holocaust with Tisha B'Av. The traditional Jewish outlook has been that for *our* sins the Temple was destroyed. Few Jews feel that this is true about the Holocaust. The tradition's demand that we be self-critical, that we accept responsibility for our own failures in order to learn how to act more responsibly—this has one meaning when we have power, as we did in the First and Second Commonwealths. But did we indeed have power over our own lives in Eastern Europe? For these reasons, the relationship of Tisha B'Av to the Holocaust is not yet settled.

In an age when large numbers of Jews and of other peoples have become refugees, it is possible to see both the explicit verbal content and the ritual practice of Tisha B'Av as ways of experiencing what it means to be a refugee. Hungry, thirsty, unwashed, exhausted in the heat of summer, without chairs to sit on or light to see by—survivors walking on the Death March to

Babylon, to Rome. Reminding us how it is to be a refugee as the Pesach Seder reminds us how it is to be a slave—and to be free.

The emergence in the last century of a more personal and individual dimension to Judaism, responding to the individualism of modern civilization without totally surrendering to it, has also led to some new ways of experiencing Tisha B'Av. It can be seen as not only the zero point of Jewish peoplehood, but a representation of the zero point for individuals. It can be taken as the occasion for individuals to re-experience their own burning sense of the loss of love and meaning. To feel their own bellies burn with the grief of knowing how they themselves have acted so as to drive away their loved ones, send themselves into exile from their friends, shatter loving connection in the world. In some *chavurot* (participatory congregations or fellowships), time has been set aside after the reading of *Eichah* for individuals to focus on their own griefs, sometimes silently and sometimes to share with others in the community.

Finally, there is an aspect of Tisha B'Av that reaches out beyond the Jewish people. Since Tisha B'Av falls in late July or early August, it often comes close to or actually falls upon August 6 or August 9, the anniversaries in the Western calendar of the atomic bombings of Hiroshima and Nagasaki. Several small synagogues and *chavurot* have treated this confluence of dates as an occasion to recognize the danger of world destruction. As the Temple symbolized the Presence of God on earth and its destruction sent God into exile, so the human race carries the Image of God within it—and the destruction of humankind would send God's Presence into exile from the earth. Ceremonial acts that have accompanied the recognition of this connection have included chanting (in English, but using the mournful broken melodies of *Eichah*) passages from books describing the sufferings of Hiroshima and Nagasaki. On one occasion in 1981 when Tisha B'Av actually coincided with Nagasaki Day, the occasion was marked by a sizeable number of Jews who undertook a traditional observance of Tisha B'Av while being present near the White House and the Soviet Embassy—buildings symbolic of the nuclear super-powers.

❖❯❯❯ GO AND STUDY ❮❮❮❖

Morris Silverman and Hillel E. Silverman have compiled a booklet for *Tishah B'Av Services* (Prayer Book Press, Media Judaica, Bridgeport, CT.) See also *The Authorized Kinot for the Ninth of Av*, ed. by Abraham Rosenfeld (Labworth, London); Arato Osada, *Children of the A-Bomb* (Putnam); David Roskies, *Nightwords* (B'nai B'rith Hillel Foundations); and several Tisha B'Av poems useful for individual self-examination in Diane Levenberg, *Out of the Desert* (Doubleday).

See esp. *Midrash Rabbah on Lamentations* (Soncino) and *Pesikta de Rab Kahana* (Jewish Publication Soc.), pp. 272–285 for some powerful commentaries on the Destruction.

◆>>> THE LAST TISHA B'AV— <<<◆
A CHASSIDIC TALE

To the little town of Safed, where the air is clearest and it is possible to see the furthest in all the Land of Israel, long ago there came a Chassid, visiting from Vitebsk to see his Rebbe. For his Rebbe had chosen to settle in the Land of Israel.

The Chassid stood at the door of a pale and quiet synagogue: so pale, so quiet that the pastel paintings on its walls and ceiling stood out as though they were in vivid colors.

The visitor frowned, twirled his beard, and turned to ask the Rebbe: "What is this painting just above the *bimah*? It looks like the Dome that the Ishmaelites, the Muslims, have built above the rock where Abraham bound Isaac. The giant golden Dome that they have built where stood the Temple. I have just come from Jerusalem . . . It looks . . ." He stopped.

The Rebbe's eyes turned inward.

"I have seen . . ." he said, and paused. "I have seen . . ." he said, and paused again. "Our rabbis teach us that when Messiah comes, he will rebuild the Holy Temple in the twinkling of an eye.

"How can this be? Messiah will be extraordinary, yet still a human being merely . . . But I have seen . . . Well, let me tell you:

"At the foot of the Western Wall, the Wall where God's Presence weeps and hides in exile, I have seen hundreds of thousands of Jews gathered, singing. Messiah has come!—and they are singing, dancing, as the Great Day dawns.

"Messiah touches the Wall. He tucks one last petition between the great carved stones. He says a sentence to the crowds; I cannot hear it. As if his words have brought forth a river from the stones of the Wall, a stream of Jews flows up the stairway that rises to the Temple Mount. The river pauses for a moment on the steps, to read a wrinkled, tattered piece of paper, signed by the rabbis of that day. It warns all Jews to go no further, lest by accident they walk—God forbid—into the space set aside as the Holy of Holies.

"Messiah looks. He reads. He laughs. He tears the sign to shreds. The stream of people shudders into a higher ecstasy, the flow resumes.

"The crowd cascades from the stairway onto the great stone pavement of the Temple Mount. Their singing turns to the thunder of a great waterfall as they look toward the other end of the Mount—toward the great golden Dome of the Rock, the rock where Abraham bound his son for sacrifice . . .

"Surrounding the Dome are thousands of Muslims. They are not singing. They are shouting, furious, stubborn. 'Not here!' they shout in unison, 'Not here!'

" 'You will not tear down our Holy Mosque to build your Jewish Temple!'

" 'But that is the place . . . No doubt, no doubt, the ancient studies tell us that it is the place,' the people mutter.

"Messiah is quiet. The sea of Jews falls to a murmuring, falls silent. They turn to watch him. He looks, gazes, embraces with fond eyes the Holy Space. His eyes move across the Dome, its golden glow, the greens and blues and ivories of the walls beneath it. 'So beautiful!' he whispers.

"The Muslims too are silent now. The stillness here, the stillness there—so total that they cleave the Holy Mount in two.

"Messiah raises one arm, slowly, slowly. The Muslims tense, lift knives and clubs and shake them in the stillness. The Jews tense, ready to leap forward with their picks and shovels. The peoples vibrate: phantom ram's horns in the silent air, wailing forth a silent sob to Heaven.

"Messiah points straight at the Dome. He speaks quietly into the utter quiet: "This is the Holy Temple!"

"He drops his arm. I blink.

"For seconds, minutes, there is not a sound.

"Then I hear a Muslim shout and see him raise his knife: 'No! No! You will not steal our Holy Mosque to make your Jewish Temple!'

"He throws his knife. It falls far short. No one stirs. The other Muslims turn to look at him. They look with steadfast eyes: no joy, no anger. They just keep looking. He wilts into the crowd; I can no longer see what he is doing.

"Messiah steps forward, one step. Everyone, Jew and Muslim, breathes a breath. One Jew calls out: 'You must not do this. You must not use their dirty place to be our Holy Temple. Tear it down!—We need our own, we know how wide and tall, it is not this!' He takes a step toward Messiah, lifts an axe to brandish it.

"The man beside him reaches out a hand and takes the axe. Just takes it. There is a murmur, but the murmur dies. The man holds the axe level in both hands, walks out with it into the no-man's-land between the crowds. He lays it on the pavement, backs away.

"There is another time of quiet. Two Muslims reach out from the crowd, toss their knives to land next to the axe. The pause is shorter this time. Then on every side weapons come flying through the air to land beside the axe, beside the knives. There is a pile. Someone walks forward, lights a fire. The pile begins to burn. The flames reach up to Heaven.

"So I have seen," the Rebbe said, "Messiah build the Temple in the twinkling of an eye. And so there is this painting on the ceiling."

The visitor took breath again. "And why?" he said. "Why would Messiah do this dreadful thing?"

The Rebbe twirled his own beard, this time.

"First for the sake of Abraham's two sons.

"Second for the sake of the circles of the Dome.

"Third for the sake of the Rock beneath the Dome.

"And fourth for the sake of the twinkling of an eye."

"And why did the people burn their weapons?"

"For the sake of the burnt offering. It is written, 'Choose!' You. Or the Temple. Or the things you use to burn each other with."

◀>>> AFTERWORD AND FOREWORD <<<◀

Tisha B'Av is the last link in the circle of the year—the link that moves from exhaustion to renewal. It is also the link in the history of the Jewish people that moves from disaster to renewal—from the disaster of the Destruction of the Temple to the renewal that was the Talmud, the beginning of the whole period of rabbinic Jewish thought.

And so Tisha B'Av may be for us today the model for how to move from our own disaster to our own renewal—from the disaster of the decline of Jewish tradition in the face of modern thought, and the disaster of the Holocaust, to the next great renewal of the Jewish people and of Torah.

The great cycle of the Jewish year is a model, a metaphor, of the great cycle of life—and of the life of the Jewish people. Over and over, we move from birth to maturity to fulfillment to what seems to be a death—but is really the seed of a new birth, a new life. So it seems fitting to end this book with a beginning—to see that Tisha B'Av can teach us how to make a new beginning.

When the Holy Temple was destroyed, the Jewish people could have given up. Look at the Book of Leviticus. At a surface reading it seems clear enough: without the Temple and its sacrifices, there is no touch with God. But the rabbis did not let the Torah come to nought. Instead, they did *midrash*: that is, they searched within the Torah text for deeper meaning, for words that would speak to a day when sacrificial animals could not be offered up. Study and prayer, they concluded, were a deeper sacrifice, a fuller contact. They found within the tradition a way to transcend the tradition. We all have died, we all have found new life.

Or the rabbis could have given up another way—by keeping on. They could have found a new place for the sacrifices. They could have preserved a Biblical remnant and rejected all the elements of Hellenism. Instead, they absorbed the best of Hellenism and then—as who they *newly* were—went back to wrestle with the Torah. Out of that wrestling sprang new Torah-truths and a gigantic new interpretation of the Torah: Talmud and the whole rabbinic tradition.

But they did not see the Talmud as brand-new. They saw it as what they called the oral Torah, the spoken words that lay invisible between the lines of the written Torah, the words that Moses heard on Sinai and passed by word of mouth to all the generations. So for them the Talmud did not replace Torah; the Talmud *was* Torah. The new truths were old truths waiting to be unveiled when the time came.

Or the rabbis could have taken the Destruction of the Temple as a merely military fact: "It was a building. It was burnt by an invading army. The Hellenists have gained in strength. Once before, when they called themselves 'Greece,' they defiled the building. We raised an army and we threw them out. Then we rededicated the building. Now they call themselves 'Rome,' and they are stronger. This time they actually burned the building. We will rebuild it when we throw them out again."

They did not do that either. Instead they made the Destruction a cosmic fact: "The *Shechinah*, God's Presence in the world, has fled into exile. The world itself is shattered, alienated." We mourn on Tisha B'Av not a military defeat, but our deep alienation from the flow of life. And if our mourning can be deep enough, our tears flow free enough, then we can touch the flow again, pour our tears into the stream. Our alienation begins to end. Messiah is born.

From the darkness of our mourning comes the night vision, the dream, welling up from our unconscious, of new life. From the blankness, empty white space that surrounds the letters of the Torah, from that fluidity and openness, comes new direction. It is not empty blankness, but white fire around the black fire of the letters. From the tiny crowns and thorns upon the letters—at once so precise and so meaningless—come whole worlds, whole worlds of meaning. The oral Torah.

The *Beit-Mikdash*, the Holy Temple, was a *beit*, a letter of the *aleph-beit*. It was the *beit* of B'reshit, "In the beginning," the letter that begins the Holy Torah.

But the Temple, the *Beit-Mikdash*, was no ordinary *beit*. It was no two-dimensional letter written down on parchment, but a four-dimensional letter. For the Holy Temple existed in three dimensions of space and also in the time-dimension, expressed through the sacrificial calendar of holy days.

When the Temple burned, when the *beit* went up in fire, the flames were crowns and thorns upon the letter: white flame from which sprang old-new Torah. When the Temple space stood empty, there was blankness. The rabbis turned the blankness into white fire, new Torah.

On the supernal heights of Sinai, above the earthly heavens, how did Moses distinguish the forty days and forty nights? During the day God taught him written Torah: visible, definite, organized, chronological, and logical. At night a dreaming God taught a dreaming Moses oral Torah: invisible, fluid, anarchic, psychological. Dreamlike.

For centuries the oral Torah remained a Dream. But then the Holy Temple burned. On Tisha B'Av we became our own psychoanalysts, we did our own interpretation of dreams. We turned our Dream, our Nightmare, into our waking Life-Path. We turned what was fluid and dreamy into specifics: *Halacha*.

What Messiah was born that Tisha B'Av? On the day the Temple was destroyed, the Exile was born and the Talmud was born. One became the body and the other the soul of the old-new Jewish people.

Now, today, as earlier Jews were conquered by Hellenism, so we have been conquered by Modernism. Not only conquered from without, by physical force—but more important, conquered inwardly. Persuaded.

There are attractions, truths, in Modernism as there were in Hellenism. There are truths to science, industrialism, liberalism, socialism, nationalism. Their central truth is that the human race can master its destiny, master the world. But it is only a partial truth. We are persuaded—but not wholly. It is also true that acting with total mastery will destroy our dominion—and thus annul, annihilate, our mastery. Acting totally as masters will total the world.

Objectify Earth, she will objectify us.

Poison the world, she will poison us back.

So we have become Modernists who know another truth: that to be only Modernists will destroy the world and ourselves. We need God-given Torah: the knowledge that we do not own the world. God does. There must be limits. There must be cycles. There must be pauses—Shabbos and Jubilee.

So we need to wrestle with Torah as the rabbis wrestled with Torah. As they searched in the white flame for new understanding, so must we. As they plunged into the darkness and the blankness to grasp the oral Torah, so must we. As they turned the Destruction from a military or a cultural event into a cosmic event, so must we.

But not—as some theologians would have it—the cosmic event that ends the covenant between God and Israel. Instead, the cosmic event that demands we renew the covenant in some new way. Not Sinai, but the burning bush: the flame that marks both outcry and response.

How do we know this? Because in our generation, the victory of Modernism brought disaster, but not only disaster. The victory of Modernism took three forms: the disaster of the Holocaust, the blessing of the state of Israel, and the blessing of the free American Diaspora. These simultaneous upheavals of hope and hopelessness should signal us: human mastery is not utterly evil, not wholly good. The covenant is not utterly dead, not wholly alive. It all depends on us. It is we who will have to search for God. It is we who will have to find new Torah.

We can learn from Tisha B'Av what we can do.

Through Tisha B'Av, the rabbis simultaneously faced the death and celebrated the rebirth of the Biblical era. They did this not only by what they *said* of Tisha B'Av—that it was both a day of disaster and a day of extraordinary birth, Messiah's birth. It was also by *doing* Tisha B'Av. For by mourning the Temple with such sorrow, they were accepting the death of the whole Biblical pattern in which the Jewish people lived freely in its own land and sacrificed to God the products of that land in its own Holy Temple. Yet by the very act of mourning on Tisha B'Av the rabbis were incorporating the content and process of the Biblical era into something new. To mourn a death is always to assert a rebirth: the dead do not mourn.

What is born on this day? When the rabbis say Messiah is born on Tisha B'Av, one way to hear them is that hope is reborn. For they speak of Messiah's birth, not of fullness, not of the shattered world made whole again, but only of a birth, a beginning, a hope.

If we wish to learn from Tisha B'Av, we can face the "death" of the Talmudic era in its age-old form. And by doing this we can preserve its seed, bring it to birth again. If in the generation of the Temple's Destruction what was "born" was the Diaspora and the Talmud, then we must notice that in our own generation what has already been born is both the State of Israel and a free Diaspora. What was born in this generation is the new Jewish people who lives both in Diaspora and the Land of Israel, with political power and freedom in both places; a new Jewish people that is both secularist and religious.

What is yet to be born in this generation? A new path of Jewish life, a new dream-Torah that can transform our daily practice, that can preserve a seed from the Biblical era, preserve a seed from the Talmudic era, embody the new Jewish secularism, and go beyond them by continuing the Torah process.

If we wish to learn from Tisha B'Av we can read *Eichah*, the Book of Lamentations. We can read with joy the verse of Lamentations: "Chadesh yamenu k'kedem. Make new our days as of old." Make new the days of the year, as we circle back to Rosh Hashanah. Make new the generations of our people, as we circle forward to the Third Age of Jewish peoplehood. Not "Give us back the good old days," but "Make our days full of newness, as You did long ago."

FROM GENERATION
TO GENERATION

Today, as I complete this book, is perhaps the strangest of all the seasons of our joy—for it will not come again for twenty-eight years. It is the day of the Blessing of the Sun—*Birchat Ha-Chamah*. On that day, according to the Talmud, the sun returns to where it was in the Heavens on the fourth day of Creation. That was when God set the sun and the moon to "serve as signs for the seasons." (Gen. 1:14). So today it is in a sense the season of the seasons, the cycle of the birth of all our cycles.

Why today? Because alongside the view that the Creation of the World occurred in Elul and Tishri, at Rosh Hashanah time, the Talmud preserves another view: that the Creation occurred in Nisan, the first of the months, in spring. Evidently to the rabbis it felt particularly apppropriate that the birthday of the sun should be at the spring equinox, when the sun emerges from the womb of winter and crosses the Equator coming northward. The Torah teaches that the sun was created at the beginning of the fourth day—Tuesday evening, to use our present labels. So the moment when the sun is again where it was at the beginning comes in a year when the equinox—as the rabbis defined it—comes on Tuesday evening in Nisan.

Then why are we celebrating today—the eighth of April? Surely it is not the equinox! The rabbis' calculation of the length of the year was a few minutes off—and in 2,000 years that has added up to a few weeks.

And why only every twenty-eight years? By assigning Tuesday evening as the moment, the rabbis made the moment hard to come by. For the year does not divide into four equal seasons of full days. There is a day-and-a-quarter left over. So if the equinox comes on a Tuesday evening this year, it will come next year a day-and-a-quarter later. It will take four years for it to come 'round to the evening again—and then it will be five days away from Tuesday. Only after seven *times* four years will the moment come back to a Tuesday evening.

By working out this cycle of twenty-eight years, the rabbis accomplished something else: by celebrating the sun only once a generation, they gave us a way to look ahead and look back that is worthy of the sun. Of all the specific objects in our created world, the sun and planet Earth are the most crucial for the life and well-being of the human race. So a celebration of the sun's creation is a good moment to ask ourselves: what have we done with the sun's light, warmth, energy, in this past generation? What do we intend to do in the next generation?

So this morning at 5:43 a.m., at sunrise, at the Jefferson Memorial on the shores of the Tidal Basin in Washington, under the windy, tattered cherry blossoms, several hundred Jews recited "Baruch atah Adonai eloheynu melech ha-olam oseh ma-aseh b'reshit. Blessed are You, Lord our God, Ruler of time and space, Doer of the deeds of Creation." And danced in circles, sang songs like "Here Comes the Sun" and "Morning Has Broken" and psalms about the sun, rising in strength and joy and radiance like a bridegroom coming forth to his wedding.

And we signed a scroll to be saved for the Blessing of the Sun in the year 5769 of the Creation, on April 8, 2009:

In this day that begins the 206th cycle of the sun since the Beginning,
We pledge ourselves to make a new beginning:
To hand on to the next generation an earth that is washed in sunlight,
   not poisoned by waste;
To see in the sun's light the light of Torah;
To feel in the sun's warmth the warmth of the human community;
To use through the sun's energy the strength of the One Who Creates.
Blessed be the Doer of Deeds of Beginning.

And we sent greetings to Jews at the top of the Empire State Building, in front of Independence Hall, on the shores of the Atlantic in New England and in Florida, at Golden Gate Bridge and in the Redwood Forest, in the prison yard at Attica and at the Wall in Old Jerusalem, who were also joining in our prayers.

I would like to end this book with that look back and forward. When the sun was blessed twenty-eight years ago, there were far fewer Jews who knew about this festive day or took joy in doing it. The renewal of our tradition has been one of the great works of this past generation. It is still beginning, still gathering strength. May the renewal of Jewish peoplehood and Torah be so strong that in 2009 this whole book needs to be rewritten: rewritten out of a deeper and broader understanding of the festivals, out of a more profound mourning for what is gone in Jewish life and a more intense joy in what is growing, out of new ceremonies and studies that grow authentically from wrestling with the old ones.

In my own life and wrestling, I have had teachers and comrades in the inner work that lay behind the working of this book:

Michele Alperin, Brad Blanton, Everett Gendler, Lynn Gottlieb, Liz Lerman, Diane Levenberg, Jeff Oboler, Rosalie Riechman, Zalman Schachter-Shalomi, Carol Simon, Esther Ticktin, Max Ticktin, David Waskow, Howard Waskow, Shoshana Waskow, and Rena Yount. Two of these people, Max Ticktin and Zalman Schachter-Shalomi, for years and years have been for me extraordinary teachers of Torah and *menshlichkeit*.

For specific contributions to one or another particular aspect of the book, I thank Richard Siegel and Joelle Delbourgo for encouraging me to write it; my son, David Waskow, for compiling the dates in Appendix V; my mother, Hannah Waskow, for supplying almost all the recipes (after some consultation with *her* mother, Rose Gertz); Rose Sue Berstein, for providing the vegetarian Pesach recipes; Joan Benjamin-Farren and Martin Farren for the illustrations; Joan Matthews and Judy Davis for turning my multi-colored scrawl into a manuscript; Jacob Agus, Carol Simon, and Max Ticktin for reading and criticizing large parts of it; and Nessa Rapoport for a tough, sensitive, and sensible job of editing.

My work during the last few years as editor of *Menorah*, a monthly journal of Jewish renewal, has helped me feel out how to respond to the Jewish community's sense of the festival cycle. One of *Menorah*'s main concerns is to renew and enrich these celebrations. I would welcome readers of this book as subscribers, writers, and artists for *Menorah*.

I also welcome readers into a conversation of *shylahs* and *tshuvas*, questions and responses, about the meaning of the holy days and seasons. Enclosed in this book is a questionnaire—please use it! Or write me at *New Menorah*, Reconstructionist Rabbinical College, Church Road and Greenwood Avenue, Wyncote, PA 19095, with your questions, comments, and responses.

My life in Fabrangen, a Washington *chavurah* or participatory communal congregation that has now for ten years taught me and engaged me in the cycle of the seasons, made the book possible. My discussions with the students in several years of classes at the Fabrangen's Jewish Study Center made the book far richer.

I remain responsible for its mistakes, its wanderings, and its transgressions.

L'hit-ra-ot—till we may see the sun once more together, in the joyful season of its cycle.

Avraham Yitzchak Yishmael ben Chanoch v'Chana
Arthur I. Waskow
4 Nisan 5741
April 8, 1981
On the first day of the
206th cycle of the
sun since the Creation.

◆»» APPENDIX I «««◆

THE SECOND DAY
OF FESTIVALS

All the festivals but one require that the night of the New Moon of their month be firmly established. (The one exception is Shavuot, which is dated by counting fifty days from the second day of Pesach.) But the astronomy available to the Jews during the Temple period and the early Talmudic period (up to the fourth century C.E.) did not permit being absolutely certain, in advance, of when the New Moon would actually appear. Sometimes it appeared twenty-nine days after the previous one; sometimes thirty. Its actual appearance was what mattered, and witnesses had to appear before a court to testify they had seen it.

In the days when the Temple stood, the Sanhedrin in Jerusalem would hear testimony and proclaim the new month. Then special torches were lit and ceremonially waved on the mountaintops, sending the news from one hill to another as well as ritually celebrating the New Moon. By this means the word quickly reached even the Diaspora in Babylonia. But there was growing animosity between the official Jewish community and the Samaritans, who had an independent sacrificial rite; and the Samaritans began to light torches on other nights in such a way as to confuse the far-flung Jewish communities.

As a result, the Diaspora Jews began to observe Rosh Chodesh—the New Moon—on both days on which it might occur. And of necessity they began to celebrate two days of festival—two days of Rosh Hashanah, which indeed came on the new moon itself; two days of rest at the beginning of Sukkot, two days of Sh'mini Atzeret at its end; two days of rest at the beginning and two at the end of Pesach; and two days of Shavuot. The other holidays—Hanukkah, Purim, etc., which did not require rest—were not doubled; and Yom Kippur was not because it would be too hard to impose a total fast for forty-eight hours.

Some have suggested that since the second day arose out of doubts over the correct date, the second day can be seen as a day to celebrate and honor doubt and skepticism—as the first day honors faith and certainty. The deepest faith can arise only after we have faced all our doubts.

Even when Jewish astronomy became expert enough to know in advance when the New Moon would appear, the distinction between the Palestinian community and the Diaspora was preserved and the custom of the forebears was honored by continuation of the two-day celebration in the Diaspora alongside the one-day celebration in Palestine.

The two-day celebration of Rosh Hashanah, however, took on a special aspect. The rabbis agreed that the two days should be treated as one long day for various legal purposes. Rosh Hashanah was probably felt to be exceptional because it was the only festival that fell on the New Moon itself, and so the uncertainty was especially strong. Perhaps as a result, when a large group of Jews from Provence (the Mediterranean coast of what is now France) settled in Palestine in the eleventh century, they insisted on celebrating Rosh Hashanah for two days. Their numbers were great enough, their prestige high enough, and their insistence strong enough that they swallowed up the one-day Rosh Hashanah that had been practiced by Jews in Palestine; and the result was that for all Jews everywhere Rosh Hashanah became a two-day festival. (It may be that an underlying desire to celebrate the day of doubt as well as the day of certainty and faith helped bring this result; or even that the desire to hear the shofar blown on Rosh Hashanah was so great that a two-day celebration seemed a good way to make the shofar blowing possible if one day of Rosh Hashanah fell on Shabbos, when the shofar is not blown.)

In the past generation, Reform Judaism formally annulled the second day of the festivals in the Diaspora (and many Conservative Jews grew weaker in observing the second day). The Reform decision applied even to Rosh Hashanah, though many Reform synagogues continue to observe both days of Rosh Hashanah.

As visits between the Diaspora and the modern Israeli Jewish communities became more frequent, it became necessary to define the personal obligations of individual Jews. The general rule is that Diaspora Jews who are visiting Israel but have not decided to move there should celebrate both days; and Israelis who are visiting in the Diaspora observe the second day when they are in company, so as not to cause a scandal or controversy over the legitimacy of the second day.

⬖ ➤➤➤ APPENDIX II ⬅⬅⬅ ⬖

THE MOON

Since this book focuses on the cycle of the year and the changing seasons of the year, we have addressed the changing festivals that celebrate these seasons. But in any Jewish year, there are also the undertones brought out by shorter rhythms. In the context of the year, these rhythms emphasize repetition rather than change.

The first of these is the rhythm of the day—with its prayer times at dawn, afternoon, at dusk, and (privately) on going to bed. These four seasons of the day may be analogous to the four seasonal festivals of the year and of the month of Tishri—with the bedtime saying of the Sh'ma almost invisible, like Sh'mini Atzeret.

The second is the rhythm of the week, crowned by Shabbos—the seventh day, over and over and over the seventh day, the day of rest that celebrates both God's rest in the creation of the universe and the repose of free men and women when they break out of slavery. Since Shabbos is not marked by any special change of the sun, moon, or earth, it depends entirely on the human act of counting and the human will to observe it.

The third is the rhythm of the moon. We have seen that Jewish tradition treats the seventh month with great distinction; but the coming of every month is celebrated specially. On the Shabbos before Rosh Chodesh, head of the moon-renewing, the day of Rosh Chodesh is announced with great fanfare during the Torah service, and the congregation asks God to make the new month one of life—life for blessing and joy and peace. If that Shabbos happens to be the day just before Rosh Chodesh, a special *haftarah* is read that recounts the love and friendship between David and Jonathan, how they made a covenant together on the eve of Rosh Chodesh, and then had to part forever because of King Saul's hostility toward David (I Samuel 20:18–42).

Some traditional Jews treat the day before Rosh Chodesh as a small Yom Kippur, when they fast and consciously turn away from their misdeeds. This custom arose among the mystics of Safed in the sixteenth century, who saw the waning of the moon as a symbol of the exile of the *Shechinah* (God's Presence in the world) and of the alienated, shattered state of human and cosmic existence. Rosh Chodesh for them was a symbol of renewal and hope.

Then on Rosh Chodesh itself, the day becomes a minor festival. In the *amidah* prayer, a paragraph is inserted like that on the festivals; and the same kind of partial *Hallel* is sung that is chanted on the later days of Pesach.

Among traditional Jews, women did not work on Rosh Chodesh. The folklore says that God gave them this special gift as a reward for refusing to worship the golden calf at Sinai. This legend may be a way of recognizing an ancient special relationship between women and the moon arising out of the similarity of the lunar and menstrual cycles, or even out of comparing the lesser light of the moon and the paler, less assertive role assigned women by Jewish tradition.

In recent years, American Jewish women who are specially interested in encouraging the full and equal participation of women in Jewish religious life and who also want to infuse the tradition with the spiritual experience of women have developed a number of ceremonies for the celebration of Rosh Chodesh by women in separate groups, and sometimes by women and men together. These ceremonies have included the lighting of a candle set afloat on cork or wood in a bowl of water, the chanting and telling of old and new *midrash* about women in the Bible, and the weaving of new and old feelings and expectations about the tone of the month that is beginning.

Some women have suggested viewing as a parable of the history of roles and relationships of women and men, the Talmudic legend that God originally made the sun and moon equal in light, reduced the moon to secondary status but viewed it as a misdeed to have done so, and promised that in the future the moon would again become equal to the sun. In this orientation, Rosh Chodesh becomes a renewal both of God's Presence in the world—the *Shechinah*, a female aspect of God—and of the female side of the human race and the human soul.

When Rosh Chodesh itself falls on Shabbos, to the regular Torah portion of the week is added a recitation of Numbers 28:9–15, about the sacrifices offered on Rosh Chodesh when the Temple stood. The regular *haftarah* is replaced by Isaiah 66, which evokes images of God as a Mother bearing and suckling Her child Israel and concludes:

And it will come to pass
That New Moon after New Moon
And Shabbos after Shabbos,
All flesh will come to worship before Me,
Says the Lord.

Shortly after Rosh Chodesh there is a traditional ceremony for *kiddush levana*, hallowing the moon. In the month of Tishri, this is usually done in the evening after Yom Kippur (the beginning of the eleventh of Tishri); in Av, on the evening after Tisha B'Av (the beginning of the tenth of Av). In the other months, it is done anytime between the fourth of the month, when the moon is clearly perceptible, and the fourteenth, when it appears full. The hallowing of the moon is always done outdoors, and only if the moon can actually be seen.

This ceremony was also developed by the Kabbalists of Safed, and explicitly mentions their hope that the moon will be renewed in the future to be as bright as the sun.

Blessed are You, Lord our God, King of the universe, who created the heavens by your command, and all their host by Your mere word. You have subjected them to fixed laws and time, so that they might not deviate from their set function. They are glad and happy to do the will of their Creator, the true Author, whose achievement is truth. He ordered the moon to renew itself as a glorious crown over those He sustained from birth, who likewise will be regenerated in the future, and will worship their Creator for his glorious majesty. Blessed are You, O Lord, who renews the months.

Blessed be your omnipotent Creator, O moon!

Even as one cannot touch the moon, so may my foes be unable to harm me.

May terror and dread fall on them; may they be motionless as a stone under the sweep of your arm.

Long live David, king of Israel!

The worshippers exchange greetings:

Shalom aleichem, peace be with you!
Aleichem shalom, peace be unto you!
May we and all Israel have a favorable omen and good fortune. Amen.

The voice of my beloved! Here he comes, leaping across the mountains, bounding over the hills! My beloved is like a gazelle, like a young deer; here he stands, behind our wall, gazing through the windows, peering through the lattice.

This, and also the reference to King David, forebear and model of Messiah who is yet to come, and the passage from the Song of Songs all evoke the hope of the Messianic days of peace, justice, and spiritual wholeness.

APPENDIX III

GLOSSARY

amidah   standing prayer, quietly murmured, that is part of each daily service.
bensch   say a blessing; over the *lulav*, or over food, etc.
bokser   carob.
bub   chickpeas.
chavurah (chavurot)   lit. fellowship(s); small and intimate participatory congregations or study groups, free-standing or part of a synagogue, creatively traditional, egalitarian between women and men and the learned and learning.
chevra   friendship group, smaller and less formal than *chavurah* (same root).
chol hamoed   ordinary part of the festival—days in middle of Pesach or Sukkot when work is allowed.
Diaspora   the widespread network of Jewish communities outside the Land of Israel.
dreidl   spinning top for playful Hanukkah gambling; Yiddish for *s'vivon*.
etrog   citron fruit for use in Sukkot ceremony.
Fabrangen   name of a *chavurah* in Washington, DC; modification of *farbrangen*, a coming together of Chassidim to hear their rebbe teach Torah.
Gemara   vast body of rabbinic commentary on the *Mishnah*, edited and brought together into an authoritative text by fifth century C.E.; together with the *Mishnah*, makes up the Talmud.
haftarah   Prophetic passage read on a given Shabbos or festival.
hak-heyl   assemble-ceremony of reading parts of Torah every seventh Sukkot.
hakkafah   circle-dance (one circuit) with the Torah scroll.
Hallel   a group of Psalms chanted as special praise of God.
Hoshanah   chant of "Save us, Lord," said while carrying Torah in procession.
Jubilee   every fiftieth year, land lies fallow and land ownership is totally redistributed into equal family shares.
Kaddish   blessing of God's powers and attributes in a prayer used for internal punctuation of prayer services into various parts, and also used as a memorial prayer for the dead.
Kapparot   ceremony of transferring sinfulness to a scapegoat just before Yom Kippur.
ketubah   (ketubot)—written contract(s) of marriage.
kibbutz   highly participatory, unbureaucratic collective farm (in Israel), with shared income and voluntary membership.
kiddush   blessing over wine used to hallow a holy day; by extension, a light meal after the wine.
kinah   (kinot)—poetic dirge(s).
kittel   white robe.
kvitl(ech)   petitionary prayer(s) on pieces of paper tucked between stones of Western (Wailing) Wall in Jerusalem.

latke   pancake (Yiddish).

Levites   tribe of ceremonial-religious functionaries.

lulav   palm branch, bound with willow and laurel for Sukkot ceremony.

Machzor   prayerbook for Rosh Hashanah and Yom Kippur (and sometimes other festivals).

maftir   last part of Torah reading on a given Shabbos or festival.

maoz chittin   wheat money—charitable gifts at Pesach so the poor can buy matzah.

Maariv   evening prayer service.

megillah   scroll; esp. (Megillah) the Scroll of Esther; by extension, any long story.

menschlichkeit   decent human behavior.

midrash   the search for deeper meaning in some text of Jewish tradition, which may lead to a reinterpretation that itself becomes part of the tradition.

mikveh   pool of water for ceremonial immersion.

Minchah   afternoon prayer service.

Mishnah   law code governing all aspects of life, based on Pharisees' and rabbis' interpretation of Torah; codified in second century C.E.

mitzvah   command from God; a good deed.

musaf   additional prayer service for Shabbos and festival days.

nahit   chickpeas.

Neilah   closing of the gates service at end of Yom Kippur.

omer   sheaf or bushel of grain.

parah adumah   red heifer—special sacrificial animal.

payot   corners; therefore, earlocks of hair.

Pharisees   religio-political faction in late Second Temple days that wanted to develop Judaism through prayer, study of Torah, and *midrashic* interpretation of Torah; forerunners of the rabbis.

piyyut   poetic prayer.

Purimshpiel   parodic play for Purim.

Rosh Chodesh   New Moon, first day of month.

Sadducees   religio-political faction in late Second Temple days that focused on priestly functions and the sacrificial system.

schnapps   whiskey.

Shabbos, Shabbat   Sabbath.

Shacharit   morning prayer service.

shalom   the fullness of peace and harmony.

Shechinah   God's Presence in the world—among mystics, seen as female aspect of God in relation to male distant, transcendent aspect of God.

shmitah   release—the seventh year in which the land lies fallow and debts are released or annulled.

shofar   ram's horn, blown to make an eerie sound.

shul   synagogue.

Siddur   prayerbook.

S'phirah (S'phirot)   emanation(s) from the ultimate, infinite, indefinable Godhead toward the palpable world; aspects of God.

sufganiyot   doughnuts.

sukkah   leaky-roofed hut.

s'vivon   spinning top for playful Hanukkah gambling; Hebrew for *dreidl.*

Ta-anit   a section of the Talmud on Fasts.

tallit, tallis   prayer shawl with ceremonial fringes on four corners.

tallit katan   small prayer shawl; a special undershirt with four corners each bearing *tzitzit*.

Talmud   vast collection of rabbinic thought, stories, law, etc., from the period 200 B.C.E. to 500 C.E.

Tashlich   casting; ceremonial casting of crumbs into water on Rosh Hashanah.

tikkun   repair; the all-night Torah study on Shavuot that repairs the world.

Torah   (1) the Five Books of Moses; (2) the whole process and content of all of Jewish tradition; (3) lit., teaching.

tshuvah   turning; repentance, turning one's life back toward God and holiness.

tzaddik(im)   righteous person(s).

tzedakah   righteous action toward the poor; obligatory charity.

tzitzit   ceremonially knotted fringes to be worn on all four-cornered garments.

ushpizin   guests, especially mystical guests in the sukkah.

yetzer   impulse; *yetzer ha-ra*, impulse toward evil.

yizkor   memorial service for the dead.

Zohar   Splendor—a thirteenth-century mystical text.

◆≫≫ APPENDIX IV ≪≪◆

GO AND STUDY

When someone asked the great teacher Hillel to teach him the whole Torah while he stood on one foot, Hillel said, " 'Love your neighbor as yourself.' This is the whole Torah. Everything else is *midrash*—commentary. Go and study!" The hasty learner was, for the moment, satisfied—but Hillel's answer was something of a put-on. "Go and study!" means, "Spend the rest of your life at it." For indeed everything else—*everything* else—is *midrash* on the Torah, waiting to be connected and understood anew in Torah's light.

Therefore: go and study! Most of the best study of the festivals comes from experiencing and observing them, and observing yourself while you experience them. But reading helps. The books noted below are those I have found most useful in my own study, in addition to those noted at the end of every chapter. All are in English.

ULTIMATE SOURCES

The Torah (Jewish Publication Society) has the basic commandments for the most ancient festivals. *Chumashim* (the Five Books of Moses divided into Shabbos and festival sections, with the connected Prophetic *haftarahs*, all in Hebrew and English) are especially useful for our purposes if they present the festival readings in a clear way. The best along those lines is the J. H. Hertz *chumash*, *The Pentateuch and Haftarahs* (Soncino, London); see especially pp. 943–1043. The translations are archaic, and the Hertz *chumash* might best be used with the newer translations of *The Torah* and *The Prophets* (Jewish Publication Society) in the other hand. When the Everett Fox retranslation of the Torah is available from Schocken Books, it will be an extraordinary advance.

The Five Megillot and Jonah (Jewish Publication Society) has excellent introductions to each of these extra readings for the holidays, each presented in Hebrew and English, all in an unusually attractive format at little cost. Herbert Danby, ed., *The Mishnah* (Oxford University Press), pp. 99–216, has many rich passages on the festivals in Second Temple days.

The Talmud has comments on the holy days scattered all through it; but by far the most of these are concentrated in *Seder Moed*, the large section devoted to the festivals and seasons. In the English edition (Soncino, London), this is four volumes totalling more than 3,600 pages. It rewards both browsing and intense study.

Of rabbinical *midrash*, one classic collection available in English is organized in such a way as to help in study of the festivals, because it follows the Torah readings, for festivals and festival-related Shabbosim, in order from Hanukkah around the circle of the year to Sh'mini Atzeret. This is *Pesikta de Rab Kahana*, ed. by William G. Braude and Israel J. Kapstein (Jewish Publication Society). Its quality is very high.

The abridged version of the Shulchan Aruch now available in English, the *Code of Jewish Law*, ed. by Solomon Ganzfried, transl. by Hyman E. Goldin (Hebrew Publishing Co.) is useful for a bare-bones outline of Orthodox practice in Eastern Europe and its American transplants during the past century.

I have found two *Siddurim* or prayerbooks (in Hebrew and English) most useful for the festivals: David de Sola Pool, *The Traditional Prayer Book for Sabbath and Festivals* (Behrman House), with exceptionally beautiful translations, clear explanations, and the festival Torah and *haftarah* readings; and Philip Birnbaum, *Daily Prayer Book: Ha-Siddur Ha-Shalem* (Hebrew Publishing Company), with an extraordinary coverage of special festival services and prayers that are sometimes ignored.

MODERN INTERPRETATIONS

For me, the two most thought-provoking interpretive books on the festivals have been Theodore Gaster's historically/anthropologically oriented work, *Festivals of the Jewish Year* (Morrow) and the section on the theology of the festivals in Franz Rosenzweig's *Star of the Redemption* (Holt, Rinehart and Winston), pp. 265–335. Eliyahu Kitov's *The Book of Our Heritage* (Feldheim, 3 vols.) is very rich in both details of practice and midrashic interpretation, in presenting the pattern for Orthodox celebration of the festivals. David Rosenberg's *Chosen Days*, with art work by Leonard Baskin (Doubleday) is a fusion of explicit interpretive comment with interpretation that is implicit in his poetic and *midrashic* renderings of some of the major readings for the festivals.

Hayyim Schauss, *The Jewish Festivals from Their Beginnings to Our Own Day* (Union of American Hebrew Congregations) and Bella Chagall's *Burning Lights* (Schocken) with drawings by Marc Chagall, are both helpful in giving a rich description of the celebration of the festivals in Eastern Europe and (in Schauss) other eras of Jewish life.

Many many entries and essays in the *Encyclopedia Judaica* were very helpful. So were a number of articles in *The First Jewish Catalog*, ed. by Richard Siegel, Michael Strassfeld, and Sharon Strassfeld (Jewish Publication Society).

Very interesting, but less useful for me, were Julius Greenstone, *Jewish*

Feasts and Fasts (Jewish Publication Society), Yaacov Vainstein, *The Cycle of the Jewish Year* (World Zionist Organization), and Abraham P. Bloch, *The Biblical and Historical Background of the Jewish Holy Days* (Ktav). Alex J. Goldman's *A Handbook for the Jewish Family: Understanding and Enjoying the Sabbath and Holidays* (Bloch) might be useful chiefly for its songs, since they are supplied with musical notation.

The Festival *Anthology* series of the Jewish Publication Society, whose individual volumes on Rosh Hashanah, Yom Kippur, Passover, etc., I have mentioned in specific chapters, could be of great help to anyone planning a celebration of the festivals. So could the series of Festival *Guides* by Irving Greenberg, pamphlets published by the National Jewish Resource Center in New York City.

Extraordinary tape recordings of chants, songs, stories, and interpretive remarks on some of the festivals by Zalman Schachter-Shalomi are available from B'nai Or in Philadelphia.

Two cookbooks are organized according to the festival cycle, and contain dozens of good recipes: Fanny Engle and Gertrude Blair, *The Jewish Festival Cookbook* (Paperback Library) and Joan Nathan, *The Jewish Holiday Kitchen* (Schocken).

Continuing articles on reinterpretations of and new ways of celebrating the holy seasons are carried by *New Menorah*, the journal of Jewish renewal that I edit. I have often referred to *chavurot*, the intimate and participatory congregations or fellowships that are developing many new approaches to the festivals. My books *Godwrestling* (Schocken) and *These Holy Sparks* (Harper & Row) describe the process and content of the *chavurot* in depth.

Since 1981, when I finished writing the first edition of *Seasons*, several important books have become available to those who wish to "go and study." Gunther Plaut's annotated edition of *The Torah* (with the prophetic *haftarahs*) has been published by the Union of American Hebrew Congregations (1981), and its readings for the festivals follow the practice of Reform synagogues. The first volume of Everett Fox's annotated translation of the Torah, entitled *In the Beginning* (Schocken, 1983), has appeared and is extraordinary. A new *Machzor* for Rosh Hashanah and Yom Kippur, *On Wings of Awe*, edited and translated by Richard N. Levy (B'nai B'rith Hillel Foundations, 1985), includes remarkable poetic English renderings of many prayers and a serious effort to use language inclusive of women as well as men in the English (not in the Hebrew). Michael Strassfeld's book *The Jewish Holidays* (Harper and Row, 1985) is a very useful guide with especially creative marginal comments by several Jewish teachers. *The Shalom Seders* (Adama Books, 1984) brings together three unusual haggadot focussed on peace, justice, and freedom.

THE FESTIVALS
AND THE FUTURE

As we have shown in this book, the Jewish festivals shape time into spirals—spirals of months, years, cycles. It is the festivals that give shape to these spirals, define the curves that make time into spirals. But the process works in the other direction as well—and it is this reverse flow that I want to discuss at the "end" of this book. (For this end is also a beginning, as in a spiral.)

What is the reverse flow? It is that the festivals not only define the spirals but *are defined by them*. That is, there are bigger and deeper spirals of change—bigger even than the fifty-year Jubilee cycle. These spirals are so profound that they may force us to transform our understanding of the festivals themselves.

We ourselves, in this very generation, are in the midst of a great curve in this great spiral of profound change—and we are therefore present at the moment of deep change in the meaning that some Jews find in the festivals and in other elements of Jewish life. I want to share here my own sense of those changes.

In the spirals of time that we have looked at so far, we have seen the new moons spiral into years; we have seen the years spiral into seven-year sabbatical cycles and twenty-eight-year "Blessing of the Sun" cycles and fifty-year Jubilee cycles. Surely this is enough?

No, for there is still a grander spiral—the procession of the great Eras of Jewish History:

• First, the Biblical Era, which was born from a courageous response to the breakdown of some dimly seen pre-Israelite society and which was followed by doubt and disintegration in the face of Hellenism;

• Second, the Rabbinic Era, which was born from a courageous response to the triumph of Hellenism and which was followed by doubt and disintegration in the face of Modernism; and

• The Third Era, as yet unnamed, to which we are now trying to give birth—by responding to the triumph of Modernism.

In this Third Era, what are the great changes? We can point to the emergence of the State of Israel and of the free Diasporas of North America—that is, to Jewish communities that in different ways have created real political power for themselves. We can point to the emergence of women who are seeking and achieving full equality in all areas of Jewish life; who are now carrying their own spiritual experience into traditional Judaism; and who are in this way transforming it. We can point to the shudder with which Judaism confronts the Nazi Holocaust and its efforts to begin confronting the danger of world-wide nuclear holocaust.

Indeed, all these changes can be seen as aspects of one great change: The Jewish people, amid the human race, now have much greater power to shape history than we have had before. Once we knew that only God had power to destroy all life on earth; now we humans hold that power in our hands. Once we knew that only God could restore the Jewish people to the Land of Israel; now we have taken that power into our own hands. Once we knew that only God could restore women and men to their Edenic equality; now we have begun the task.

Yet, this change has taught us to begin to make another change. For this change alone is the lesson of modernity—that we humans have enormous power. The *new* lesson is that there is an enormous danger in this knowledge: the danger that if we use our power without self-control, we will destroy ourselves and all life on earth. If we act as if we are "totally in control" of this planet, we will "total" the planet—proving that we are not really totally in control. So we have begun to draw again on the pre-modern religious traditions which teach us that there is a Mystery within us and beyond us. By spiraling forward, we have also spiraled back—to the knowledge of limits, of Mystery, of God. Spiraled back to what the festivals themselves have tried to teach us.

What does all this have to do with the festivals, the seasons of our joy? The festivals themselves have been different in these different eras. Different and yet the same—as in a spiral we return, yet find ourselves in some place different.

In our Biblical Era, the festivals were a way of asserting with great political power that the Jewish people were a band of runaway slaves—just liberated from Pharaoh. For when hundreds of thousands of Israelites gathered at the Temple in Jerusalem to celebrate Pesach, or Sukkot, their presence in such numbers was itself a challenge to Pharaoh—not only literally to the Pharaoh of Egypt but also to imperial monarchs of Assyria and Babylon and to miniature pharaohs in Canaan itself.

By the "late Second Temple" period, there had evolved a version of the festival cycle that said with special power that the people of Israel continued to be a band of runaway slaves, ever celebrating its freedom anew. For the cycle had become understood as a reliving of the liberation—of the exodus from Egypt. Not only was Pesach a moment to relive *in the present* the delivery from Pharaoh, but Shavuot was the moment when the headlong rush of slaves away from their slavery was checked; when they came face to face at Sinai with a Presence that mirrored their own, that forced them to reflect upon themselves, to become a community with a center rather than just a line of march. And Sukkot, it was said,. represented the extraordinary time of traveling in the wilderness with God's Presence in the people's very midst.

So whenever the people gathered, it recalled itself to the covenant of slaves determined to be free. It gathered in huge numbers to exemplify its own freedom, to defend it, and to accord freedom to others—for "you were slaves and strangers in the Land of Mitz-ra-yim."

In the Rabbinic Era of our history, this lesson was preserved—and transformed. For now, scattered in Diaspora, the Jewish people could not show its political power by gathering in one place. Only in the nooks and crannies of the Roman Empire, Babylonia, and then of Christendom and Islam could the Jews relive what it meant to be liberated. So the Pesach Seder became an event in myriad homes—and the Sukkah a hut that was built outside myriad homes and congregations. Indeed, the rabbis encoded this very fact of "nook and cranny" into the heart of the Seder; for they took the form of a Hellenistic symposium dinner, a philosophic discussion intertwined with two cups of wine before dinner and two cups afterward, as the form of the Seder. They turned its symbolism upside-down in the direction of freedom by having the least learned person present ask the questions—not the most learned, as in the symposium. And in the very crannies of the conqueror's culture, they asked the celebrants to say *both* that in every generation a destroyer rises up, and that in every generation we, today, are liberated.

Thus the Seder itself, in its sardonic subversion of the conquering power, became a moment of freedom in dispersion. The new form of freedom was not found in the ability of the Jewish people to transform the world by publicly showing its collective freedom, but in its ability to preserve its own identity and values under pressure and conquest.

This is the model of the festivals that we have inherited: the model from Rabbinic times that accepts the limits on Jewish power. We have power to make ourselves just, peaceful, holy; we do not have power to transform the world.

But it is precisely this model that no longer defines the Jewish people. Traumatized by a modernized super-pogrom that destroyed one-third of us, we decided that we *must* have enough political power to protect ourselves. In one generation, we have built that power—and a surplus that is enough to have an impact on the rest of the world besides. Not only in Israel but in America the Jewish people have such power. We do not rule the country but we can make a difference.

We are free to be both as fully Jewish and as fully citizens as we choose to be—and that is, like Israel, a new event. Even in the Soviet Union, where we are *not* free to be both fully Jewish and fully citizens, the Jewish community has, against all odds, become the arena of the feistiest questioning of governmental power.

So now we are able to ask ourselves again: can the Jewish traditions, experiences, values that are embodied in the festivals be brought into the public world? Can a *new form* of power—not military but militant, not violent but vigorous—be expressed through public observance of the festivals?

Is this what—all unconsciously—Soviet Jews in the late sixties were doing when they carried their Torah-dancing for Simchat Torah into the public streets? Is this what American Jews were doing in the late sixties when they invented "Freedom Seders"? For these new versions of the Haggadah intertwined the ancient Exodus with such modern struggles as the Warsaw Ghetto uprising and the work of Nat Turner, Martin Luther King, Henry David Thoreau—and thus made it possible for Jews to join with black civil rights workers and anti-war activists to do Pesach Seders in the public sphere.

Such responses of Soviet Jews and American Jews to crises in their lives came "from the gut"—unplanned, untheorized. But as the movement for Jewish renewal gathered more strength and self-awareness, by the early 1980s networks of Jews all across North America were *consciously* drawing on Jewish tradition to carry the meaning of the festivals into public awareness.

The first of these efforts drew on a "festival" that was totally new to Jewish life—though the basis for it was extremely old. As Jews began to wrestle with the danger of a world-wide nuclear holocaust that might destroy all life, one element of Torah that rose up for them was the story of the Flood, when almost all life on earth was destroyed.

This tale is unique in all the tales of Genesis in that there are specific dates given for the events. "On the seventeenth day of the second month," says the story, the rains began to pour; the Flood began. One lunar year and eleven days later ". . . on the twenty-seventh day of the second month . . . ," after exactly one solar year, the earth is dry again. Noah and his family leave the Ark, and God sends the Rainbow to be a sign of the convenant that all life will continue: "Seed time and harvest, cold and heat, summer and winter, day and night, shall not cease."

From the Creation to the Exodus from Egypt, the Torah gives no dates—except for the Flood. Why did Torah preserve the tradition of these dates when it did not provide any dates for such important events as the departure of Abraham and Sarah from Ur at God's command, or Jacob's wrestle with God in which he took on the name Israel—"Godwrestler"? What are we to make of these dates?

For many other dates—the date of the Exodus itself, for instance; the date of the destruction of the Temple; the date of Esther's triumph over Haman—we know what to do. We turn these dates into Pesach, Tisha B'Av, Purim—moments to re-experience liberation, disaster, turning the tables. We relive the moment from our history, in order to draw on the ancient experience for the sake of our own lives.

But we have never done this with the dates of the Flood and the Rainbow. Why not? Suddenly, to many Jews who were involved in efforts to "renew" Jewish life, it seemed clear that these dates had never become times of observance because no generation had ever faced the danger that all life might be destroyed, or the necessity of consciously joining in a covenant to act to preserve all life.

No generation—until our own. So now these dates leaped off the scroll of Torah, to come alive for the first time in Jewish practice.

What to do? First of all, a curious debate that began long ago among the rabbis of the Talmud had to be resolved. When was "the second month"? Most of the rabbis said, in the fall—the month of bitter Heshvan—counting from Tishri, the month of Rosh Hashanah, as the first. But Rabbi Yehoshua said—and "the sages of all the other nations" agreed with him—that the Flood began and ended in the spring, counting from Nisan, the month of Pesach. By this count, the Flood began on 17 Iyyar and ended one year later on 27 Iyyar.

Which month to choose for an observance? The community decided to honor the unusual fact that for this debate, the Talmud cited the opinions of the sages of all nations. Usually their views could have no weight in the interpretation of Israel's Torah. But for *this* text, their understanding mattered. For the Flood affected every nation; it and the three-sided covenant between God, all living breathing beings, and Noah's family, was the archetype in Jewish thought of what was universal danger and deliverance.

Thus, facing the universal danger of nuclear holocaust, it seemed appropriate to side with Rabbi Yehoshua and the sages of all nations. And so, beginning in 1982, first dozens and then hundreds of Jewish communities began to observe the time of Rainbow Sign. They drew on the full eleven-day period from 17 Iyyar to 27 Iyyar as the holy time, so that any Shabbos or any Sunday in the period could be used to celebrate.

They developed new ceremonial forms to recognize the season. These included reading the Torah passages about the Flood and the Rainbow (especially Genesis 8:14-22 and 9:8-17) and as Prophetic haftarah, the passage from Hosea about renewing the covenant with all of life and breaking "bow, sword, and battle from the earth" (Hosea 2:20-25).

The ceremonies often included the lifting of a human "rainbow" to the sky by releasing multicolored balloons. Some communities sang the traditional song about the Flood: "Rise and Shine and Give God the Glory, Glory," with two new verses at the end: "So Noah he sent out/ Sent out a dovey, dovey./ She stayed out/But sent back her lovey lovey/ Children of the Lord"; and "God gave to Noah a Bow/With colors seven;/ Peace on earth/as in the highest Heaven!/Children of the Lord."·

Other groups have chanted specific psalms, especially Psalm 69: "Save me, O God! For the waters have risen up to my neck . . ." and the end of Psalm 29: "Yah will sit above the Flood—God's reign will never cease. For God will give the people strength and bless the world with peace." Some have invited those present to name aloud a place on Planet

Earth that needs special healing from impending destruction, and then chanted "Eyl na r'fa na lah!"—"Please God, heal her!"

Most of the celebrating communities have invited a speaker to address the connection between the Flood story and the danger of nuclear holocaust—a "Flood of Fire," as the rabbis warned might still be possible. Some have asked for two speakers or a double focus: one on the danger (the Flood), the other on new possibilities and hope (the Rainbow). One more element of the observance of Rainbow Sign that might be noted: many Jewish communities and congregations have invited other religious and ethnic groups to share in this particular observance, simply because the ancient story is a universal one and the present danger is a universal one.

Another festival that has become a focus of concern about the danger of nuclear holocaust is Sukkot. Drawing on the prayer "Ufros alenu sukkat sh'lomecha"—"Spread over us the sukkah of Your peace"— The Shalom Center in Philadelphia and hundreds of congregations and other Jewish groups have created Sukkat Shalom. The sukkah-booth itself is so open, so vulnerable that it is precisely the opposite of a fallout shelter; it proclaims that the only security in the world today comes from all peoples' sharing with each other the knowledge that everyone is vulnerable. Just as the sukkah is open to every wind and rainstorm, so under the rain of nuclear weapons, no roof, no "shield," can make any nation safe.

In 1980, sukkot bearing this message were built in Lafayette Park, between the White House and the Soviet Embassy in Washington; and also in Independence Park in Philadelphia, Boston Common, Daley Plaza in Chicago, and in many other cities. These Sukkot Shalom acted as gathering points for public discussion and rallies; in some, the homeless and the poor came as guests (ushpizin) to eat; in some, the "70 Nations" were invited to embody the ancient tradition that 70 sacrifices were offered at the temple during Sukkot, on behalf of peace and plenty for all the 70 nations of the world.

Many families and congregations dedicated their own sukkot to shalom; and in many religious schools, children helped decorate the sukkah with symbols of peace. Even non-synagogue groups joined in Sukkot Shalom celebrations.

Then the Sukkot Shalom committees began to realize that in every even-numbered year, Sukkot will come a few weeks before an American national election. Most participants felt that it would be Jewishly inauthentic to turn Sukkot into an electioneering time for this candidate or that party. But most of them also felt it was perfectly authentic to make Sukkot a moment in which the Jewish community could remind itself that no Jew should enter an election booth without the *issue* of shalom foremost in their minds. *"From harvest booth to voting booth,"* one activist said, "there is a difference, but the path from one to the other should be clear and well walked. It would be a profanation to fit Sukkot into the rhythm of American elections, but it would be an affirmation to fit American elections into the rhythm of Sukkot."

The development of Sukkot Shalom raised questions that its originators had not expected about the relationships of religious communities to the state. When sukkot were built on public space, some Jewish organizations committed to the separation of religion and the state raised a flag of opposition: was not this state entanglement in, and support of, religion? Some participants replied that confronting the state was utterly different from depending on it, and that neither the First Amendment to the U.S. Constitution nor Jewish values would forbid religious communities to use their own deepest symbols to challenge government policy. Some sukkot were built in this spirit. On the other hand, in response to this dialogue some Sukkot Shalom were erected in private space, were moved for the space of a single day to public space in order to serve as the focus for a rally, and were then dismantled or moved again at the end of the day. This approach underlined the sense that the sukkah was not a creature of the state, but of the people who dwelt in and around it.

These new issues stemmed from the new outlook on what the festivals might mean in the "Third Era" of Jewish life. Increasingly, as new aspects of Jewish renewal unfolded into experiment and experience, excitement grew about what it meant to carry profound meanings of the festivals into the world.

Perhaps the most basic of these—and perhaps the most crucial corrective of the "modern" perspective—is simply the teaching that some time is holy; some days are sacred; some rhythms are central to the meaning of life.

In a world in which any moments of rest, celebration, meditation— the festivals of any religious tradition or spiritual orientation—are often seen as "a waste of time" because they detract from productive work, it is crucial to remind ourselves that work is not the only valuable behavior. *Doing,* making, producing, must be part of a rhythm in which *being* also has its place.

This is the ultimate message of the seasons of our joy: that there *is* joy in the seasons themselves, in our very decision to join in noting them, in celebrating them, in walking the spiritual path—the spiral— that they make.

—ARTHUR I. WASKOW
Wyncote, Pennsylvania
November 21, 1985
8 Kislev 5746

ABOUT THE AUTHOR

ARTHUR WASKOW grew up in Baltimore during the 1930s and 1940s. After taking a doctorate in U.S. History, he served as a legislative assistant in the U.S. House of Representatives and became a leading activist in the anti-war movements of the 1960s. Waskow did research at the Institute for Policy Studies and at the Public Resource Center, writing six books on such issues as American foreign policy, race relations, and energy policy.

In the midst of the social upheavals of 1968, Waskow began to feel deep stirrings of Jewish identity and started to wrestle with the meaning of Jewish tradition and thought. Out of this experience he wrote two books:

The Freedom Seder, which intertwined traditional Passover texts with modern passages on freedom and slavery, and *The Bush Is Burning*, an examination of the meaning of Jewish identity in our generation. He became part of the *Havurah* movement of small, joyful and participatory congregations of creatively traditional Jews. He wrote the book *Godwrestling* about how his rediscovery of Torah was both helping him remake his own life and casting new light on how to deal with the crises of American society.

In 1979 Waskow founded a journal of Jewish renewal that is now called *New Menorah* and is published by the B'nai Or Religious Fellowship, with Waskow as editor. He began teaching at the Reconstructionist Rabbinical College in 1982, and in 1984 published *These Holy Sparks*—stories and histories of the movement for Jewish renewal.

Together with his son, David, and his daughter, Shoshana, he wrote *Before There Was a Before*—new and delightful stories of the Seven Days of Creation.

Waskow reunited three of the major strands in his life—his commitments to peace, to Judaism, and to the lives of his children—when in 1983 he became Director of The Shalom Center, a resource and organizing center for Jewish perspectives on preventing nuclear holocaust.

ABOUT THE ARTISTS

MARTIN FARREN and JOAN BENJAMIN-FARREN met in 1967 when they were graduate students at The University of Iowa. Joan graduated in 1969 with a Master of Arts degree in Art and Martin graduated two years later with a Ph.D. in Music.

Since that time they have collaborated as artists in the fields of theater and music, as well as the plastic arts, with that collaboration reaching its most intense expression in the art of Jewish papercutting.

They approach their art from a highly literary point of view and express the words and ideas of Jewish tradition in visual terms which are rich in detailed symbolism. Their work has often been described as a kind of visual *midrash* (commentary).

They write: "We have tried to create a work of art which is not only beautiful to the eye, but when 'unpacked' of its symbolic meaning will be beautiful also to the heart."

Joan and Martin have lectured widely on their work and the history of Jewish papercutting, and have exhibited throughout the United States and in Israel. Their papercuts are in private collections in this country as well as in Europe and Israel, and are held in the permanent collections of such major museums as the Wolfson Museum at the Seat of the Chief Rabbinate in Jerusalem and the H.U.C. Skirball Museum in Los Angeles, California.

The Farrens make their home with their two children, Shoshanna and Yosef, a few miles south of Boston, in Sharon, Massachusetts.

TO: Arthur Waskow
     6711 Lincoln Drive
     Philadelphia, PA 19119

Dear Arthur Waskow—Shalom!

☐ I have a question about the festivals. Please write
me your reactions.

☐ Please keep me up-to-date on creative yet
traditional ways of celebrating the festivals, as
presented in your journal *New Menorah*. Please send
me a one-year subscription (six issues) for the *special
price* of $12.00. I enclose a check made out to *New
Menorah*.

Name _____

Address _____

City/State/Zip _____